QUESTIONS OF SEMITIC LINGUISTICS
ROOT AND LEXEME. THE HISTORY OF RESEARCH

QUESTIONS OF SEMITIC LINGUISTICS

ROOT AND LEXEME

THE HISTORY OF RESEARCH

by
Gregorio del Olmo Lete

translated by
Wilfred G. E. Watson

CDL PRESS
2008
Bethesda, Maryland

LIBRARY OF CONGRESS CATALOGING-IN-PUBLICATION DATA

Olmo Lete, Gregorio del.
  [Questions de linguistique sémitique. English]
  Questions of Semitic linguistics : root and lexeme, the history of research / by Gregorio del
  Olmo Lete; translated by Wilfred B.E. Watson.
     p. cm.
  Includes bibliographical references.
  ISBN 978-1-934309-15-5
  1. Semitic languages—Morphology. I. Title.
  PJ3027.O4613 2008
  492—dc22   2008025370

ISBN 978-1934309-155

CONTENTS

ABBREVIATIONS

AAL	Afroasiatic Linguistics (Malibu, Calif.)
AEPHE	*Annuaire de l'École Pratique des Hautes Études* (Paris)
AIDA	Association Internationale de Dilectologie Arabe
AION	*Annali del Istituto Orientale di Napoli* (Naples)
ALSC	G. Deutscher, M.J.C. Kowenberg, eds., *The Akkadian Language in its Semitic Context: Studies in the Akkadian of the Third and Second Millennium BC* (PIHANS 106), Leiden 2006.
ALUOS	*Annual of the Leeds University Oriental Society* (Leeds)
ANLR/M	*Accademia Nazionale dei Lincei, Rendiconti/Monografie* (Rome)
AnOr	*Analecta Orientalia* (Rome)
AOAT	Alter Orient und Altes Testament (Münster)
AOS	American Oriental Series (New Haven)
ArOr	*Archív Orientálni. Quarterly Journal of Asian and African Studies* (Prague)
AS	Assyriological Studies (Chicago, Ill.)
AStThHLSc	Amsterdam Studies in the Theory and History of Linguistic Science (Amsterdam/Philadelphia, Pa.)
AuOr	*Aula Orientalis* (Sabadell [Barcelona])
BALM	*Bolletino dell'Atlante Linguistico Mediterraneo* (Venice)
BBB	Bonner Biblische Beiträge (Bonn)
BEO	*Bulletin d'Études Orientales* (Damascus)
BFAO	*Bulletin de l'Institut Français d'Archéologie Orientale* (Cairo)
BSLP	*Bulletin de la Société Linguistique de Paris* (Paris)
BSOAS	*Bulletin of the Society of Oriental and African Studies* (London)
CANE	J.M. Sasson, ed., *Civilizations of the Ancient Near East*, 4 vols., New York, N.Y. 1995.
CBQ	*Catholic Biblical Quarterly* (Washington, D.C.)
CILTh	Current Issues in Linguistic Theory (Amsterdam/Philadelphia)
CJL	*The Canadian Journal of Linguistics* (Toronto)
EI	*Erets Israel* (Jerusalem)
FoL	*Folia Linguistica. Acta Societatis Linguisticae Europaeae* (Berlin)
GL	*General Linguistics* (University Park, Pa.)
GLECS	*Groupe linguistique d'études chamito-sémitiques* (Paris)
HdO	Handbuch der Orientalistik (Leiden)
IELOA	Instruments pour l'étude des langues de l'Orient Ancien (Lausanne)
IOS	Israel Oriental Studies (Jerusalem)
JAL	*Journal of Afroasiatic Languages* (Leiden)

JCS	*Journal of Cuneiform Studies* (Ann Arbor, Mich.*)*
JNES	*Journal of The Near Eastern Studies* (Chicago, Ill.)
JRAS	*Journal of the Royal Asiatic Society of Great Britain and Ireland* (Cambridge)
JSS	*Journal of Semitic Studies* (Manchester / Oxford)
LinAeg	*Lingua Aegyptia* (Göttingen)
LLMA	*Langues et Littératures du Monde Arabe* (Lyon)
LOAPL	*Langues orientales anciennes: philologie et linguistique* (Louvain)
MEAH	*Miscelánea de Estudios Árabes y Hebraicos* (Granada)
MUSJ	*Miscellanea de l'Université de Saint-Joseph* (Beirut)
NELS	*Proceedings of the Annual Meeting of the Northeastern Linguistic Society* (Amherst, Mass.)
OLA	*Orientalia Lovaniensia Analecta* (Leuven)
Or	*Orientalia* (Rome)
OTS	*Oudtestamentische Studien* (Leiden).
PBSCS	*Proceedings of the Barcelona Symposium on Comparative Semitics, 11/ 19-20/2004 (AuOr 23, 2005), Sabadell* (Barcelona) 2005.
PPPIK GNS	*Pis'mennye pamjatniki i problemy istorii kul'tury*, Godičnaja naučnaja sestsija (Narodov Vostoka).
PWPL	*Penn working papers in Linguistics* (Philadelphia)
QuSem	*Quaderni di Semitistica* (Florence)
RA	*Revue d'Assyriologie et d'Archéologie Orientale* (Paris)
RES	*Revue des études slaves* (Paris)
RGGU	*Rossijskij Gosudarstvennyj Gumanitarnyj Universitet* (Moscow)
RHPhR	*Revue d'Histoire et de Philosophie Religieuse* (Strasbourg)
RSO	*Rivista degli studi orientali* (Rome)
SPJASt	*St. Petersburg Journal of African Studies* (St. Petersburg)
StSem	*Studi di semitistica* (Rome)
StSLL	*Studies in Semitic Languages and Linguistics* (Leiden).
TL-LC	*Al-Tawāṣul / Linguistica Communicatio* (Fez)
TL/SM	*Trends in Linguistics: Studies and Monographs* (Berlin/New York)
UCPL	*University of California Publications on Linguistics* (Berkeley, Ca.)
VIAAUW	*Veröffentlichungen der Institut für Afrikanistik und Ägyptologie der Universität Wien* (Vienna)
VTS	*Vetus Testamentum Supplementa* (Berlin)
WdO	*Die Welt des Orients* (Tübingen)
WZKM	*Wiener Zeitschrift für die Kundes des Morgenlands* (Vienna)
WZMLU	*Wissenschaftliche Zeitschrift der Martin Luther-Universität* (Halle-Wüttenberg)
ZA	*Zeitschrift für Assyriologie* (Berlin)
ZAH	*Zeitschrift für Althebraistik* (Berlin)
ZAW	*Zeitschrift für Alttestamentliche Wissenschaft* (Berlin)
ZDMG	*Zeitschrift der Deutschen Morgenländischen Gesellschaft* (Stuttgart)

PREFACE

The first four chapters of this book correspond to a course given at the Collège de France (Paris) from May 18th to June 4th, 2001. A fifth chapter has been added that did not form part of the lectures but its premises and basic considerations (problems of etymology and semantics) underlie the first four. At a time when comparative Semitic lexicography is about to make a final leap that will enable it to catch up to and even go beyond its past delay, it has seemed opportune to take stock and provide the reader with an overview of its most important trends. In fact, it was while making a survey of the theories of my predecessors that I constructed the background upon which are drawn the lines I am actually following in my own research on comparative Semitics. In this field there has been a certain tendency to closed and even exclusive attitudes. Often, Assyriologists, Semitists, and Arabists have ignored each other in their research on Common or Early Semitic, not to mention the language barrier created in the case of Eastern European scholars. The marvellous openness of spirit and wide scientific horizons of Orientalists at the end of the nineteenth century has been followed by a certain narrowing of perspective in our own time. It seems to me that knowing and putting together the various contributions and different points of view were an indispensable preliminary to achieving the most complete summary possible of the data from the whole field of Semitics. The undertaking was complex and very broad; I fear that perhaps I have failed to mention some contributions that were worth including. Nevertheless, I hope to have succeeded at least in offering a representative and even adequate view of the position as it is today.

Here I wish to express my gratitude to the Assemblée des Professeurs du Collège de France, who kindly invited me to lecture there, at the suggestion of Prof. Jean-Marie Durand, to whom I am particularly obliged. In their invitation, the Assemblée had the kindness to ensure the publication of these lectures once they had been edited, a decision for which I am doubly indebted. Prof. Javier Teixidor was kind enough to accept the text in the collection "Antiquités sémitiques." I offer him my deepest gratitude for this new demonstration of a friendship by which I have always felt honored.

I must express my appreciation of those who had the kindness and patience to revise the French text of my lectures. My heart was set on preserving it in its original form, in homage to a language and a culture toward which we Semitists are always indebted. In a very special way, then, I thank first of all Prof. Jean-Marie Durand for his generous and patient help. I am also particularly grateful to Dr. Arnaud Sérandour, of the Laboratoire des Études Sémitiques Anciennes (CNRS-Collège de France), who was kind enough to revise the original text. My thanks go to Dr. Wilfred G. E. Watson, who translated the revised French text of these lectures and also corrected the proofs.

At a different level, I wish to express my gratitude also to Prof. Leonid Kogan, of Moscow, and to Dr. Jana Kořínková, of Prague, whose invaluable help enabled me both to acquire and understand the contributions of Russian and Czech Semitists and Orientalists. It was a question of gaining access, even if in a provisional and rudimentary fashion, to two areas of Semitic research that, to a large extent, were closed off by a language barrier. As I said above, the aim of these pages is to assist in bringing together in mutual recognition all those engaged in research on Semitic linguistics who are interested in the converging aspects in this vast field, from different but complementary points of view. I hope to have made a contribution to it.

INTRODUCTION

For a long time it has been acknowledged that Semitic philology lags behind Indo-European philology, especially in the domain of lexicography, both with respect to etymology and comparison.[1] I have felt this delay, which entails lack of precision and, therefore, uncertainty of choice, as a heavy burden during the long years devoted to the interpretation and understanding of texts in the Ugaritic language that could be explained only by constant reference to other Semitic languages. In many cases this has been to experience the void and the lack of academic assurance that had to be compensated for and overcome every time, assuming the risk of the provisional nature and the lack of perspective that the disorganized aspect of this reference entails. The multiplicity of "etymological" options offered by various scholars, some of them marked by desperation, clearly showed a lack of basic academic consensus.

This state of affairs has often given Ugaritology the appearance of being a discipline that allowed anyone at all, armed with an elementary knowledge of Semitic philology (usually biblical Hebrew), to devote himself to the frenetic pursuit of phantoms.

Now that in principle I consider my study of the Ugaritic texts to be at an end, the experience has led me to undertake a global study of Semitic lexematics that may make good, even if only in a preliminary and provisional way, the delay in question and in this manner provide a certain guarantee to the interpretation of texts requiring reference to comparative studies and ultimately attempt to put some order into the lexico-semantic organization of Common Semitic. I do not claim to set out to discover *terra incognita* or to be a pioneer and innovator. In this respect the first essential task, as it wa stated in the Preface, is to survey and compare to each other the studies that various Western specialists (Arabists, Assyriologists, and Semitic scholars in general) have undertaken, often independently, without forgetting the important contributions of the Slav scholars devoted to Semitic studies, often misunderstood and insufficiently taken account of in the West.

As a starting point, I compiled a *Bibliography of Semitic Linguistics* (1940–2000), arranged by theme, in which are collected studies of strictly linguistic scope, leaving out all other problems (literary, textual, historical, cultural, etc.) related to common and comparative Semitics, as well as to various specific languages. At first only the record of the classical and literary language was considered, but given the importance attained by studies of the contemporary dialects of these languages, in the end I decided to include them as well. As reminders, I have included also some fundamental studies that are prior to 1940, since they are still valuable and comprise a reference point for earlier work.[2]

One section of this bibliography refers to the "structure of the Semitic root," and it is on this that the summary that I wish to present in the following chapters is focused. In this respect, two aspects need to be considered: the current state of the art and the evaluation of the results that inform my own opinion in the present state of research.

At the same time, this aspect of research on the general question mentioned was accompanied by a direct and personal analysis of three lexematic series that I consider to be fundamental for organizing the Semitic lexicon, beginning with the monemes that prove to be the simplest. Of course, neither in this case nor in my later lexicographical research, did I ever have any intention of developing a glottogonic enquiry according to the mathematical model recently proposed by M. Nowak and D. Krakauer.[3] In principle, it is an empirical lexematic inquiry, starting with the simplest elements in terms of phonology, that only envisages a reconstruction of the proto-Semitic lexicon. We will consider this topic later.

This reconstruction, as will be seen below, should include proto-phonetics as well as proto-morphosyntax alongside proto-lexematics. The invention and utterance of the very first "word" in the proto-language already supposed a certain structured "grammar," even if minimal, that is, a correspondence of lexemes. It seems clear that in the beginning there was the "word," but at the same time it had a range of meaning and an "actantial" function, however implicit. At all events, the proto-Semitic level cannot be considered as a glottogonic model suitable for explaining the origin of language. The level in question is already fully organized and derived.

The series mentioned are as follows: the monoconsonantal lexical series,[4] which is basically deictic and functorial; and the series on personal pronouns[5] and numbers[6], which are also deictic, the first with an agglutinative structure and the second triconsonantal in origin. However, our attention was drawn in particular to the biconsonantal series of both nouns and verbs, and to their later expanded forms, which we are dealing with now.[7]

This combined study of the different theories, on the one hand, and direct and independent analysis of the linguistic data, on the other, has enabled us to make progress in systematizing them and also testing the validity of our own appraisals. In fact, study of the biconsonantal series was an aim in its own right, not only from the aspect of lexematics but also from the aspect of sociolinguistics.[8] This is why the series pays particular attention to the semantic field (paradigm, associative field), which enables the simplicity of the phonological structure to be contrasted with the well-known elementary nature of the sphere of reference, i.e., of the signified (*signifié*). In this way I hope to contribute some order into the world of the Semitic lexicon and at the same time discover its process of explicit expansion toward the triconsonantal series, which, in any case, is unavoidably the functional structure of Semitic grammar.[9]

The aim of this analysis of the biconsonantal base is not to defend or confirm "the possibility of the assumption of an original biliteral character of the Semitic root"[10] or to lay the foundations for a "biliteral theory." It is an empirical analysis of bases and roots that essentially seem to be (from the graphemic point of view) biliteral or biconsonantal or articulatory binary (CvC-, CvC̱- > CvCC-) and their diffusion by implicit intensification, epenthesis, or glide (C$v̱$C-, Cw:yC-), and also of bases expanded by prefixation, infixation and suffixation (Xv-CvC-, Cv-Xv-C-, CvCv-X-). Those models are generated by phonetic intensification of one of their components (vowel or second consonant) or by morphemic extensions (/ ʾ, h, l, m, n, r, s, t, w, y /) and can be defined as expansions of the primary root or consonantal cluster. For the moment we are not concerned with related semantic "groups," accepted by many scholars as "biconsonantal" with a free and different third radical, called a "determinative," "complement," "increment," or "modifier."[11] These possible expansions, aside from the mentioned morphemic extensions, will be studied only systematically and comprehensively at a later stage, starting with analysis of the duly established biliteral morphemes, which will ensure that they are true roots/bases and not simply triconsonantal alternatives or allotheses due to other phonetic factors. In this way it will be possible to resolve the issue of their original independent existence, generally called into question (see below pp. 79f.).

I do not claim, then, to reduce triconsonantal roots to biconsonantal ones. On the contrary, I consider triconsonantalism as structural in the Semitic system and as primordial as biconsonantalism, and that will be our conclusion. From the aspect of historical linguistics, both have an equal claim to be original. I do not believe there was a stage in the Semitic lexicon (for the moment we are not considering other levels) in which all the roots would have been biconsonantal and from which there emerged all the triconsonantal roots by a process of expansion. I only assume and also record the existence of a certain number of biconsonantal roots/bases susceptible of expansion by intensification of their components, as I mentioned above, which can result in the assumption of a triconsonantal form under the influence of this pattern. Once this form is verified, the apparently biliteral forms that are produced by inflection do not necessarily mean that the root originally had a biliteral form. These forms depend entirely on general phonetic laws.

In this perspective, I pay as much attention to phonology as to semantics, which often is an unexpected or insufficiently nuanced aspect. Concepts such as SSR ("Strong Semantic Relationship"; French RSF: "Relation Sémantique Forte") or WSR ("Weak Semantic Relationship"; French RSL: "Relation Sémantique Légère") are not precise analytical tools of diachronic semantics. In this respect, generative semantics, induced by phonological restructuring of the base by means of expansion through intensification, has to be distinguished from analogical semantics, produced by a shift in actual meaning, due to the complexity of the *signifié* (metaphorization/lexicalization) and its extra-linguistic (supra-segmental) functionality on the same phonological base. The two realizations have their own laws that are sufficiently uniform and univocal. To speak of the original or primitive structure of the Semitic lexical morpheme (pre-)supposes admitting the existence of a single configuration, valid for the whole lexicon of the linguistic family, at least at its primitive or original stage, from which would be derived all the more complex patterns that are perfectly verifiable in their morphological development. Such a structure must inevitably be "phonological," that is, phonetic and semantic at the same time. This leads us initially to examine studies concerned with the inventory or original system of basic phonemes (consonants and vowels) of the Semitic languages, to identifying and classifying them, some of which are hotly debated today. Next, opinions on their sequential coordination or "symphonic compatibility," that is, their empirical realization, have to be collected, first in syllables and then in "bases," from the aspect of the consonantal component (mono-, bi- or triconsonantal) and primitive vowel syllable (mono-, disyllabic, etc.) together with their apophonies. In this regard, emphasis has to be put on the lack of interest shown by Semitists in general to deal with the primitive Semitic vowels, especially in the West, to the extent of creating the belief that the Semitic languages formed a family of "consonantal" languages, making the whole of the semantic meaning consist in this sole element. Finally, in third place, we will have to arrange the many contributions concerning the fundamental subject of biliterality/triliterality (bi-, triconsonantalism), around which the more general theme of the "structure of the Semitic root" has polarized and which, to some extent, includes the other points. At the close, we will take our bearings on studies of comparative and etymological Semitic lexematics, using the opportunity to tackle the topic of reconstructing proto-languages. As I have stated above, the discussion will not be merely informative in nature. I will also present my own point of view with respect to each of these questions, as well as the results of my own research.

In principle, my perspective is limited to the field of Semitics, even though I am well aware that claiming to reconstruct the proto-Semitic level leads unavoidably beyond it, to the Hamito-Semitic or Afro-Asiatic level. I will not shrink from taking this step, but only in order to look for confirmation of the results obtained from the Semitic data, not to establish them.[12] In this respect, contributions from Egyptian, the only "classical language" among the non-Semitic Afro-Asiatic languages, will be highly appreciated.

I

WHAT IS A ROOT?
THE STATE OF THE ART (1940–2006)

1. General Survey

This section is a wide-ranging survey (including Afro-Asiatic) of research completed after 1940 on the structure of the root and related problems. Some of these studies take up the question from its beginning, that is to say, after the Mediaeval period, or refer to scholarship of the first half of the twentieth century, two aspects that I will leave to one side.

Over the years, other scholars, of course, have provided "states of the art" of comparative Semitics in general. In order to prepare my survey, it seems prudent to examine general studies—which inevitably tend to repeat each other— and to select the most important. I here provide a list of them together with a brief summary of the problems and periods discussed. Unfortunately, several of these summarizing articles omit reference to some significant, previous contributions. This is the first barrier to overcome: lack of mutual recognition. This list does not include presentations of general Semitics, such as B. Spuler et al. (*Semitistik* [HdO], Leiden, 1964), G. Garbini (*Le lingue semitiche*, Naples, 1972), D. Cohen ("Les langues chamito-sémitiques," in *Les langues dans le monde ancien et moderne*. Part III, Paris, 1988), and J. Huehnergard ("Semitic Languages," in J. Sasson, ed., *Civilizations of the Ancient Near East*, vol. IV, New York, 1995, pp. 2117–34), that often provide an historical outline of the history of research. I have also omitted general studies on comparative Semitics (Fleisch, Kramers, Rinaldi, Moscati, Garbini-Durand, Lipiński, Bennett, Stempel,[1] Kienast).

1.1. E. Ullendorff, "Comparative Semitics," in G. Levi della Vida, *Linguistica semitica: presente e futuro* (StSem 4). Rome, 1961. Pp. 13–32.

A short historical outline from the Middle Ages[2] to the present, with a summary of the most important contributions in the various languages; tasks to be completed are also noted. In addition, a general survey of the problems of Semitics is provided in his article "What Is a Semitic Language?" *Or* 27 (1958), pp. 66–75: "root / pattern," "consonantism / vocalism," "biliterality," "classification."

1.2. J. H. Hospers, "A Hundred Years of Semitic Comparative Linguistics," in *Studia Biblica et Semitica Th. C. Vriezen dedicata*. Wageningen, 1966. Pp. 138–51.

The author presents the development of the methodology and studies of comparative Semitics since the nineteenth century, with a brief glance at earlier stages. At the center of this historical survey, which is divided into three periods, is Brockelmann's work, with the *Introduction* by S. Moscati et al. at its apex. He also outlines the tasks to be completed: comparative lexicography and syntax, attention to modern dialects, Hamito-Semitic comparative studies.

1.3.   B. S. J. Isserlin, "Some Aspects of the Present State of Hamito-Semitic Studies," in J./Th. Bynon, eds., *Hamito-Semitica. Proceedings of a Colloquium...* The Hague and Paris, 1975. Pp. 479–85.

An evaluation of the situation at that time (1975) and his suggestion to use a non-linguistic approach, i.e., material or archaeological, to deal with the problems of comparative linguistics.

1.4.   W. Vycichl, "L'état actuel des études chamito-sémitiques," in P. Fronzaroli, ed., *Atti del secondo congresso internazionale di linguistica camito-semitica. Firenze 16–19 aprile 1974* (QuSem. 5). Florence, 1978. Pp. 63–76.

A brief outline of some twenty very varied questions of morphology, lexis, and classification related to the Hamito-Semitic languages.

1.5.   K. Petráček, "La méthodologie du chamito-sémitique comparé: état, problèmes, perspectives," in J. Bynon, ed., *Current Progress in Afro-Asiatic Linguistics. Papers of the Third International Hamito-Semitic Congress* (AstThHLSc. Series IV; CILTh 28). Amsterdam and Philadelphia, 1984. Pp. 423–61.

A classified and complete bibliography up to 1984 on basic topics: method, classification, and comparison of languages; typology and morphology; reconstruction and diachronic development; problems and future tasks. Slav scholars are included.

1.6.   M. Goshen-Gottstein, "The Present State of Comparative Semitic Linguistics," in A. S. Kaye, ed., *Semitic Studies in Honor of Wolf Leslau...* Wiesbaden, 1991. Pp. 558–69.

A short and unimportant reflection on well-known facts of the history of comparative Semitics and suggestions for the future; on this topic see also his "Ethiopian-Chaldean and the Beginnings of Comparative Semitics in Renaissance Times," in P. Fronzaroli, ed., *Atti del secondo...* 1978, p. 149: on the term "Chaldæan" in the sixteenth century; also "Comparative Semitics," in *Essays in Honor of the Seventieth Anniversary of the Dropsie University*. Baltimore, 1979. Pp. 14ff.

1.7.   J. Huehnergard, "New Directions in the Study of Semitic Languages," in J. S. Cooper, G. M. Schwartz, eds., *The Study of the Ancient Near East in the Twenty-first Century. The William Foxwell Albright Centennial Conference*. Winona Lake, Ind., 1996. Pp. 251–72.

A good summary of the contributions to the descriptive grammar, classification, and the diachrony of the Semitic languages, but, above all, it is a program of *desiderata*. The author insists on the "developmental approach" and "nodal" reconstruction for branches in general Hamito-Semitics as a task for the future, on the application of general linguistic theory to Semitics, on historical linguistics. and on the use of electronic techniques in the study of Semitic languages and the compilation of their lexical data.

A new survey has been offered by the same author: "Comparative Semitic Linguistics," in Sh. Izre'el, ed., *Semitic Linguistics: The State of the Art at the Turn of the Twenty-First Century* (IOS 20). Winona Lake, Ind. 2002. Pp. 119–50.

1.8. S. A. Kaufman, "Semitics: Directions and Re-Directions," in J. S. Cooper and G. M. Schwartz, eds., *The Study of the Ancient Near East in the Twenty-first Century. The William Foxwell Albright Centennial Conference.* Winona Lake, Ind., 1996. Pp. 273–82.

This is a rather harsh critique of the failings and lack of open-mindedness of modern Semitic scholars, both philologists and epigraphists, with an avowed nostalgia for the great masters of the past (such as Albright) and a long list of questions to revise and tasks to carry out, none touching on our problem.

1.9. A. Zaborski, "Comparative Semitic Studies: *status quaestionis*," in *PBSCS* (*AuOr* 23 [2005]), pp. 9–15.

A short but very illuminating paper that gathers and revises contributions made mainly after 1961, including not only general syntheses but also significant studies on Semitic phonology, morphology, syntax, lexicography, and the reconstruction of Proto-Semitic. Particular attention is given to the reconstruction of the Proto-Semitic verbal system. Interesting insights are offered regarding the classification of the Semitic languages, which are viewed as a dialect *continuum*. Zaborski writes in favor of the Hamito-Semitic perspective in comparative Semitic studies. He advocates the creation of a journal and supplement series devoted to comparative Afro-Asiatic linguistics.

2. Thematic Studies

What does "root" mean in Semitic and what are its components? The question may seem simple and self-evident, but, in fact, there is no unanimity on the subject and the different answers stem from attitudes that derive from divergent theories of the general problem of the structure of the Semitic root.

2.1. J. Cantineau, in two short articles (1950),[3] based the interpretation of all Semitic morphematics (morphology) on the concepts of "root" (consonantal components, e.g., /b-y-d/) and "pattern" (phonic silhouette, e.g., /'abyad/). He defended (against Brockelmann) the idea of "root" as a valid and functionally very useful "abstraction." "So there are two great intersecting systems, enclosing within their network the whole mass of Semitic vocabulary" (see Cantineau 1950(a), p. 123; 1950(b), p. 74).

This is the well-known classic point of view, found in the grammars of the various Semitic languages and is claimed to be put into practice, justified, and analyzed in its lexical and grammatical implications.[4] In this sense, the second article, which reproduces part of the first, tries to identify the consequences that a change of pattern could have from a grammatical and lexical point of view, as can be seen in some Semitic languages (dialectal Arabic and Syriac); he finds in masoretic Hebrew the culmination of this change. Classical Arabic, instead, presents the more complete and more stable list of lexical patterns in Semitic. The semantic load, at least the primary semantic load, is applied to the consonantal root, while the pattern only entails derivational and grammatical modifications. This point of view is still followed today by many scholars.[5]

In our time, the distinction has also been applied to the analysis of Egyptian morphology (*root-and-pattern*), even though it has its own characteristics. In pure Cantineau mode, C. Reintges states (1994):[6] "I will show that the morphological component of this language is organized around relatively abstract form-meaning representations (*roots*) and physically interpretable surface forms (*stems*)." The generative process of derivation is organized as moving from one level to the other. The problem of transformations, both of patterns and of roots, was studied a few years later (1984) from the same viewpoint by L. Galand,[7] in connection with the Touareg language. Although the system holds up well in general, it still presents deformations in that language, which could well be the rule for the whole of Afro-Asiatic.

Cantineau proposes an interesting distinction between root ("essential common radical element"), which underlines the changes in the vocalism, and base (unmodified common radical element, sometimes simply called "radical"), which includes it. Instead, for Brockelmann and Indo-European scholars, the base is a simple fundamental form that once had, or still has, its own existence (in fact, it is a "base word") and the root is an abstraction that is simply taxonomic and didactic, but not scientific. For Cantineau the root is not an ancient "historical" form but definitely an "abstract" concept although operative in Semitic, often in the guise of homophony, i.e., with differing semantic meanings. It is clearly present in the Semitic lexicon as a formal unit (consonantal group) that is also a semantic unit. In other words, as "a linguistic sign" composed of "signifier" (*signifiant*) and "signified" (*signifié*) in Saussure's terminology. The pattern attains this same characteristic of a sign, also carrying form and its own meanings.

As can be seen, it is a question (root-pattern) of the lexico-morphological evidence of Semitic languages that is difficult to avoid, but that remains on this side of the question of the original or primitive structure of the Semitic lexical morpheme (the "root") and does not affect either its basic constitution—even consonantal (with one, two or three components)—or the "radical" nature of the vowels. The dominant triconsonantalism is assumed to be the norm. These articles by a renowned Semitist are evidence of what research had undertaken in its earlier stages, careful to be precise and based on evidence. (In pp. 14–15 I shall describe my own position with respect to this terminology, where other concepts, such as "stem," mentioned by Reintges, will be brought into the discussion.)

2.2.   Some years later (1965/1970), in an article that I will comment on later with regard to the structure of the root, I. M. Djakonoff again raised this question, including the vowels as well, beyond considering it as only having consonantal structure. "The notion 'root' is certainly no more than an abstraction with no real content unless under the conditions existing in real words."[8]

Clearly, the root that Djakonoff is studying, and that he will distinguish into two separate groups, "nominal" and "verbal," is closer to the concept of "base" than the one proposed by Cantineau. Now the problem is to find the structure of this root morpheme in the empirical base. The division into two groups harks back to ancient tradition and was to be accepted by many modern scholars. These are matters to which we will return.

These ideas were first formulated in his general work on the Hamito-Semitic or Afro-Asiatic languages (1965, 1967, 1988). In the last edition to appear,[9] a complete chapter is devoted to our specific topic: "Root and Word Formation," which summarizes his 1970 article.

In a review of this work, D. Cohen (1972) expresses his reservations about this theory on the structure of the Semitic root.[10] He defends the classical concept of its "abstract" character, which has to be applied also in the case of nominal roots with their own vocalization according to Djakonoff, as against verbal roots, which were the preferred object of study in classical theory. His concept of an "historical base" of the derivation the Russian author uses when speaking of original nominal roots also includes, according to Cohen, a "pattern," which as the root of derivation functions uniquely from its consonantism.

The same ideas were repeated by Cohen in a later contribution (1978),[11] which emphasizes that the functionality of the "root" is evident even in loanwords. This restatement, however, did not seem satisfactory to Djakonoff, who once more insisted on his point of view: "in all these cases we have every reason to consider as roots the forms *kalb-*, etc." (p. 45).

We are dealing with two different points of view, depending on whether or not they admit the original vowels to have "radical" significance, an issue we will later discuss.

2.3.   At the same time, and in relation to Semitic lexicography, P. Fronzaroli (1973) re-introduced the question of the need to accept original nouns or nominal bases with unmotivated vocalization alongside the concepts of "root," "pattern," and "stem" (Cantineau), and precisely in opposition to the latter, understood such base as "the interdigitation of a discontinuous morpheme in the root."[12] Such bases (and only triconsonantal bases are in question here) whose vocalic variation can be explained in the various languages by means of phonetic changes or analogies of derivation coexist, differentiated from (verbal) "roots" in the preliterary phase (common Semitic), without submitting to the laws of incompatibility and derivation / extension (since prefixes are not accepted). But for the verbal root one can also foresee an unmotivated original vocalization, which is different for action verbs (forms with prefixes) and for state verbs (forms with suffixes), even though its general function is apophonic by preference. At all events, a phase preceding Common Semitic cannot be excluded where this unmotivated lexical vocalism can be explained.

2.4.   In a survey (1974),[13] K. Petráček also raises the issue of the structure of the root in Semitic and, in a summary fashion, its historical treatment within the Hamito-Semitic family. As a decisive factor for a typology of Semitic roots he points to the presence or absence of a vowel, a hotly disputed matter as we have just seen: "From it one could deduce the often-cited thesis that the original vowel has been replaced by a vocalic pattern with a grammatical function" (p. 116), in agreement with the occurrence of this feature in Hamito-Semitic. In the Semitic family, the vowel is missing from verbal roots and present in nominal roots that also lose it through change. Petráček formalizes his system, playing with the concepts of "root," "pattern" (vocalic pattern), and analytical "stem" (root + pattern) and synthetic "stem" (the root alone). Consonants and vowels, whether or not bearing semantic and grammatical functions, in agreement with the various "patterns," also have a role. In this sense, the role of internal inflection and the correlative derivation become determinative. One can classify the various Hamito-Semitic languages in terms of how each realizes the model. As a result, one might conclude that the Chadic and Cushitic languages represent its oldest stage. "But what is really characteristic of the Hamito-Semitic languages is the delimitation of semantic and grammatical functions by vowels (V) and consonants (C) and, at the same time, the development mentioned of the structure of the RP type (R: consonantal root; P: vocalic pattern) from the root CV" (p. 119).

2.5.   S. S. Majzel' (1983) devotes two chapters, in his posthumously published book, to the question of the Semitic root (see below p. 83), in which the tradition of the Russian school is retained, at least up to a certain point.[14] Vowels (extra-short vowels) serve only for the pronunciation of the consonants. In addition, triconosontalism becomes the premise for removing vowels from the root, of which the basic element is the consonantal component. Thus, from the aspect of phonology, this component appears abstract, but remains no less real and semantically concrete than the Indo-European consonantal-vocalic root. However, he criticizes the theory of the "biconsonantal cell" defended by Jusmanov (see below pp. 72–73) within the framework of his exposition of theories of the origin of the Semitic root.

2.6.   In a very interesting study that is polemical—even belligerent, one could say—which I will discuss in connection with the issue of biliterality, R. M. Voigt (1988) proposes a new analytical method that enables the deep level of the various morphemes to be reached:[15] "In Semitic, in fact, the phonemes are organized into a morpheme by a root and a (nominal or verbal) pattern. We refer to root and pattern as monemes. Both consist of phonemes and by intersecting produce morphemes. Monemes and morphemes belong to the category of pleremes. Therefore, monemes can be referred to as discontinuous pleremes" (p. 17 and n. 4).

Thus, Voigt accepts Cantineau's terminology, but from the perspective of structural analysis according to a "one-dimensional layering" (namely, according to the sequence: "sentence, morpheme, moneme, phoneme, distinctive feature," p. 18) in two directions: one ascending (*"Morphemisierung"*) and the other descending (*"Monemisierung,"* pp. 36f.), a very important concept for our perspective, that is to say, etymological inquiry. It belongs to Voigt's perspective only to the extent that it justifies his pan-triliteral theory, especially in the case of so-called "weak" verbal roots. In any case, it constitutes a necessary tool for the description of the Semitic languages. "Monemisation of the open morpheme class represents a kind of segmentation by root and pattern. Monemisation means the analysis of the nuclear morpheme classes into two opposing pervasive discontinuous units, which are called root and pattern" (pp. 36f.). We will have the opportunity to return to these ideas and the author's peculiar concept of weak "roots," in the composition of which vowels can take on the "radical" function / position of consonants.

Another interesting contribution by Voigt that must be taken into account is the distinction he borrows from Jungraithmayr of "functional / synchronic" and "etymological / historical" root (pp. 164f.), which he uses to justify his own etymological inquiry *"Monemisierung"* of weak roots, but which is valid more generally.[16]

2.7.   In opposition to the generalized morphological typology, which by now had become classic, of the "interdigitation" (= intersection) of the discontinuous root morpheme (semantics) and the vocalic pattern (grammar), G. M. Schramm (1991) shows the violence effected on many nouns when they are reduced to verbal "roots," especially "tiny" or short nouns.[17] Instead, it is necessary to suppose two different types of Semitic roots, one linear or continuous and the other discontinuous. Continuous roots derive from continuous bases by the bias of apophony; the other roots, which are verbal, come from a root that would generate a base from which the future form proceeds and then all the other forms. Once again, the vowel is inherent in the root. This verbal base has the form /ABvC/ in strong verbs; the weak verbs have one or more glides instead of consonants. The verbal base corresponds to the imperative, from which all the others are derived by means of prefixes, suffixes, and apophony in a fixed and predictable way. However, the formalization of this derivation does not concern us at the moment.

2.8. In the same sense, but focusing on the structure of the root in Arabic, some years later (1993) G. Bohas[18] presented a study based on the phonological theory formulated by J. J. McCarthy (1979).[19] In the representation underlying the Arabic, he distinguishes the "vocalic melody," the "consonant melody," and the "skeleton," in combination with the syllabic component in which they are conjugated in linear association from left to right (McCarthy). Taking this kind of association into account, the biliteral character of so-called geminated roots, as well as the impossibility of reduplicating the first consonant, is deduced by reason of the OCP ("Obligatory Contour Principle"), which will be discussed later. In this way we can have biliteral "roots" and triliteral "patterns" or skeletons and attain a more direct analysis of the root structure or consonantal melody. As is easily seen, the analysis corresponds basically to Cantineau's (root-pattern) analysis, but, in line with the recent trend noted above, it has the merit of including in the analysis of the underlying representation of the root the vocalic component. In addition, Bohas distinguishes the diachronic level of the original base and its grammatical development, or what amounts to the same thing, the generation and extension of the triconsonantal pattern imposed by lexematic expansion. He then tries to explain this in every case possible by various principles: directional association (McCarthy), association of the margins with fillers and diffusion (Yip), epenthesis and free association (Guerssel-Loewenstamm), and theory of government (Kaye-Loewenstamm). But all this belongs rather to derivational morphology and it will be discussed later in connection with the generation of triconsonantal patterns.

In another article in the same publication, G. Bohas (1993) discussed specifically Cantineau's binomial, "root"/"pattern," and their intersection, as an explanation of Semitic morphology.[20] He thinks that this binomial is inadequate and that a third "larron" (gap or link) is missing "which is only another pattern" (p. 46). Accordingly, account must be taken of the nature of certain phonemes in the root and of the grammatical semantic function of the forms in order to determine the distribution of the patterns. That is, there is no mechanical intersecting of root and pattern, but instead hierarchy and pre-determination, starting from the *maṣdar*, following the opinion of Arab grammarians and against the opinion of modern scholars such as Yip and McCarthy (p. 53). This clarification is very interesting because it introduces apparently a vocalized base into the heart of the lexical system, but I think that it is incorrect with respect to Cantineau's aim. He puts the *"croisement"* (crossing, intersection) between root and pattern at a synchronic and empirical level, not at the generative or diachronic level of morphematic distribution that can be predicted: for him these variations are just other patterns.

G. Bohas (1997, 2000) hardened the implications of his theory, already suggested in the studies mentioned, in a new and radical direction.[21] It is as an extension of his earlier opinions on the components of the root in Semitic, with the new concepts that he had introduced. In the first study he literally repeats the studies cited above (and others on biliteralism that will be cited below) in connection with the structure of the Semitic radical morpheme and its phonological shape, but incorporated into new developments. For example, he accepts Djakonoff's suggestion in respect of base-nouns, which he would like to be able to link to his general system explaining the root of Semitic biliteral lexis, admitting for all an extension by suffix, as Djakonoff proposes for the category of wild animals (/-b/). Even the "irreducible" nouns (cf. pp. 186f.) would thus form part of a uniform (pan-)biliteral base system. The structure of this base, in connection with the consonantal melody, has three levels: matrix, etymon, root. The first represents "a non-ordered combination of two areas of articulation"; the second, "a non-ordered combination of two phonemes"; the third is the etymon (root) lengthened by diffusion / addition (triliteral in principle) and ordered. It is at the third level that empirical (not original) vocalism appears and where grammar to its fullest extent becomes operative. The semantic load linked to the three becomes progressively more specific.

Bohas concluded: "In this system there is no room for the triconsonantal root" (p. 9). I will return to this question later as well as to the more disputed aspect of the "non-ordonnance" (or reversibility) of matrices and etymons. For the time being it is enough to note that, even though operating with ideas that had previously been formulated, this approach is completely original in its systematic development. In connection with our present subject of the arrangement of the "root" it implies actually two levels of the idea of "root," which could be called respectively "generative" (matrix and etymon) and "functional" (root), and does not consider the existence of an original vocalization. This means that the concept of "base" does not appear, as matrix and etymon are "abstract realities," which he readily admits. The very concept of "root," since the "root" is itself a derived element, remains dissolved in the other two. In other words, we are back to the consonantal "root" (the etymon is a root, but biliteral) and to morphological "patterns," but set now at different levels.

In his second and most recent work (2000), Bohas insists on these ideas, adding as the main novelty, in connection with what we are now discussing, the concept of the "matrix" as a combination of "two phonetic features," not of two areas of articulation (pronunciation). A series of these binary combinations and general topics related to the expansion of the root are developed in this work. These will be discussed later.

2.9.   While accepting as valid Cantineau's theory on the intersection of "root" and "pattern," G. Goldenberg (1994) prefers to speak of the "interdigitation" of two discontinuous morphemes as the basis of morphological derivation.[22] But one must also take into account other elements besides the pattern, such as augments and extensions. On the other hand, root and etymon (base) have to be distinguished. The etymon is mono-morphemic (Dressler) and includes a root vowel, whereas the root is a discontinuous morpheme required for derivational morphological analysis, the primitive vowel being secondary in this respect. Even if the scholar's interest is focused on the derivational process, his comments are very relevant for an exact understanding of the "lexical morpheme" at the original or etymological level.

2.10. A final study, by A. R. Bomhard (1999), although focused on analysis of the structure of the root in Proto-Indo-European and Proto-Afro-Asiatic, presents an interesting approach for the problem concerning us.[23] He starts from a definition of "root" ("the base form of a word") and of "stem" ("an inflexional base"), where one can clearly see that he distances himself from Cantineau's abstract concept of "root."

2.11. Finally, in the same perspective, D. Baggioni and P. Larcher (2000)[24] again take up the notion of "root" in its various acceptations (Indo-European, Semitic, the acceptations of various Arab grammarians) as "reconstruction" or "abstraction," starting especially from the formulations of Cantineau and Cohen, as well as that of Benveniste: root and pattern, nominal and verbal roots, derivation by denomination, deverbation by expansions / consonantal affixes, and the semantic function of each of these elements. They point out the difficulties that such formulations create, especially for the morphological analysis of Arabic. These scholars favor replacing "root" by "radical," following Indo-European usage, since it is more relevant in the derivational and verbal system, especially of Arabic (by affixes and apophony). Thus, it is not a matter of doing without the vowels—which would be unthinkable in Indo-European—even if here we also have multiple apophonic forms with the same consonantal group. Similarly, the root must not be considered as the principle of verbal "derivation." For Arab grammarians, as Bohas notes, this derivation comes from *maṣdar* and *ism ǧāmid*. Derivation from the root is an incorrect idea and contrary to the diachronic flow.

Once again we see the extent to which the inclusion of the vowel in the radical lexical morpheme has made headway in generic studies on the structure and componential analysis of the root. Later, when discussing this structure itself, we will deal with the topic directly. Undoubtedly it is an item of information that has to be considered.

2.12. A close discussion of the terms and notions here involved has recently been carried out by J. Sanmartín (2005).[25] He analyzes the functionality of the interdigitation model (base and theme) in language acquisition, as well as its semantic potential. Both elements intimately related and each one with its semantic valence makes up the (mono-morphemic) root. Pre-eminence goes to the theme: "it may be said, that the theme, while interdigitating with the base, works on it like *forma* on *materia*: it bestows conceptual (and therefore linguistic) reality on the base" (p. 73). It works as a "semantic formalizer." A future task will be the study of "the semantic relationship of both with some primary semantemes and lexical universal" (p. 77).

3. Appraisal

After considering all these opinions on the root we can take stock and retain some ideas that seem to be compelling in a coherent way. First of all, two levels of application of the concept of root have to be distinguished.[26]

The first is the functional level, the level of synchronic or morphological analysis. In this domain, the use of the root as an abstract morpheme by intersection or "interdigitation" with the pattern is completely valid, not only as a method of teaching but also as an operating system that has become structural at the derivational level (Cantineau, Cohen, Goldenberg, etc.). As Rosén states:[27] "The root in Semitic and in Indo-European, as well as most likely in other genealogical entities, is a real, living functional unit with a given normal phonemic patterning, which furthers a tendency for those radical units, that do not show it originally, to assimilate themselves to it."

Voigt's systematic use of this pattern may be accepted at this level, even if we think that he uses the phonological functions of the base in an illegitimate, or at least equivocal, way. In any case, for him this explanation is not merely a superficial explanation but reaches the deep structure of the lexeme (at the level of the moneme).[28] If a biliteral structure is accepted as probable in certain cases, as accepted by him, his claim of wishing to sketch out a universal triliteral pattern has no purpose and, therefore, neither has his recourse to the distortion of phonological concepts that that entails. Later we shall return to a more detailed critique of Voigt's thesis.

The second level is generative or diachronic, the level of primitive or "etymological" forms. At this level I prefer to speak of "base"/ "stem" (either on its own or as supporting inflection) rather than of root, which remains reserved to the first level. At all events, the concept of "stem" is not univocal. For some scholars, "stem," as opposed to "root," is the actual form at a superficial level, that is to say, an interdigitated "pattern," whereas for others "stem" is the lexical "base" as a mono-morpheme, acting as a support for inflection and derivation, a view I share.[29] Starting from or within this base, both nominal and verbal patterns are generated by affixation and apophony,[30] in agreement with the functions of internal and derivational inflection.

On the other hand, this means assuming the vowels of both the nominal and verbal bases as radical constituents, leaving the consonantal abstraction for the functional level mentioned above. This concept of base is, to a large extent, very much like the one used in Indo-European and at this etymological level, enables one to speak of a "continuous radical mono-morpheme."[31] As we shall see later, this is, in fact, the opinion defended by Djakonoff in his study of the structure of the root in Semitic, which I will analyze in detail.

As for the contribution of G. Bohas, it must be noted that if it proves to be valid for Arabic it must also be valid for the whole Semitic family and even for the Afro-Asiatic super-family, given the level of pure phonological realization, where the matrix structure is located (this may even include the Nostratic or long distance comparative macro-family and would become the definitive proof (!) that it existed as a language). In fact, this theory is open to this universal linguistic perspective. But it is precisely this perspective that makes it suspect and leads to the greatest reservations about it. It has to be submitted to minute analysis, which I will attempt later. For the moment, we remain on the level of what Bohas calls the etymon or a combination of articulatory phonemes.

On the other hand, he does not take full account of the role of radical vocalism, as he had originally in his 1993 writings. In his later work he views its structures as only consonantal from the aspect of phonology and semantics. Consequently he maintains attitudes that are, to some extent, obsolete. His matrices and etymons turn out to be "abstract roots." One could say that it is a problem that does not worry him, as his interest lies in proving the original biliteralism of the Semitic languages.

In fact, the Semitic "root" or original lexical morpheme is a historical linguistic reality with a complex phonological composition that is "symphonic" (consonant + vowel) and has a specific semantic meaning. It is the "base" (degree zero, in Djakonoff's terminology) or "stem" (inflected degree),[32] from which the syntagmatic correlation with other lexemes takes place, resulting in a unit of communication of meaning, the sentence or clause. This dynamic concept of the "root" implies that we should speak not only of the radical or thematic vowel but also of the "complement" of inflection, which originally was vocalic. It is to Djakonoff's credit to have postulated for the primary nouns this twofold degree of realization: 0 / inflectional.[33] For reasons we will present later, and in a hypothetical way, one could think that the original lexematic alternation was not degree 0 / inflection, but "absolute" or indeterminate state (neutral vowel /ə/) / determined state (oppositional vowel /u:a/). This would be the first degree of "grammatical" or morphematic development.

The two degrees represent each of the original historical Proto-Semitic realizations in agreement with the various functions of the syntagmatic relation. As previously stated, a pre-inflectional stage of the lexeme is a simple abstraction that cannot be verified, which is prehistoric in Semitic and refers at least to the pre-Proto-Afro-Asiatic level, when this constituent feature of the group (inflection) had not yet been developed. As far as we can prove, that is to say at the Proto-Semitic level, and even at the Proto-Afro-Asiatic level, "in the beginning was the word" (*horribile dictu!*), i.e., the morphosyntagm, not simply the "root." It is not a question of a linguistic stage of pure lexicality, if that can be imagined. In quoting Coseriu we can say that even at this level "in a language, by every lexeme used in a speech-act, sentence functions are expressed at the same time."[34] I postulate this union of lexematics and syntagmatics not only at the level of the "word," but also at the level of the "base"/"stem."

If etymology claims to carry out research on the proto-lexeme, what it finds, in fact, is a proto-morphosyntax, an original proto-grammar, set in motion by elements that are even more primitive (the morphematic functorial series and the deictic pronominal series) than lexical morphemes, The "deixes" seem to be "older" than "words" and the only ones as such that can end in a (non-inflectional) vowel. In this sense one can agree with Cantineau's classical system, according to which semantics is linked to the "consonantal skeleton," just as grammar is linked to the "vocalic melody," a value that is not only functional and synchronic but also primitive, provided that one accepts the "continuity" of the two elements (consonant and vowel) in the structure of the original lexical mono-morpheme. That means that the original "consonantal skeleton" must include radical vowels also (pure consonantal articulation is impossible) and the "vocalic melody" must be complemented with consonantal elements in its organization of the grammatical development (inflection), leaving aside the morphological expanded patterns of second degree.

II

THE STRUCTURE OF THE SEMITIC ROOT
GENERAL PROBLEMS

After setting out my own views on the general organization of the root as a lexical morpheme in its components, as well as my preferred perspective or generative horizon, we now examine the more concrete matter of its structure. Even if our viewpoint is limited to the field of Semitics, the primary level within which our research is conducted always makes it necessary to move beyond this limit, which in any case is not precise, and to refer constantly to Afro-Asiatic and sometimes to Indo-European. The Semitic family is definitely not the universal primitive language, "the language of Adam," but rather a relatively recent cultural development within the linguistic evolution of humankind. This means that it shares with other families, called Afro-Asiatic, many linguistic epiphenomena at a very remote genetic level. In other words: the proto-level of a language is common ground to all its related languages.

1. The History of Research

1.1. At the core of the Russian tradition, continuing the work of Jušmanov (see below p. 54), are the writings of V. P. Starinin (1963).[1] He is not concerned with the structure of the "root" but rather of the "word," that is, the question of "inflection," both internal and derived. Starinin reflects on the nature of the Semitic root, which he considers to be consonantal and clearly separable from derivative affixes, especially nominal bases, making these Semitic languages appear to be agglutinative. These are different from their Indo-European counterparts. Without dealing directly with the problem of root structure, his writings provide evidence of the traditional interest of Russian Semitists in basic problems of Semitic lexico-morphology.

1.2. I. M. Djakonoff (1970) has made what may be considered the most important global and innovative contribution so far to the question of the "structure of the root" in Proto-Semitic.[2] Emphasis is laid on triliteral (nominal) morphology, without discussing the existence of biliteral roots, which are equally accepted, or their structure. He reiterates his previous proposals (1965, 1967),[3] which would be summarized in a later publication (1988).[4]

The first task to be faced in this research, according to Djakonoff, is to set out its frame of reference. In fact, research on the structure of the Hamito-Semitic root and its proto-forms can be begun only from Semitic, given that it is the only linguistic family providing enough data for this purpose, as Egyptian is attested only in consonantal form. The other families, including Egyptian, according to Djakonoff, can contribute only elements of confirmation and support. Nevertheless, research on Proto-Semitic, given its primary level, certainly leads beyond the Semitic horizon, as we shall see and as Djakonoff himself later admits. In his work, then, there is a degree of tension in delimiting the horizon of work for research on Proto-Semitic: he acknowledges that only Semitic data offer a scientific guarantee, but, at the same time, he senses the need to go beyond that.

As his starting-point Djakonoff makes a distinction between verbal "roots," with functional apophonic vocalization, and primary nominal (not "deverbal") "bases," with fixed vocalization that is not semantically determined. Their apophonic variations with respect to state and number must be taken as secondary developments. In this connection, Northwest Semitic and Akkadian provide the most reliable models. As a result, the vocalization is definitively included in the structure of the root, beyond considering it as pattern / consonantal melody. This consonantal "root" is a simple "abstraction," "with no real content unless under the conditions existing in real words" (1970, p. 455). The issue is how the root morpheme actually fits the "verbal base," especially as regards its vocalization.

The collection of nominal root morphemes is viewed as a closed system. Their vocalic structure is completely different from the classical Proto-Semitic structure of six vowels (a/ā, i/ī, u/ū). In this structure the long vowels are missing and /u/ results from apophony of /ī/ on contact with labials, palatals, and the laryngeal / ᵓ/ (p. 455 n. 9). As a result, the new vowel system remains reduced in the contrast / binary opposition /u::i::a/, as happens in the reconstruction of Indo-European. In addition, the vowel /a/ can equally become /i/ for reasons of stress and intonation. On the other hand, one notices in this system the special role of the so-called "sonant" phonemes (/l, m, n, r, ᵓ, h/) and "semi-vowels" (/w, y/). In this manner certain phonemes are considered to have two functions: vocalic in the /SC/ position (a position in which the vowel /a/ forms a diphthong with the sonant) and consonantal in the /SV/ position, in agreement with the inflection and the syllabic structure of the root morpheme. Taking these data into account, Djakonoff formulated a series of laws and models of syllabic incompatibility that govern the structure of the nominal root morpheme, agreeing with laws that are considered unbreakable in Semitic phonology, i.e., a syllable cannot begin with a vowel nor can it either begin or close with more than one consonant (except in contiguous syllables). It is also necessary to presuppose that "a primary nominal root morpheme may contain either two or three different consonants, and either one vowel or two" (1967, p. 456). In the case of a nominal morpheme of three consonants and one vowel, its possible structures would be / CvCS/ or else /CaSC/, that is, one of the two final consonants must be a sonant.

This diagram of the subsystem of nominal root morphemes, which comprises two vowels and seven sonants, reflects a stage preceding Proto-[Hamito-]Semitic with six vowels, and should be defined as Pre-Proto-Hamito-Semitic, in any case earlier than Proto-Semitic. By this means we clearly leave the perspective set out in the title of his paper, since Proto-Semitic refers beyond itself, as is also the case in Indo-European. In fact, this vocalization remains tied to the syllabic structure of Semitic in general and to its law of the formation of only two possible types of syllable: /CV/, /CVC/,[5] but taking into account the twofold function of "sonants." One must exclude the juxtaposition of two consonants or two vowels in the same syllable. As a result, Djakonoff gives the descriptive list of possible syllables, excluding those that are impossible: /CV/[= SV, CS, SS], /CVC/[= CVC, CSC, CSS, SVS, SSC, SSS]. To this must be added the law of syllabic contact, which excludes the coincidence, at the boundary between two syllables, of more than two consonants and, therefore, "that a sonant cannot precede or follow a cluster of two non-sonorant consonants" (1967, p. 458).

Furthermore, it must be considered, as I noted in the first chapter, that the Proto-Semitic noun can occur with the case/degree 0 or else with suffixation of vocalic inflection, which later has the vocalic polarity of the base mentioned above, as can be seen by its functions in Akkadian (and even in Egyptian): /ə(i/u)::a/. In fact, its radical structure as a morpheme has to obey this twofold realization according to the phonological laws just mentioned. This supposes that no nominal root morpheme can end in two consonants or in a vowel. This, therefore, excludes, in principle, the possibility of having primitive monoconsonantal Semitic nouns, as I discovered empirically, independently of Djakonoff, when studying the monoconsonantal lexical series in Semitic.[6] The few examples that are usually cited (/g/, /š/, /p/, /m/) are probably loans or else biliterals at the Proto-Semitic level. As a result, all nouns of the type /CvCC/ must be considered (1) as secondary or deverbal, following Djakonoff (and the same must be said of /Ci :uSC/); and in this situation, the role of sonants (2) with their twofold function, is completely decisive, in both monosyllabic and disyllabic morphemes. In this manner we have five possible types of nominal root morphemes: /CS/, /CvC(C)/, /CVCS/, /CvCvS/, /CvCCvC/ and equivalents (permutations with /S/). Moreover, these morphemes can have expansions by suffix with their own semantic meaning: /-am/, /-(a)b/, /-(a)r:l/, /-(ā)r:l/ /-y/, /-t/.

Djakonoff seeks to note, verify, and explain the apparent exceptions to his outline of the structure of the nominal root morpheme. Thus, he first established that (1) very few of the primary nouns, apparently, present a long vowel [/bāb/ < /baʔbaʔ/, /dā:am/ < rhythmical analogical formation (*Analogiebildung*) of /CaSC/, /ʔilāh:'il/, /ʔinās/]; and (2) only a small number present a vocalic alternation [i/u]—the /u/ occurs before and after only the labials [/b, p, m/]) and the velars (/g, q, k/) and (/ʔ/). Djakonoff lists these primary nouns with the vowel /u/, originally /ə/ in the various Semitic languages, which in turn present their own historical phenomena of phonetic transformation (change). Despite insufficient lexical material, it is possible to verify some constancy in the realization of the primitive vowel /ə/ [u:i] in these sequences, depending on the language, for example, */-am-/: Akk. ʔum, Heb. ʔim, Aram. ʔim, Ar. ʔum.

The vowel /a/, characteristic of the nominal root morphemes and the disyllabic bases (/CvCvC(+v)/, /CvCS(+v)/) occurs under "phonotactic conditions" peculiar to each language, so that it is sometimes difficult to determine the lexical pattern (for example /CvCvC-/ // /CvCC-/) or whether they are nominal or verbal roots. At first, the presence of pharyngeal phonemes (/ᶜ, ḥ/) produces the well-known "coloration" in /a/ and does not permit the original vowel to be identified in certain cases /ə::a/, which is recognizable as primitive despite the treatment peculiar to Arabic and Akkadian in this case. In other cases, there is a weakening of these phonemes in first position with unstable vowels in the various languages. The other root morphemes and their extensions by the afformative suffixes mentioned above are divided into two groups: those with a stable vowel /ə[i/u]/ or /a/ on contact with the pharyngeals *H {<ᶜ}, the others with unstable /a/ in the first syllable, as can be seen in the various languages: in Arabic and Hebrew, normally /a/, in Akkadian, Aramaic and Ethiopic, /i/.[7] Each language develops its own historical phonology; for example, Arabic would have /i/ in first position if the second vowel is long, but /a/ if it is short. The position of the stress (*accent grave*) undoubtedly plays a decisive role in determining the stability of the vowels: /ə/ > /i/ (/u/ before a labial); /a/ > /aːi/.

From these data Djakonoff illustrates the realization of the five models of nominal root morphemes established above, and the claimed function of "sonant" phonemes in their composition, with a long list of examples that occur in more than one language (/CS/, /CvC/, /CvCS/, /CvCvC/). There is, however, some confusion in this regard. Are the roots or bases of the /CSC/ type, which are alternatives to the /CVC/ type, biliteral or triliteral in origin? Is the sonant / semivowel [w:y] vocalic, that is, a strengthened vowel, or does it form a diphthong? How does it enter the root lexeme, as a simple glide? Thus the limit between vocalism and consonantalism remains somewhat blurred and his distinction seems inadequate.

Djakonoff analyzes also some dubious forms and patterns, such as forms extended by rhythmical analogy (*dām, māʾ, šāʾ*) or cases of 0 (zero) inflection, which can produce changes in the vocalization, especially of groups with sonants, as in Assyrian and Aramaic, and generate confusion and a mix of patterns. Most often, the pattern /CvCS-/ becomes /CvCvS/, following the model /CvSC-/ → /CaSaC-/, and there occur vocalizations of the diminutive type (/CaCiC-/, /CəCiC-/). The anomalies are multiplied in the derived forms, both nominal and verbal, especially in languages where internal (plural) inflection is very predominant. Account has also to be taken of original variant radicals (allophones).

Lastly, Djakonoff deals with the problem of the subsystem of verbal roots and their derivation, considered to be different from and later than nominal inflection. He postulates a system of six vowels, essential for its diachronic apophonic development (Kuryłowicz). In this case, the reconstruction of the pre-Proto-Semitic level is much more difficult and hypothetical. There is no need to include a sonant in its triliteralism and its original vocalization is almost indefinable. Supposedly, *a priori*, it is provided by the /yqtl/ form, but its vocalization reveals itself as apophonic from its origin. Now, if verbal inflection supposes the system of independent pronouns from which the verbal affixes emerge, "in this case there is no reason to believe that the root morpheme with verbal semantic (*sic!*) would formally differ in any way from that with nominal semantic; this brings us to the necessity of reconstructing the primary verbal root morpheme as, in principle, identical in pattern with the primary (*nominal*) root morpheme; which means that it must have included a vowel" (p. 476 n. 110).

The force of this logic should lead even further, even as far as imposing the abolition of any lexematic distinction between the two groups, reducing them to one: object and action coincide originally from the phonological and semantic aspects, even if to do this one must discard certain discriminating distinctions that are required in nominal root morphemes, as, for example, the necessary presence of a sonant in monosyllables. This unification means also lengthening the list of primary nouns / verbs (or, in short, "roots" / primary or "nominal" bases," in effect, all of them).

It is necessary to inquire into the form that verbal root originally had, because, as such, it must form part of an empirical system and "abstract roots" should not be looked for. After excluding other forms, Djakonoff considers that one can start from the stative participle (/CaCa:i:uC-/) or else from prefixed forms of the type (C:Sv-) (in fact, they have sonant prefixes: *ma-*, *ya-*) that accept suffixation and also the alternation 0/vowel. By applying the same laws of syllable formation valid for the first sub-system, four possible models result. In every case it can be ascertained "that the conditions of existence of the verbal root inside a word do not contradict the possibility of its including three consonants, none of which is a sonant, even if two of them are in contact" (p. 477). Now, *a priori*, all these models are proved historically in Proto-Hamito-Semitic: /ya-CəC-/, /ya-CCəC-/, /ya-CaC-//, /ya-CCaC-/, /ya-CaCaC-. It seems that here a process of standardization and contrastive opposition is activated with semantico-functional value (intransitive / transitive, transitory / durative) that absorbs as internal inflection the initial suffixing of the nominal model (/a/ // /ə/). That it is "usually impossible to establish any particular vowel as belonging to the [verbal] root" (p. 476) does not mean that it is negligible or that Djakonoff dispenses with it.

According to Djakonoff, this is how the Semitic verbal system has been generated and could serve as the basis for the formation and triconosonantal expansion by means of non-sonant and weak consonants. The later influence of rhythmic analogy (long vowels) and the differentiation of vowel /ə[i-u]/ have favored the creation of the rich apophonic system of nominal and verbal formations and inflections and the polarity of vowels and consonants on the stable base of the consonantal root. In this case, as well, the most original derived models will be those that correspond to the nominal models seen already (/faᶜl/, /fiᶜl/, /faᶜal/).

This amounts to acknowledging the identity of formation of the nominal and verbal roots, with some priority, even if only apparent, of the nominal base. This also amounts to admitting the original syntagmatics/grammar of the verbal base just mentioned. But the allusion to simpler nominal types will lead, as will be seen later, to looking for original verbal forms that are simpler than those adduced by Djakonoff, which, in fact, suppose a more complex and later derivational process based on the combination of the verbal base with the already developed sub-system of the pronominal series.[8]

In this way a theory of the formation of the Semitic root is created, considered by Djakonoff himself as hypothetical and requiring proof. In order to do this, a question at the more general level must be posed, without losing sight of the Hamito-Semitic perspective, when possible.

This is what Djakonoff himself has done in a further summary article (1975)[9] and in a longer study that projects these ideas to the Proto-Afro-Asiatic level (1991–1992).[10] In fact, they had been formulated first in the successive editions of general studies on the Hamito-Semitic or Afro-Asiatic languages, as we have noted above.[11]

1.3.   Within an even wider perspective, the development of the concept of "root" in Semitic has been linked, since the twentieth century and especially after Brockelmann, with its development in Indo-European.

For example, K. Petráček, after a general study, tackles the problem in the comparative perspective of the root in Indo-European and Afro-Asiatic (1982).[12] He shows the differences of original conception and gradual methodological and structural closeness in relation to, for example, primitive vocalism, to the influence of internal inflection in morphological transformation/change (with a long bibliography), and to the respective apophonies. The primary system of roots seems to be composed of the types /CC/ and /CCC/, with reciprocal pressures for lexical reasons (semantic fields), morphological reasons (inflections), and phonetic reasons (some groups disappeared). This state of affairs poses the problem of the shift of these types from one to the other, with the famous question, unresolved in its full complexity, of "complements" or "determinatives," to which we shall return later. On the other hand, the syllabic and, therefore, vocalic character of the Semitic root is increasingly being accepted (for example, a type with a predominantly monosyllabic base, according to Djakonoff), which brings the two language systems closer together. The Semitic consonantal system presents a specific problem, namely, its incompatibilities, which have been studied extensively, with respect to both nominal and verbal roots, each behaving differently. But in any case, it is a trait that to some extent they share with the Indo-European languages. The closeness of the two systems has been increased by the introduction into the field of Semitic phonetics of the group of sonant phonemes (Djakonoff), as well as the pharyngeals (Petráček, Bohas) with their specific role in the organization of the root due to their later vocalic-consonantal change and their function as glides. These phenomena must be considered in determining the etymology of "roots."

This may help to explain, in each system, the shift from biconsonantal to triconsonantal roots. In this way a reconciliation between the two theories has been reached, which Petráček summarizes in eight points, at the same time noting the tasks that have to be completed: the explanation of their convergence due to a genetic or areal relationship, as well as the agreement in the structure of their phonetic set. "There arise the following tasks of comparative Semitics, if one wishes to deepen comparative study of the root in Semitic or Indo-European: a comparative dictionary of the Semitic or Hamito-Semitic languages…and a new model of the phonetic and phonological development of the Semitic languages" (pp. 401f.).

The merit of Petráček's study is to have defined the root as a real and complex linguistic fact, which is phonological (including its vocalism), semantic, and grammatical, and also to have set the comparison with the Indo-European system, invoked since the nineteenth century, in a correct perspective.[13]

Two years later, K. Petráček (1984) devoted yet another article to the principal questions of method raised by Hamito-Semitic linguistics, with a very lengthy bibliography on this topic, starting from the postulates of the "Prague School."[14] It comprises very interesting reflections, but because of their generic nature (in large part, it is a review of the state of the question) for the moment we will leave it to one side.

The short note by the same author, published a year later, can be considered a bibliographical addition to the previous study.[15]

1.4. A more general and somewhat confused discussion, also comparing Indo-European and Semitic, has been provided by H. B. Rosén (1987).[16] It is a very useful comparison and explanation of both sets, conducted from the historical aspect of the very concept of "root" (minimal, /Cv/, /C(C)vC(C)/: Ammer, Kuryłowicz). However, the structure of Indo-European is different, as shown by the special role played by the sonants and by its peculiar syllabic structure with respect to Semitic (tri-) consonantalism and its internal inflection. Yet one can appreciate a strong concurrence of linguistic phenomena in the expansion of biliteral roots. We have already quoted his point of view on the functionality of the "root" (see p. 14).

1.5. V. Blažek (1989) has paid particular attention to this topic as part of his studies on "Nostratic."[17] After a short survey of the question, he analyzes a series of morphemes common to Indo-European and Semitic (metathesis of /n/, prefixing of /s/, /t/ and /mV-/, the glide /w/). These are not only typological but refer to the common structure of the "root," which has the basic pattern $/C_1C_2-/$ or $/C_1C_2C_3-/$. In this structure can be found certain apophonic and even sequential variations due to the presence of sonorants.

1.6. By combining the theories of Kuryłowicz and Benveniste, A. R. Bomhard (1996) has formulated a more refined pattern that is closer to Proto-Afro-Asiatic—with which Proto-Indo-European is thought to have coincided originally (Nostratic)—summarized in five principles that govern all the nominal and verbal roots, simple and extended.[18] In fact, these are the laws of syllabic formation. In this way, three basic stems (nominal, verbal, and indeclinable pronominal), are generated, of which only the last can end in a vowel. Stress appears as a differential or grammatical element, which acts on all the vowels, making them stable or disappear, creating from them two types of lengthened stems extended either by suffixes or determinatives. As for Proto-Afro-Asiatic, he starts from the opinions of Djakonoff and Ehret on the Semitic biconsonantalism of the base. The structure of the root, moreover, agrees with what has been said about Indo-European: a single initial consonant, two basic syllabic forms (CV, CVC), a radical or extended stem, and vocalism of the nominal stems. In agreement with the classical theory, meaning is ascribed to the consonantal component and the grammatical function is attributed to the vowels.

1.7. Lastly, as is the custom in manuals on comparative grammar, E. Lipiński (1997) summarizes the question, concentrating on the nominal monosyllabic patterns /C/, /CC/ and /CCC/ in distribution with the three basic vowels /a:ā/, i:ī, /u:ū. It is more a synchronic and comparative approach, not radical or "etymological."[19] Even so, his conclusion remains valid: "The morphological analysis… reveals a relative stability of radical vowels, which should therefore be regarded as forming part of the root. In other words, Semitic roots are *continuous* morphemes which are instrumental in derivation but subject to vocalic and consonantal change in this process which is based on continuous and discontinuous 'pattern morphemes,' both lexical and grammatical" (p. 202).

2. Radical Vocalism

We have seen how the inclusion of the vowel in the radical lexical morpheme has made its way into general studies on the structure and analysis of the components of the root. Now it is necessary to refer to a series of studies that have presented it in detail as an autonomous element—concerning which the Russian School has been in the forefront (Gazov-Ginsberg, Grande, Djakonoff, Orel, Belova, Stolbova, etc.). I shall leave aside the issue of apophony, which is more related to derived morphology and does not directly affect our problem, even though it is crucial for defining Semitic vocalization in general (Kuryłowicz).[20]

2.1.   B. Kienast (1962) was concerned with thematic verbal vocalization and its *Ablaut* in Akkadian with respect to the so-called "weak" verbs, from a rather morphological perspective.[21] Nevertheless, his comments on the position and length of the root vowel in the various verbal types (PIS, PSI, PŪS, but excluding the type APS → ᵓP[roto-]S[emitic]) are important for the emphasis on the role of the vowel in (biliteral) verbal roots.

2.2.   One of the first studies devoted to this problem from the point of view of Common Semitics was that of P. Fronzaroli (1963).[22] Common opinion accepts Cantineau's system for the consonantal nature of the lexeme, but various data require posing "the problem of an original presence of the vocalic element in the lexeme" (p. 120). The data include primitive or primary nouns, semantically unmotivated and not apophonic, with a structure similar to that of Indo-European nouns. "In itself the vowel of unmotivated nouns is a simple vowel of the lexeme" (p. 123). Also verbs exhibit an indeterminate, non-apophonic vowel in the prefixed forms and in the imperative of the simple theme of action verbs, while their possible semantic value remains doubtful. The stative verbs in their suffixed forms refer, in turn, to original adjectives with an unmotivated lexematic vowel. Thus, an unmotivated primitive vocalism prior to historical or even contemporary apophony is postulated in the cases of prefixed forms of verbs of action, an opinion we share.

2.3.   Almost at the same time, A. M. Gazov-Ginsberg (1965) was defending a strict "monovocalism" of the Semitic root.[23] The vowel is certainly necessary as one of its components, but it is indeterminate and unstable, phonetically neutral and with no phonemic value. The Semitic root, then, is a "proto-phoneme" (morpheme?) of which the consonantal component is the only determinant from the semantic point of view. The consonantal group, relatively rich from the phonetic aspect and also very stable, acts on the monovowel by developing different vocalic phonemes, which, in turn, share in the formation of an "algebraic" or "symbolic" system (see below pp. 57, 68, 82, 118–20) of Semitic inflection. From this perspective, the Semitic root is different from the Indo-European one. Thus it impossible to reconstruct the vocalic element in primitive nouns, as certain theories would wish. The Semitic root is also a very ancient witness to the language of *homo sapiens*.

These ideas are taken up again in another book, according to which two levels can be distinguished in Proto-Semitic vocalism.[24] In the first, there is no "zero/vowel" opposition; in the second, the opposition operates between "a vowel (a[?])/zero vowel." This undefined state can be seen in the vocalism of primitive nouns, where the nature of the vowel is defined by the phonetic characteristics of the consonants. On the other hand, the increase of the vowels cooperates in the formation of the plural, while the opposition /u(w):i(y)/ shares a semantic symbolism: masculine / feminine, size marker (diminutive / augmentative).

This theory of semantic symbolism is formulated even more radically in another work (1965) in which the author analyzes the supposed "expressive" character of Semitic phonemic consonantalism and its combinations through a great deal of evidence of "Proto-Semitic." [25] This is clearly a glottogonic perspective that was to emerge again in our own day (see below p. 83 [Bohas]). From this basis, the Semitic root would be constructed in a very stable way, based only on consonantal components. The vocalic component is again shown to be random and variable, without any meaning due to its position. Each consonant can be accompanied by any vowel at all. The final part of his book is devoted to the problem of the variation of roots, specifically to the reduction of quadriliteral roots and to the variation of homorganic consonants, and lastly to the interweaving of roots among themselves and with suffixes. Many of these ideas have a parallel in the work of Majzel' and earlier in Jusmanov, on whom both depend.

This extreme opinion on vocalism refers, on the one hand, to the classical theory that considers the consonantal pattern as the only one to bear the semantic load and, on the other, reflects the difficulty in defining the nature of Proto-Semitic vocalism. However, the solution proposed takes no account of the vocalic oppositions that are very well defined and well documented in Common Semitic, nor of the clear function assumed by vocalic differentiation in the inflectional system with its apophonies.

2.4.   Furthermore, the vocalism of the original lexical base is an essential element in Djakonoff's theory, as we have seen, as well as in those of others (for example, Voigt, Orel, Belova) on the structure of the Proto-Semitic root. Let us recall his opinions in this regard (see p. 29). Djakonoff presents a special system opposed to the classical Semitic vocalism of six short and long vowels (1970), which I have discussed.[26] For him, the original Semitic vocalism or, rather, the Proto-Hamito-Semitic vocalism had only two vocalic phonemes: an allophonic vowel /i:u/ [/ə/] and a fixed vowel /a/ (p. 456). In fact, the allophony of /u/ occurred only in contact with certain consonantal phonemes (labials, velars, the glottal stop) just as the phoneme /a/ also changes to /i/ in certain positions. The situation, then, is similar to primitive Indo-European vocalism, for which only two vowels are postulated. This situation can be found also in the primitive inflectional system of Old Akkadian, Egyptian, and even Cushitic (pp. 459, 478 n. 113, 480), which would argue in favor of the secondary character of /u/.[27]

2.5.   R. M. Voigt is also of the opinion that one must "fit the characteristic vowels of the perfect and imperfect in succession into one basic form" (1988) as against earlier (Schultens) and modern opinion (Travis) that wishes pure consonantalism to be at the base of every Semitic lexeme.[28]

2.6.   V. Orel (1994) systematizes the data of his *Hamito-Semitic Etymological Dictionary* (1995) (in collaboration with Belova) in connection with the issue of apophony (*Ablaut*) documented in certain cases (/a-i-u/) in Afro-Asiatic:[29] "The Ablaut types (/*a- *i/, /*a- *u/) are quite numerous in primary nouns of CVC-pattern" (p. 162), but there are others. However, he is not concerned in this study with the origin of the phenomenon and its connection to radical vocalism.

2.7. A. G. Belova (1996), resuming earlier studies relating to Afro-Asiatic and Egyptian,[30] notes the irrelevance in our day of the strictly apophonic function—meaning morphological function— of vowels as against the lexical function of consonants and the presence of an unmotivated non-morphological vocalism of primary "themes" (nouns).[31] The same situation can be observed in the primary verbal themes, specifically in the theme of the simple imperfect of the type $/C_1C_2VC_3/$ in Arabic and Akkadian, with a semantic reflex, although some exceptions can be found. These are motivated by the phonetic environment and by analogy. This is proved on the basis of biconsonantal verbal themes in Arabic, lengthened by one of eight complements /ʾ, h, w, y ; s, š ; m, n/ (types CvCC, CvC, CCv) and triconsonantal verbal themes in Arabic and Akkadian. This problem of the vocalism of verbal bases / themes, as we have seen, is one of the most lively currently being debated. Belova concludes: "In comparing the facts examined, one comes to the conclusion that the vocalism of primary verbal themes is related to the structure of the root" (p. 86). In the case of verbal themes lengthened by complements, one could think of "two degrees of radical vowel: short and long" [u/ū/, i/ī] (p. 87). Belova (1993) treated the issue of verbal vocalization in a very thought-provoking article that is based upon a comparison of Arabic and Akkadian.[32] This allows her to reconstruct a radical vocalism independent of grammatical function. The necessary lexical opposition, based on vocalism, is provided by a certain number of biliteral roots, an opposition that sometimes finds confirmation in other Afro-Asiatic languages, especially Egyptian.

2.8. T. Frolova (2002) discusses the reconstruction of radical vocalism, this time of the "strong" triliteral prefixed verbal base $/-/C_1C_2VC_3-/$ as a morpheme that is conditioned neither by function nor by grammatical aspect according to the explanation usually applied to Hebrew and Aramaic.[33] The inquiry is limited to Akkadian and Arabic, given that these two languages are the only ones that provide the three short vowels in vocalizations of the verb. After a detailed examination of 138 Arabic and Akkadian roots that are clearly related, arranged in seven classes, starting with Akkadian (/a,u/, /u,u/, /a,ʾ/, /ʾ,u/; transitive /i,i/; intransitive /i,i/; transitive-intransitive /a,a/) and a comparison to their Arabic equivalents, he concludes that only the transitive verbs in /u/ provide positive evidence of original vocalization. Less clear is the evidence provided by the transitive class in /i/. A positive conclusion cannot be reached concerning the intransitive verbs, due in large measure to the morphological changes operative in this category.

3. Appraisal

Of all the studies on the actual phonological structure of the Semitic root, the most significant remains Djakonoff's due to his bold concept and his systematization. Even if one is prepared to accept many of his approaches, there are a certain number of presuppositions that deserve to be reconsidered.

First of all, the distinction between nominal roots and primitive verbs, assumed by other scholars, has to be refined. In principle the distinction seems to be secondary, that is, semantic, even though it is evident phonologically.[34] From the point of view of proto-language, one can even state that it marks the limit between common Semitic and Proto-Semitic, or even better, pre-Proto-Semitic (= Proto-Afro-Asiatic), the true etymological horizon. It is valid at the level of inflection, either of the theme or the stem, but not at zero level of the base.[35] At this level, nouns and verbs coincide phonologically; they are differentiated at the level of syntagmatic organization, which, as we shall see below, cannot be later in time. In this sense, both seem to be and must be considered as primary at the same level, but with distinct functions. The action noun and its object (possible original type /QvTL/) recall each other, and it is precisely their expression that is the origin of "grammar," which appears in this way. A primary noun cannot be articulated as a verb/agent, given its character as object. It can generate only de-nominations.[36] Nevertheless, in the development of their syntagmatic structure, the system of verbal inflection, probably taking as its model the nominal model or simply coinciding with it, gives rise to the system of epenthetic thematic vowels (internal inflection), while the radical vowel does not change in the noun, since its inflection is external and linear. Thus, there is no specific "radical verbal" vowel and it is a fictional object of research, just as finding it in the forms of the imperative or the jussive is a mirage produced by their elemental character. This research may well be educational but does not necessarily lead to the original form (*maṣdar*).[37] same time nominal forms. These elementary morphs (imperative-jussive and infinitive) may be considered to carry the original verbal vowel in as much as they are at the same time nominal forms. Thus, one has to renounce as well the futile controversy concerning the priority of the noun with respect to the verb and *vice versa*.[38] The distinction between them as primary lexemes will arise again later in connection with the various phonetic incompatibilities that seem to affect their patterning. It is precisely this common origin of the two types of root that makes it completely unlikely that there was a different phonological system for each. It is a point of view that is becoming more and more common.

The nominal or verbal character of the primary root lexeme comes from its own referential structure. This is built from a relationship of interest of the "referring" subject, the man who speaks. He can refer to his surroundings statically, paradigmatically, objectively; or dynamically, syntagmatically, actively / actantially. By the first set he is placed in his context, taking his place there, and arranges it. By the second set he acts on it and controls it; he profits from it or reacts against it, as the concept of "interactive property" of modern semantics supposes. "To name" is not only "to label" but "to interpret," to bestow a meaning in relation to my perception and its repercussions on me. Things and their aspects "are" such in function of their usefulness and their value for me. To name something is thus "to delimit" a perception of the values of the object mentioned or referred to. It is the activity that is supposed to have been carried out by Adam: "and whatever name that Adam called the animals, that was their real name" (Gen 2:19). Things, then, can have unsuitable or "useless" names, according to the suitability of interpretation man has give them in keeping with his own interests.

The two types of reference co-exist and no order of priority can be established between them. The first type produces "primary nouns" ("*Primärwörter*"), which are synthetic or global references, and "adjectives," which are analytical or partial refer-ences and become "stative verbs" as immanent references to the subject. The second produces noun-verbs that define the environment as the object of the action, both with the same "signifier" (object-noun and action-noun). The identity that is evident in the case of stative bases between nominal / adjectival form and verbal form must also be supposed in the case of "active / actantial" forms.[39]

It is interesting to note the original identity between the infinitive (the "construct infinitive," of course, as the absolute infinitive is only a morphological apophony) and the imperative, as is clear in Hebrew (and in several Indo-European languages). The descriptive or referential form also expresses action: "eating" was originally also "to want to eat," "eat!" So in English "(the) say," "(to) say," "say!" (though in this case by a sort of reduction of the diachronically developed pattern, a kind of coming back to the sources).

Thus, two lexical sub-systems are formed from the semantic point of view: the system of referential naming (objective) and the system of ergative naming (active), which, in turn, can become "instrumental," "transitive," etc. This differentiation then gives rise to the specification of the verbal system as an inflected system through inter-nal and external inflection, where the function of the vowels becomes decisive. The level of etymological reconstruction one reaches when speaking of lexical "roots" or "bases" finds this system already well established. However, this semantic differen-tiation neither authorizes nor requires any phonological differentiation. Object-nouns and action-nouns have the same consonantal and vocalic structure, as can be verified also in other Afro-Asiatic languages, especially in Egyptian, at least from the graphe-mic point of view. In fact, one can regard this state of affairs as harking back to a (pre-) Proto-Semitic (= Proto-Afro-Asiatic) level.

In this connection, the obligatory presence of a sonant in the formation of primary nouns, allowing all the rest to be considered as nouns derived from verbs, cannot be proved. I think that it is going too far to apply, in this case, the model of the root of certain Indo-European scholars (Benveniste) to Semitics. There are certainly some "specific" primary nouns that do not generate verbs, but nothing forces us to grant them their own determinism/phonetic limitation. Phonology is not conditioned by referential semantics. In fact, many nominal-verbal bases that, as such, do not need to have a sonant in their phonological composition, according to Djakonoff, are also primary or primitive, like the nouns that are considered as such. This means, then, that the radical structure without a sonant can be valid also for primitive nouns. Besides, the phonological character of sonants does not seem clear in Djakonoff's account. It even seems to have a certain contradiction as to whether or not they have a syllabic function (see pp. 474 and 457 of his article summarized above p. 17). At the very most one could acknowledge Djakonoff's primary nominal class as a sub-class of primary lexemes with a sonant character (in second or third position). This character must be taken into account given its probable origin as a glide and its biliteral Afro-Asiatic parallels. In fact, the intensification or lengthening of vowels coincides with the epen-thesis or reduction to a diphthong of a sonant ($C\underline{v}C$/ # /CsC/). They are chance cases of expansion that each language develops as it pleases.

On the other hand, Djakonoff's theory, which postulates a twofold degree of primary lexical morpheme, is very interesting in the sense that it supposes the appearance of a structured grammar (inflection), as I have said, at the same time as the appearance of lexematics: every naming or de-signation (lexis) presupposes more or less explicitly a syntagmatic interlinking with other lexemes through vocalic inflection. In fact, this would imply that there are no monoconsonantal lexemes (the degree zero would be missing), the only one allowed being of the /CS/ type. As I said above, I have been able to verify this fact empirically by an analysis of the monoconsonantal series. However, we cannot exclude that at the (pre-)Proto-Semitic / Afro-Asiatic level, these monoconsonantal nouns could have existed, as is supposed by the "functorial" series and confirmed by the Egyptian and Proto-Afro-Asiatic (possibly also Akkadian) lexica. In that case, one would have to suppose a neutral vowel alongside those with a morphological character or else ascribe two values to one of the vowels.

It is also possible that, a long time ago, the original level had developed an anaptyctic support under the influence of the monosyllabic sub-class with a sonant (/CvCC/, /CvSC/, /CvCS/), intended to break up the final biconsonantal cluster, mainly in the case of degree 0, contrary in principle to the laws of Semitic phonology. Or else the class without a sonant in position 2/3 originally becomes disyllabic (/QvTvL/) in nouns and verbs, and must be considered just as primary as the one with a sonant, as one of the patterns accepted in this respect by Djakonoff himself. What we are seeing here, perhaps, is the appearance of a push toward a generalized implantation of triconsonantalism and apophonic systems. It is then possible to suppose quite simply that Djakonoff's law of consonantal clusters could not be applied (accepting no sonants) and that a final or anaptyctic vowel could arise, as I have just said. This could well be primitive, as some scholars suggest.

With respect to the original Semitic vocalism, the hypothesis of two original vowels, both thematic and inflectional, seems quite plausible. Beside the support found in a comparison to Indo-European, this hypothesis represents the articulatory opposition of "central # anterior-posterior" base, which, by its shift through the "upper # lower" modulation, generates the complete range of vowels (a → e → i // u → o → a). The other vowels can be considered to be variants of these vocalic basic modulations/positions, often conditioned by contact with certain consonants. On the other hand, the very frequent /u:i/ alternation is documented in the various Semitic languages, both in the primary nouns and in the active inflection of the verb (/yqtu:il/), and attests to its basic allophony, beside the shift just indicated: (/u → ü → i/) (Akkadian), (/u → ə → i/) (Ethiopic). The application to Proto-Semitic of the phonetics of tiers favors this interpretation.[40] The system with six vowels, long and short, must be considered, in agreement with Djakonoff, to be the result of contrastive morphological development.[41]

On the basis of statistics, one could suggest a hypothetical distribution of the two classes of lexical morphemes, according to which the primary nouns tend to have the /a/ sound, whereas the nouns of action verbs prefer /ə/. In any case, one must allow for the undeniable influence of analogy.

On the other hand, the final position of a radical lexeme belongs to the realm of inflection and so cannot be intensified like the preceding positions, or extended by a vowel functioning as a consonant. Any possible complement must be attached at the nominal degree zero (0) (Djakonoff) by means of a dispensable auxiliary vowel /-(a)-wa/. In the case of verbal bases, this would have consequences for the analysis of the origin of the structure of verbs with a third "weak" radical /w:y/. This radical must be understood as a (semi-)consonantal syllabic complement attached to the primary stem of the verb, already perfectly structured, and not as a lengthened vowel, as proved by Ugaritic and Ethiopic, as well as by the Arabic script.

It is noticeable that in Djakonoff's work there is some fluctuation, which is inevitable of course, with respect to lexematic levels. From an etymological perspective, all the languages that belong to the same family or super-family must be included because they all derive from it and attest to it. But the diachronic disparity, the influence of substrates and adstrates and the development of their research, make reference to many Afro-Asiatic languages more embarrassing than useful. As a result, on the one hand, Djakonoff assumes as his frame of reference "the Common Semitic material only" (p. 453), but on the other, he accepts "that our reconstructed scheme of vocalism as suggested for the subsystem of primary nominal root morphemes, i.e. seven sonants and two vowels proper, refers to a still earlier diachronic level which we may conventionally call "pre-Proto-Semito-Hamitic'" (p. 457). Some years later (1975) he claimed yet that resorting to Semitic alone is too hazardous and not very certain; it is necessary to study each of the other branches and gain a general knowledge of them.[42] Even so, for Huehnergard, even in 1996 "in the current state of the field, reference to Afroasiatic for Semitic reconstruction continues to present significant obstacles" (pp. 264f.),[43] whereas for Dolgopolsky (1999) "now time has come to realize that…deep Semitological reconstructions without Hamito-Semitic historical perspective are facing a danger of becoming increasingly unproductive" (p. 11).[44]

It is a situation without a solution. As I said when commenting on Djakonoff's work, the diachronic and documentary gap of the *corpora* of the various languages gives, in my opinion, preference to the "classical" Semito-Egyptian evidence as against a certain current fashion that tends to look for support in the other "modern" Hamito-Semitic / Afro-Asiatic languages without historical documentation. Thus, one is aware of a degree of tension in setting the frame of reference for research into Proto-Semitic: the importance of "classical" data is recognized, but at the same time also the need to going beyond it is recognized. In fact, any claim to the etymological reconstruction of Semitic, even if limited to the data provided by this family of languages, goes beyond the level of its synchronic comparison (Common Semitic), even beyond its more or less original pre-dialectal stage, to reach a deeper level, in this case called "pre-Proto-Semito-Hamitic" (Djakonoff). And it is in this sense that the etymological reconstruction of Semitic must be compatible with that of other languages of the phylum. The problem that arises here derives from the situation in which they are, with the exception of Egyptian, with no ancient documents and with serious problems of phonological and semantic adstrates and substrates. This means that normally one can resort to them in order to confirm a fact already acquired and very rarely to establish it. In principle, an adequate reconstruction of Proto-Semitic should prove to be "etymological" at the lexematic level valid for Afro-Asiatic in general, as would be the case with other languages of the phylum if they reached the adequate level of documentation and development, as may well be the case in the Coptic-Egyptian family. At the same time one must accept that none of these "family" reconstructions covers either all the primary lexicon or the whole grammar of the Afro-Asiatic family. In the same way, the phonological framework of each family must correspond (be governed by uniform laws) to those of the others, but without coinciding completely. We will return to this point.

III

As can easily be imagined, one of the basic aspects of the root in Semitic at the concrete level of its formation—once the more or less formal aspects of the base structure have been taken into account—is the aspect of its phonological set, especially its consonantal set. This has been treated by many Semitic scholars who, encouraged by common opinion, consider consonants to be the chief component of the Semitic root, from the phonological and semantic viewpoint, depriving vocalism of any meaning, relegating it to the level of functional apophony, as we have just seen.

1. The Semitic Perspective

1.1. This approach had been developed by J. Cantineau, in a study contemporary with that cited above on the structural binomial root-pattern (1951–52).[1] This article summarizes and refines previous studies that were concerned with the phonetics of certain specific Semitic languages, with frequent excursions into Proto-Semitic (1941, 1946, 1950).[2] Having shown that various scholars, since the beginning of comparative grammar, preserved the consonantal system of the Semitic languages intact, Cantineau notes certain disputed points that still await a satisfactory explanation.

The first point is phonological taxonomy and its relationship to the point of articulation of phonemes. Against Bergsträsser's opinion, he posits that spirants and occlusives (stops) cannot have the same point of articulation in Semitic. This leads to attributing to the consonantal system a number of articulation classes that are more important than usually indicated, in fact, no fewer than nine:

> labials (/p/, /b/, /m/)
> "low" apicals "à pointe basse" (/t̤ː t₂/, /d̤ː d₂ /, /t̤ː t₂/)
> "high" apicals "à pointe haute" (alveolars) (/t/, /d/, /ṭ/)
> sibilants (palato-alveolar fricatives) (/s/, /z/, /ṣ/, /š/)
> lateralized (/ḍ:t̤$^{l}_{2}$/, /ś:s^{v}/))
> palato-dorsals (/k/, /g/, /ḳ/)
> velars (/ḫ/, /ġ/)
> pharyngeals (/ḥ/, /ᶜ/)
> laryngeals (/h/, /ʔ/)

The "liquids" (/r/, /l/, /n/) and the "semi-vowels" (/w/, /y/) remain "unclassi-fied."

Of these 29 consonants, fourteen can be arranged into seven categories of voiced/voiceless, which are equivalent in the various Semitic languages according to their frequency of occurrence. The (marked) opposition occurs between the features "soft aspirated," "with open glottis" (voiceless), and "hard unaspirated" (sonorant) with respect to their "manner of articulation."

Another correlation opposes five pairs of "soft aspirated voiceless" (voiceless) and "emphatics." In this case, the difficulty lies in resolving the phonetic nature of the emphasis, of which there are two types in modern Semitic languages: glottal or ejec-tive (Ethiopic) and palato-velar (Arabic). The consonants of the first class have no influence on a neighboring vowel, whereas those of the second do. Scholars are divided as to which of these two types of emphasis is the original Semitic type. Cantineau leans toward the Ethiopic emphatic-ejective type, which is the current opinion today.[3]

Finally, we have two "nasal" phonemes, connected to the general system, one by the series of labials (/m/) and the other by the liquids (/n/).

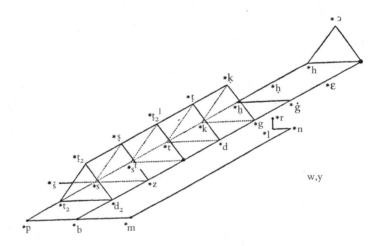

As for the system itself, Cantineau provides a diagram in the form of a trian-gular prism, in which the four famous "triads" (voiceless, voiced, emphatic) are distinguished.[4] However, in his diagram the phoneme /ʔ/ has no definitive place. This is not the only shortcoming of his work: liquids, nasals, and semi-vowels are also vague ("unclassified"). Despite this, Cantineau's analysis is important, for he summa-rizes the situation and discusses the phonological set that, up to now, has been accepted.

1.2. A direct reaction to Cantineau's work was an article by A. Martinet (1953) in which he summarized his own theory, one which Cantineau, in fact, had referred to and accepted.[5] Martinet's comments have led to a reduction and simplification of the entire system, and are based on three series (open glottis, sonority, closed glottis) and nine orders (point of articulation / localization), which are slightly different from those Cantineau proposed: labial-apical-dorsal, anterior-lateral-sibilant-dorsal, middle-dorsal, and velar-pharyngeal-laryngeal.

The differentiation is, if anything, (typo-)graphical. The three series determine Cantineau's triangular model (triads: voiceless, voiced, emphatic) and represent an "increasingly open glottis" (/t/, /d/, /ṭ/, ...). Martinet prefers representation by binary coordinates (series/order), enabling the "empty" slots to be seen more easily. For example, the slot of the consonant /p/ and of other glottalized / ejective (emphatic) consonants. The complexity of its execution (either glottalized or ejective) explains its absence from phonological models. Martinet's excellent analysis of ejection / emphasis / glottalization is noteworthy.

The phoneme /ʔ/, which was absent in Cantineau's arrangement (and in Moscati's, as will be seen below), has to be incorporated into this category as "the actual marker of the corresponding series of glottalization," just as /h/ is the marker of non-sonority (voicelessness), at the same time a special phoneme. As for the dentals and palato-alveolar fricatives (sibilants) (simplifying the peculiar typographical notation of Cantineau and his own), Martinet opposes structurally /š/ and /ḍ/ as voiceless/emphatic (open/closed glottis), or non-occlusive/continuant, as Cantineau prefers, while admitting with him, for the glottalized emphatic, a semi-occlusive or affricative character (the continuant/fricative emphatic character would be secondary in front of the [semi-]occlusive). A parallel argument, based on Hittite-Akkadian transcriptions, also favors the semi-occlusive (affricated) character of the two other phonemes /s/ and /z/: voiceless/voiced.

In this study one can recognize the expertise of the phonologist, whose remarks, made from a wider linguistic perspective, can no doubt help in going beyond the rigid character of the classic Semitic system.

1.3.   Cantineau's consonantal system has become a classic and is closely followed by other scholars, such as S. Moscati (1954)[6] and in the general outline given in the comparative grammar that he edited (1964).[7]

Analysis of Proto-Semitic consonantism "at its most ancient stage" is set out by Moscati following C. Brockelmann, but also takes into account recent phonetic and phonological developments, in a diachronic perspective.

The first section deals with the classification of consonantism depending on the point of articulation, according to the IPA as was known at that time: bilabials, dentals, palato-alveolars, velars, uvulars, pharyngeals, and laryngeals; depending on the manner of articulation they can be occlusives (stops), nasals, laterals (lateralized?), trills, fricatives, and semi-vowels. At first sight, this classification seems more conservative and less analytical than Cantineau's.

Moscati then discusses the other two features of Semitic phonemes, namely voice and emphasis. He rejects Cantineau's suggestion of a "correlation of intensity" between the two categories, as well as the aspirated pronunciation of occlusives and fricatives, without, however, explaining the opposition voiced / voiceless (sonorant / unvoiced) found, for example, in his comparative grammar. For emphasis and after evaluating the various arguments, Moscati also tends to favor the realization of a glottalized voiceless type (Ethiopic) instead of the velarized type (sonorant / voiceless) (Arabic).

His analysis of twelve groups of lexemes, derived from the combination of the point and mode of articulation (ultimately there are seventeen [p. 41]), follows general opinion, though in many cases differing from Cantineau's. For example, he displays the four famous triads; but a possible fifth triad, consisting of lateralized phonemes, is not accepted, for only two morphemes are certain, given that for him lateralization "is not a distinctive point of articulation" but only a simple correlative position, like the sonorant, emphatic, and nasal characters.

This analysis enables Moscati to arrange all the Semitic phonemes (except /ʾ/) into a diagram, presented as a correction to Cantineau's. Nevertheless, in this diagram many phonemes still remain outside a desirable phonetic symmetry. His classification retains some categories that are not very well analyzed (sibilant, hiss or palato-alve-olar fricative, liquid, nasal, semi-vowel, aspirated, soft/hard, emphatic ...) even from the aspect of articulation. Others, such as "sonance," are simply ignored.

He presents similar solutions in a study of the same date, limited to a specific language (1954).[8] Even if his viewpoint is ancient Hebrew (Massoretic and pre-Massoretic), it is open to Proto-Semitic and the Northwest-Semitic languages of the second millennium. The treatment is diachronic, but focused on a particular language. The same could be said of Cantineau's very similar study, cited above, which Moscati often quotes and corrects. The perspective opened by these studies on Semitic phonol-ogy has remained classic.

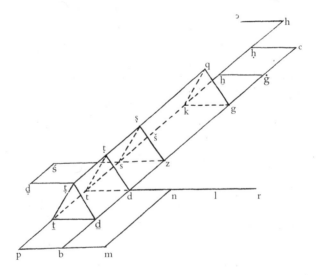

1.4. In a short contribution, W. Leslau (1957) analyzed our problem, recognizing the difficulty of reconstructing Proto-Semitic phonology on the basis of dead languages and their modern forms.[9] Here again we have the classic problems, well known since Cantineau: the twofold pronunciation of the "emphatics," triads of phonemes, only two laterals, and the aspiration of occlusives (stops). The interdental phonemes, the laryngeals, and the laterals have undergone the strongest diachronic transformation. Leslau sets out these special changes and many others for each language. It is a well-informed but elementary summary at textbook level.[10]

1.5. R. C. Steiner (1977) has written a very interesting study, even though it is limited to one particular phonological series.[11] His analysis criticizes and completes the thesis that, especially since Cantineau, argued for the existence of a series of lateral phonemes in Proto-Semitic. Apart from /l/ (liquid lateral or voiceless approximant), universally recognized as such, in this category we need to include the Proto-Semitic phonemes /ś/ (voiceless lateral-alveolar-fricative) and /ḍ/ (voiced lateral-alveolar-fricative). This means that we have to acknowledge the lateral feature in the historical realization of /š/ in Akkadian, Ugaritic, Arabic, and also, in part, Ethiopic. The study is empirical and based on the analysis of relevant cases found in each language (alternations, doublets, examples of incompatibility).

The discovery of the lateral realization of these phonemes in Modern South Arabic occurred in the nineteenth century. Thereafter, various scholars (Steiner lists the contributions) extended this realization of these phonemes to other specific languages, even to Common Semitic. Having established the symbols and phonological characters of the laterals, Steiner takes stock of the lateral phonemes in the South Arabian languages, based upon evidence from modern speakers, since there is no ancient written evidence. In Chapter III, perhaps the most interesting section, Steiner sets out a table of the correspondences between the various languages, gives a list of relevant words, and discusses their phonic realization in each language. From this point the research becomes completely empirical. After collecting the evidence from Arab grammarians on this topic, he collects the transcriptions and loans from Arabic in other languages (Iberian, Malayan, West and East African) and some especially important cases. Some of them document the lateral pronunciation of /š/ in Proto-Arabic and Akkadian. While the alternation /ḍ/ – /ś/ produces allophones of identical meaning and in some cases alternations of the type /ś/-/l/ or /ś/-/ls/, /ś/-/sl/.

Steiner summarizes and refines the phonological character of the lateral "triad." This excellent study surpasses previous essays on the sibilants in Semitic (Murtonen, Garbini, etc.) and has become a reference work for studies of Semitic phonology.[12]

1.6. An innovative and comprehensive perspective and a critical revision, applied directly to Semitic, is provided by A. R. Bomhard (1988),[13] who, at the time, was unaware of Djakonoff's work (p. 114). He retains almost the same phonological distribution indicated, at the same time seeking a wider and newer horizon: "the phonological system traditionally reconstructed for Proto-Semitic most certainly cannot be maintained, not even on the basis of the Semitic data alone" (p. 114). But curiously he then states: "The revised consonant system that emerges from this reexamination is found to resemble fairly closely the reconstruction proposed by Cantineau (1952) and Martinet (1953) over thirty years ago" (p. 115). The various categories of phonemes (emphatics, etc.) are analyzed in light of Afro-Asiatic phonology in the search for the most likely realization to emerge from this comparison. He holds the theory of four triads (p. 115) and is inclined to favor the glottal articulation of emphatics (ejectives) (with Steiner and Dolgopolsky [pp. 116f.]), voiceless occlusives probably being "breathed" / "aspirated," as Cantineau thought (p. 119). Leaving aside the categories of phonemes that are peculiar to Proto-Afro-Asiatic and that have converged in Semitic, Bomhard concludes that the classes of (bi)labials, dentals, velars, nasals, liquids, glides (semi-vowels), glottals, and pharyngeals (22 phonemes) present no problem in his reconstructions as Proto-Semitic phonemes, according to the accepted theory (p. 133). The sibilants (s, z, ṣ), however, have to be treated as dental affricates (ts, dz, ts), the classical interdentals (/t̠/, /d̠/ /ẓ/) as alveolar-velar-occlusives (t^y, d^y, ṭ^y), and /ś/ and /ḍ/ become lateralized affricates, voiceless and glottalized respectively, eight phonemes in all (pp. 133f.) that have to be renamed.

1.7.   In a more recent work from the school of Djakonoff, A. Militarev and L. Kogan (2000) provide the direct application of their teacher's etymological approach to Semitic, and, therefore, to Afro-Asiatic, as well as a discussion of some of his proposals.[14] The starting-point is the classic table of 29 simple Semitic consonantal phonemes (p. LXVII). The two scholars favor the affricated articulation of sibilants, interdentals, and laterals (see Martinet above, and Djakonoff below). After a detailed description of the diachronic phonetics of some sub-families in the Semitic languages, Militarev and Kogan study and accept certain proto-phonemes proposed recently, namely, two lateral/lateralized voiceless sibilants, affricated and non-affricated respectively, / ŝ / ← AA / ĉ /) and / ĉ$_x$:s/ ← AA / ŝ /), based on the double equivalences [s/š] given in Hebrew, South Arabian, and other modern Afro-Asiatic languages. In the case of labial consonants, in the classic table the third "emphatic" member forming the triadic symmetry already accepted (p. CV; but see below) is missing. As a result, they assume as possible the existence of a (glottalized) emphatic phoneme / ṗ /, defended by Djakonoff and others, in spite of the ambiguous proofs for it, the principal argument being the irregular /p:b/ correspondences in the various Semitic and Afro-Asiatic languages. Finally, as regards the series of labio-velar consonants [kw, gw, qw], well known in Geᶜez and usually explained as positional or conditioned mutations, later understood as analogical, without forgetting to mention the influence of the Cushitic substrate, the situation remains undecided.[15]

    To complete the frame of reference for discussion on the problem of Semitic consonantism, it should be noted that it is in the phonological table provided by Militarev and Kogan that we find incorporated for the first time the category of (re)sonants as opposed to consonants (obstruants). It is one of Djakonoff's contributions (see below) that his school has canonized. Here is the distribution of Semitic consonants as provided by these two scholars:

	Obstruant Stops Voiceless-Emph. Voiced			Consonants Fricatives Voiceless-Emph. Voiced			Resonants
bilabial	p		b				w, m
dental	t	ṭ	d				r, n
interdental				ṯ	ṯ̣	ḏ	
hissing				s	ṣ	z	
hushing				š			
lateral				ŝ	ṣ̂		l
palatal							y
velar	k	ḳ	g				
uvular				ḫ	γ		
pharyngeal				ḥ	c		
laryngeal				h			

1.8. Among other classifications of the list of phonemes, in line with new proposals of phoneticians (see below, on the Afro-Asiatic perspective), mention must be made of the nomenclature given by G. Bohas (1997),[16] as well as his insistence on the "features," that is, the classes and modalities of articulation, and not only the points of articulation, for the structuring of what he calls the "matrix." At first, Bohas (1997, p. 80) arranges the phonetics of the "matrices" (on this point see above), defined as a "combination of (two) points of articulation" with its own semantic load, in 6/7 classes of consonants, in agreement with Cantineau's more classical phonology.

But this phonological distribution of the root lexeme over three levels still remains somewhat inexact. In fact, Bohas brings into play a further specification. Alongside the matrix categories cited (generic point of articulation) he speaks of other characters that have to be taken into consideration. For example, he speaks of a "[labial]+[emphatic]" matrix (p. 175), and this aspect has not been taken into account when calculating the (number of) matrices. In fact, "features" such as "emphatic, nasal, sonorant, dorsal, voiced…" are those that, according to Bohas, are relevant for arranging the matrices and on which he has insisted in his second work (2000, pp. 17ff.), where he gives a complete table of these features, fourteen in all, based on Halle and Kenstowicz. The six or seven articulatory combinations (under this or an equivalent name) form part of this list of "features": consonant, sonant, approximative, voiced, continuant, labial, coronal, dorsal, pharyngeal, anterior, distributed, strident, lateral, nasal.

Each phoneme shares one or more of these features. Consequently, says Bohas, "we call matrices (M) the combinations of features to which common primordial meanings are attached" (p. 20).

The most significant "novelty," however, from the aspect of phonology (we have spoken above about the structural plan of the radical lexeme and its reversibility), is his discussion of the nature of the Arabic phoneme /jim/ [ǧ], found in his first work and for which he already uses analysis by features. As the basis of this lexicographical analysis, he postulates a twofold origin for the phoneme /jim/ [$\hat{g}$]: voiced uvular (/G/ # /q/) and voiced velar (/g/ # /k/) (pp. 143–52), both sharing the features "[dorsal]+[voiced]" and distinguished by the attribute [high] of the second feature. This results in roots with an identical or different semantic load, depending upon this phonological profile. In origin there was a split in the Proto-Semitic emphatic/ejective consonant /q/. We will return to this view below.

But even if it should prove correct, this remains an internal process of Arabic phonology, in the course of which the phoneme /q::k/ would have lost its emphatic nature. As a special diachronic event, it will be missing from other Semitic languages and from the contour of the Proto-Semitic root / matrix. However, it must be considered when defining equivalences of the Arabic lexicon.

1.9   The contribution by A. Murtonen (1996) has special significance with respect to the origin of the phonological system in general and the Semitic phonological system in particular.[17] He summarizes and refines his earlier and more detailed treatment, focused on Hebrew (1989/1990).[18] His starting-point is a list of ten to thirteen proto-phonemes (p. 395), common to all languages, including pre-Semitic languages, with a statistical frequency that could prove their importance in the lexicon. Starting with this list, he thinks the Semitic languages have developed a more complex system of 25 to 26 phonemes by means of a series of processes of extension in order to suit the demands of semantic diversity.

Another point to emphasize is his treatment of all the vowels and consonants. However, his lexicon continues to be constructed on purely consonantal roots.

1.10   Lastly, recent works on comparative Semitic grammar have followed more or less the classic phonological distribution, sometimes discussing some of the questions raised recently.[19]

2. The Afro–Asiatic Perspective

2.1   The pioneer work in this field was by M. Cohen (1947).[20] In addition to providing an almost exhaustive bibliography on previous research and setting out the problem in relation to the structure of the lexicon common to the superfamily of Hamito-Semitic/Afro-Asiatic, he devotes several pages to phonological analysis as it emerges from the comparative lexical corpus and defined by grouping lexemes according to phonetic categories. It is an attempt at the reconstruction of the Afro-Asiatic phonological system, but his conclusion is that, for the research of that time (1947), it was impossible to go beyond the Semitic system. It is possible, however, that one should go further in the reconstruction of the Hamito-Semitic phonological system, which is, in fact, what modern research has done. Actually, in the introductions to each one of the phonetic categories, Cohen offers interesting discussions that provide a glimpse of a much more complex situation than the classification already mentioned would allow us to believe.

2.2   The Afro-Asiatic perspective for the study of Semitic phonology was begun in a definitive way above all by I. M. Djakonoff and his school. After less well-defined discussions (1965, 1967), the last edition of his overall survey (1988) traces the phonological set of common Afro-Asiatic, based on data extracted from living languages and not from the "grapho-phonemes" provided by ancient written languages.[21] Only living languages allow "the oppositions of the semantically minimal phonological pairs" (p. 35) to be established. As such, this reconstruction lies beyond our present horizon of interest, but it is very illuminating for the new phonetic categories it introduced, for example, dentals that are fricative and affricated, palatalized and non-palatalized, plus the fricative and affricated laterals (the three groups of sibilants), the labialized velar plosives, the (post-)velar fricatives and labialized affricates, and, in particular, the introduction into the phonetic set of the specific category of "strong" and "weak" sonants (encompassing nasals, liquids, semi-vowels and certain velar-pharyngeal realizations) alongside the consonants. He lingers particularly on the explanation of the transformation of sibilants, bringing in his own hypothesis of a Proto-Afro-Asiatic phoneme /š̠/, which would be the origin of the pronominal-causative "marker" [/š/, /h/, /ʾ/, /s/] in the various Semitic languages. Lastly, Djakonoff notes the ambiguous character of the phoneme /ʾ/ as both sonant and consonant (p. 40), highlighting in this way a problem that is still unresolved in Semitic phonetics.

This short sketch has the merit of providing at the diachronic level almost all the problems presented by Semitic phonetics and will be referred to frequently in the approaches that follow.

2.3 Several years later, I. M. Djakonoff (in collaboration with Stolbova, Militarev and others) proposed a more developed reworking of these ideas, this time applied to Akkadian, more suited in this way to be considered his own interpretation of Semitic phonology (1990–1991).[22]

2.4 For other reconstructions of the phonological set of Afro-Asiatic there is an excellent summary in the introduction by K. Petráček (1989)[23] and in the lexicographical studies by A. R. Bomhard and J. C. Kerns (1994),[24] V. L. Orel and O. V. Stolbova (1995),[25] C. Ehret (1995),[26] and G. Takács (1999).[27] A recent and very graphic treatment of Semitic phonetics from the standpoint of Afro-Asiatic linguistics is that of A. Dolgopolsky (1999).[28]

However, all these studies, as well as others on the Afro-Asiatic languages that could be added, lie beyond our horizon, even though it would be very interesting to take them into account for an overall view of the phonological problem of Semitic.

3. Incompatibility

3.1 A problem connected to consonantism is the incompatibility of certain phonemes as components of the same root lexeme. The definitive discussion of the topic was by J. H. Greenberg, in an article that is now a classic (1950).[29]

The merit of Greenberg's article is that it outlined the problem in a general and systematic way, that is, in relation to all the Semitic languages, even though based on Arabic (i.e., the lexica of Lane and Dozy), because in 1950 there were no suitable reference books for the other Semitic languages. Three tables provide the complete set of triconsonantal roots (3775) of the Arabic lexicon, produced from the combination of 29 phonemes in the three possible positions. Greenberg completes a detailed analysis of the data acquired, arriving at the following general "laws':

I. In positions I–II, identical and homorganic consonants are mutually exclusive, that is, they are incompatible; the rare exceptions are idiosyncratic or phonetically secondary.

II. In positions II–III, homorganic consonants are excluded, but not identical consonants (reduplication); this is an "anomaly" that has to be taken into account for a theory of triliteral roots derived from biliteral roots.

III. In positions I–III, identical and homorganic pairs are tolerated, as is often the case in primary nouns.

Greenberg groups the series of consonants into four sections of which three / four classes or series of laryngeals/pharyngeals, post-velars, and velars comprise the first section, with back articulation. Of the remaining sections the second contains the liquids and /n/; the third, the frontal consonants with the series of sibilants, dentals, and interdentals; the fourth comprises only the labial series. In applying the "laws" mentioned to the sections, the following conclusions can be drawn:

a. The four sections of consonants are completely compatible among themselves.

b. Consonants of the same section tend to be avoided in the same triliteral root, except for velars with pharyngo-laryngeals and sibilants with dentals (the latter always in first position).

c. The incompatibility mentioned is more rigorous in positions I–II and II–III than in positions I–III.

d. There are no Proto-Semitic (verbal) roots with identical consonants in positions I–II, nor probably in positions I–III. However, they are common in positions II–III.[30]

e. These rules apply only to verbal roots, not to nominal roots, nor do they affect secondary radicals from which other morphemes derive.

In this study, which affects a field of research that he considers to be promising, Greenberg considers only triconsonantal verbal morphemes, essentially based on Arabic, whereas in the other languages the incompatibility is not so clear. A revision and reinterpretation of the subject are required based on Akkadian, Ugaritic, and South Arabic lexicography, which is now more advanced than that then available to Greenberg. Perhaps the final model will not be as rigid and more importance may be attributed to analogy and phonological transformations. Its integration is necessary within a wider perspective, which would include the problem of nominal root morphemes that, in principle, should not behave differently with respect to phonology, as well as the problem of biconsonantal roots, both verbal and nominal. Above all, it should take into account the problem of primary vocalization, not considered here. At all events, this distinction between nominal and verbal lexical morphemes is very important and has become common opinion, as we have seen in connection to more general, as well as with some other more specific, studies on the Semitic root. Since its appearance, every study bearing on Semitic lexicography, comparative or etymological, has had to compare its results to the system of phonological relationships outlined by Greenberg.

3.2   G. Herdan (1962) took up Greenberg's approach and proposed applying Shannon's mathematical information theory to Greenberg's combinational statistical method, extending it to all roots, not only verbal roots, as well as to other languages, not only to Arabic, for which Greenberg gives the number of 3775 roots, asking himself why and how they are generated.[31] Apparently the results confirm Greenberg's findings.

3.3   K. Petráček (1964)—independently, it seems, since he does not cite Herdan's article—also considers the incompatibility formulated by Greenberg in light of information theory, but without the mathematical formalization.[32] The "coefficient of distinctiveness" is studied according to the method of binary phonological analysis, proposed by Jacobson and his students, on the basis of twelve pairs of acoustic properties and the resulting quantification of the oppositions between phonemes. The comparison to Greenberg's incompatibilities gives a very similar result, with the exception of well-differentiated phonemes (belonging to different sections, following Greenberg's nomenclature) that nevertheless are incompatible (against conclusion a).

In a more classical perspective, K. Petráček (1975), in a general approach to the reconstruction of Proto-Semitic, touches very briefly on specific problems of Semitic phonology: back articulation (glottals, pharyngeals, post-velars) and the correlation of emphatics (secondary articulation), resulting from dynamism or innovation, demonstrated by Arabic, which led to modifying the accepted system.[33] This dynamism leads to the development of new phonemes, as is the case of /ġ/ and /ḍ/. "In this case it would be useless to view Arabic as the most conservative language—quite the reverse!" (p. 164). The data from Afro-Asiatic and Egyptian dynamism corroborate this possibility. The (Semitic) proto-system must be more restricted than particular attested systems. This minimalism will have to be applied even more to the reconstruction of the Afro-Asiatic system.

K. Petráček returned to the subject some years later (1988),[34] from a more general approach of the whole laryngeal-pharyngeal-postvelar-velar section, following the same statistical pattern as Greenberg, specifying groups of incompatibilities within this section both in Semitic and especially in Egyptian, a domain not yet studied systematically by him.[35] Petráček exposes the differences between the two consonantal systems, Semitic and Egyptian, and discusses the possibility of their correlation. But this is a topic that we are leaving aside for the moment. It is very interesting, however, to set down his conclusions:

a.   The Egyptian system of the incompatibility of pharyngeals is looser and, it seems, older than the Semitic system.

b.   The procedure implied here may well be related to the character of "sonants" that Petráček ascribes to all the laryngeals (glottals and pharyngeals) and the importance that this category of phonemes (glides) has, it seems, in the structure of the Afro-Asiatic root (Djakonoff).

c.   Apparently, in Egyptian the distinction between nominal bases and verbal roots is no longer operative, where nominal bases break the incompatibility laws established for verbal roots. As a result "one has to admit that the

Semitic root has developed and established itself during the specific development of inner inflexion" (p. 377).

3.4.   A completely new treatment of incompatibility in Semitic, in terms of point of view and development, was proposed by R. M. Voigt (1981).[36] After a very subtle analysis of the general framework in which incompatibilities occur and the logical discrepancies, semantic and phonological (sentence, word, lexical category, morpheme, root and pattern, loans and new formations, root and morphematic morpheme, distinctive feature of the phoneme), he tries to situate them in Coseriu's theory of "Norm-System-Rede." He then considers at length the phonematic incompatibility of the Semitic root, which tends to weaken over time, and more specifically the first law of incompatibility, which forbids a sequence of two identical root phonemes. The exceptions to this law are carefully analyzed and explained: loans and new formations, onomatopoeic words, internal phonetic developments, compound lexemes, morphematic extensions, various types of reduplication with associated phenomena, assimilation/dissimilation, reduction, etc. The second reduplicated consonant requires special attention; it is explained as a gemination or prolongation in order to make it fit the triconsonantal system, or else as a result of partial reduction. In other respects, certain special cases (the nouns for "three," "six," "sun," "root") represent assimilated forms of completely compatible primitive roots. All these phenotypes give rise to "roots" that could be called secondary, with a phonological structure that apparently goes against the law of incompatibility, although in themselves not really exceptions. Incompatibility must be considered within the more general framework of the mechanism of phonological laws and changes at work in diachronic linguistics.

3.5.   More recently, A. Zaborski (1994/1996) tried to demonstrate that, apart from onomatopoeia and loanwords, the incompatibility rules in Semitic allow of no exceptions.[37] A study of alleged exceptions shows that they are secondary innovations or denominative roots, taking possible root variants into account. At the close of the second article (1996, pp. 652–54) Zaborski provides a detailed and very useful table of incompatibilities.

4. The OCP (Obligatory Contour Principle)

The phenomenon of consonantal incompatibility uses nowadays a formulation and a very general formal development that applies the obligatory contour principle (OCP), formulated by linguists since the 1970s, "according to which two contiguous elements of a melody cannot be identical: in every series /a, b/, a # b."[38] It should be noted that "originally proposed to account for distributional regularities in lexical tone systems (Leben 1973), its role in tone was later either modified (Leben 1978), rejected (Goldsmith 1976), or limited to the phonetic level (Goldsmith 1976). The OCP has enjoyed greater success in its application to nonlinear segmental phonology (McCarthy 1979)."[39]

In fact, what seems to be merely a particular and specific case of incompatibility conceals a large number of implications and applications that seem useful to explain the structure of the root, its diachronic developments, and its morphological products. In fact, it is a principle used extensively in this domain, but has not remained free of criticism.

4.1. In a series of articles, G. Bohas analyzes the effect of OCP on structure and change in the Semitic lexicon. More specifically, in a brief squib (1990),[40] he analyzes its action on the transformation of the Proto-Semitic/Arabic phoneme /ḍ/ to Syriac /ᶜ/ when it converges with an original /ᶜ/ (in positions I/II), a convergence rejected by the OCP. The result is its fusion with the third consonant (by directional projection), its gemination, and the reduction of the lexeme to a biradical morpheme. The effectiveness of the OCP thus becomes clear at the diachronic level in the phonetic application of the Syriac system.

In another study that resumes the previous one (1993), the analysis is applied to the same phenomenon, this time in the case of the transformation of Proto-Semitic/Arabic /ᶜ/ to Syriac /ʾ/ by a restriction of the OCP, which forbids contiguous phonemes with the same articulation, now in position I/III.[41] The possible Aramaic-Syriac exceptions are explained by the persistence of the deep representation (root), the only level where OCP is strictly effective, whereas the transformation mentioned is very late. One piece of evidence that corroborates this late phonetic process appears in the transformation of /q/ to /ʾ/ in the modern Arabic dialects of the Levant and in the different vocalization (apophony) of the accomplished/unaccomplished, agreeing with the nature of the /ʾ/, whether original or not, in all positions. Also the late change of /g/ to /ǧ/ in Arabic confirms the thesis defended by the preservation of the underlying representation, which explains the apparent anomalies flouting the OCP. The nature of these phenomena has to be sought in "radical" structure (etymology), not in diachronic transformation (lexis).

4.2. The OCP has not lacked its critics, who deny it any value, as McCarthy and Bohas certified at the start. Recently, other Semitists, including R. M. Voigt (1982) and G. Goldenberg (1994), have expressed their disagreement with the application of the principle to Semitic phonology.[42]

In any case, both the OCP and articulatory incompatibility apply to biliteral roots: there, /C-C/ root lexemes, composed of phonemes of the same class or the same articulation point, are very rare.

5. Appraisal

We have seen some oscillation in the classification and definition of the table of phonemes of the Semitic languages, and as a result, of Early Semitic. Certain classical labels, which are more or less "impressionistic" (liquids, emphatics, even (re)sonants or rolls), tend to disappear. It must be supposed that this variation is the fruit of an attempt to determine more exactly the pronunciation of the phonemes in question. This determination is often made by Semitists who are not phoneticians by training and who work on historical facts (for example, descriptions by Arab grammarians) or comparative data (inter-dialectal variants or equivalences). Methodologically, these facts are not enough to establish an exact table of the characters or articulation features of phonemes, as shown by the discussions we have just examined. On the other hand, when it is a question of modern Semitic languages, proof by quantitative empirical means should be used to eliminate all ambiguity and supply exact verification, according to the parameters of the IPA (International Phonetic Alphabet) of the actual nature of the phoneme, unequivocally and beyond dispute, discarding all other intuitive or purely theoretical opinions. But the use of this material to define the original Semitic system is suspect, given the extreme degree of change and contamination experienced by these languages (Modern South Arabian, Neo-Aramaic, Modern Ethiopic in general).

Reference to a good textbook on general phonetics can provide precise data and, in fact, this is customary among Semitists.[43] There will always be, therefore, differences in the terminology that have to be taken into account, as is the case, for example, with the "coronals" of Bohas, based on the classification of Halle-Kenstowicz, which correspond, in fact, to the "apicals," sibilants, and lateralized consonants of Cantineau.[44] Generally speaking, I am more in favor of the binary opposition of features and points of articulation of phonemes, and against grouping them into "triads," the classic three or four. In this connection one could speak also of "tetrads" (sets of four).

Yet there are certain points on which a consensus has been reached. For example, the original glottal articulation of phonemes characteristic of Semitic languages called "emphatics";[45] the lateral or lateralized articulation as a category that includes several phonemes with a much discussed character even today (/l/, /ṣ/, /ḍ/...);[46] the importance of "sonants" (approximants) in the Semitic phonetic scheme, now arranged in a special category that includes all the phonemes that until now remained a little beyond the academic classification. Their meaning is perhaps decisive for the study of the original structure of roots and their morpho-lexical development, while at a historical level these phonemes have acquired a clear typology that differentiates them very little in terms of phonological function from the other consonants. This is why we can say that the importance granted by Djakonoff and his school to these phonemes, in their theory of the structure of primary nominal roots in Semitic, relies too much on the Indo-European model and risks erasing or at least blurring the limits between the phonetic functions of vowels and consonants.

Even so, with respect to the alternation of /š:h/ as a double reflex of a Proto-Afro-Asiatic /*š̌/, especially in the Epigraphic South Arabian languages, I think that it is better explained as a *Lautwandel* or phonetic change peculiar to the Semitic family. There is no need to resort to any specific original phoneme. Also its functional distribution in the lexicon (the pronominal series and causative morphematic series) with very few "radical" realizations, probably to be explained by analogical contact (for example, in Mehri, in words with a clear Common Semitic equivalence), indicates an alternation between semantically interchangeable elements (semantic calque) as Edzard suggests.[47]

Instead, the primitive nature of the phoneme /ġ/ can be considered as certain, which cannot be said of /ʔ/, whose articulatory character and binary opposition are not yet clear.[48] In this connection, note the functional and positional similarities that link this phoneme to the "semi-consonants" ([bi]labial /w/, palatal /y/, glottal /ʔ/, in progressive articulation). It fills the same slots, for example, in the glottalization /Xʔ/, that they fill in the labialization /Xʷ/ or the velarization /Xʸ/. Like them, it can assume a range of syllabic intensity (/a̲/), as a "diphthong" /aᵓ/ or as a contraction /â/ (parallel to /u̲/ → /aw/ → /ô/, /i̲/ → /ay/ → /ê/), with the double character of consonant and vowel. Lastly, like them it can be interposed as a glide in any position. Moreover, in several Semitic languages, e.g., Arabic, there is an alternation of /w, y/ /# /ᵓ/, even in first position. Perhaps they should be grouped into a "tetrad" of glides in two binary oppositions (/w, y/ /# /h, ᵓ/) in parallel / opposition to the sonants / approximants (/l, r/ # /m, n/). Finally, in regard to these note the exchanges between the two groups of "liquids" and "nasals."[49]

In the same context, the nature and phonetic role of this entire series of semi-vowels / consonants has yet to be determined, especially from the diachronic aspect.

In relation to the question of phonetic incompatibilities in Semitic, a general validity must be accorded to Greenberg's conclusions, the fruit of an empirical analysis of the Semitic lexicon, especially of Arabic. But it should be noted that they are only valid for triliteral verbal roots, which means that the vast lexicon of triliteral non-verbal roots and all the biliterals are not subject to these restrictions. Besides, these incompatibilities do not function equally in all the Semitic languages.[50]

But, in good linguistic logic, one cannot have different laws of consonantal incompatibility in the lexicon of the same language with a well-defined phonological system. Incompatibility is a phonetic rather than a phonological occurrence, which affects the general system of the phonemes of each language. If there are different systems of incompatibility within the same language, then they are due to non-phonetic reasons. Moreover, incompatibility is a statistical evaluation, not a phonetic law. All this poses the question of the unity of an original phonetics. Can a double phonetic system, one for primary nouns and the other for the remaining lexemes, one for triliteral verbal roots and the other for the remaining roots, be envisaged and justified within a proto-language? What would be the reason or the criterion that would lead to its evaluation? This question is linked to another issue, the distinction between "noun" and "verb," which we discussed earlier.

I am inclined to favor a unified phonetics for the two categories of lexemes, whose original differentiation is neither phonetic nor lexematic but functional, or grammatical if one prefers. And in regard to the incompatibilities, I take a very flexible position, while still maintaining the validity of the general rule according to which the Semitic languages (Common Semitic) tend to exclude combinations of identical or homorganic phonemes in triconsonantal verbal roots, especially in positions I–II, I–III, less so in position II–III. In this connection, it is worth remembering Petráček's conclusions (1988) mentioned above on phonetic incompatibility in Egyptian (that is, at a pre-Proto-Semitic level), which are not as rigid as Greenberg suggests for Semitic, and on the lack of a noun/verb distinction in Egyptian roots. In addition, if there is in fact a "symphoneme" (or consonant-vowel compound phoneme) in a language, whatever its origin may be, one can no longer speak of its phonetic incompatibility, but only of relative or statistical frequency. The domain of phonetics and phonology has to be unified within each lexical system.

On the other hand, one of the more significant novelties in Semitic phonology with respect to the original structure of roots, phonetic and semantic, is the introduction of an analysis of "features" instead of points of articulation. In fact, these points are considered as so many "features," which causes some confusion. (Should we distinguish between features that are points of articulation and features that are articulatory modifications, such as occlusion, vibration, co-articulation, etc.?) Taking lexematic analysis to extremes allows its proponents (Bohas, for example) a wider margin of semantic differentiation than is provided by analysis based on points of articulation.

In the specific case of G. Bohas' theory, the "matrix" or third level, the deepest, of the arrangement of the Semitic lexeme or phonetic where "features" work in binary combination, assumes a large capacity for including many specific realizations (admittedly, by combining articulatory phonemes that belong to the matrix and are the only ones empirically effective in the language) within a very wide set of semantic derivations. The starting-point for this way of viewing radical analysis was, as previously noted, the theory of "features" formulated by Jacobson-Hall.[51] But that was an analysis of isolated "phonemes" on the basis of twelve pairs of phonetic features, and Bohas applies it (with fourteen features) to the analysis of matricial lexemes (pairs of phonemes) composed of these features. There is then a certain shift of the initial theory. At all events, we have to define which are the "dominant" features in the formation of the matrix, in the Bohas sense, or whether in this respect they all have the same value in themselves and in relation to those of the other phoneme with which they combine. A single feature is not enough to define and take the place of a phoneme; an isolated feature is phonetically impossible to realize.

In addition, in each matrix there remains still implicated another pair of features, at least for each etymon (pair of phonemes), in agreement with which this can belong to another matrix. It is not too difficult to find, especially in the Arabic lexicon, another semantic load and the corresponding list of etyma that cover it. One could think that it is precisely this variety of matrices that explains homonymy and even enantiosemy.[52] But we then enter dangerous and wild terrain where anything is possible; we shall return to this question later. Leaving aside for the moment an appraisal of the theory of Jacobson-Halle,[53] it seems that in its application to the theory of matrices there is an error of method (a move from the phonetic level to the phonological level) that puts its validity into question. This shift, in my view hasty and unsuitable, from the phonetic theory of "features" to the semantic and phonological interpretation of matrices, is repeated when Bohas uses Wittgenstein's semantic theory of "family features," which this author outlined, to define the members of a "semantic" category. The phonetic features that defined the matrices of Bohas belong rather to the class of NSC (necessary and sufficient conditions) and not to the class of "family resemblance." If such a well-orchestrated theory proves acceptable for Arabic, it must be acceptable for all Semitic in general and all its families, given its radical lexematic level. But only a comparative proof can give a reply. Otherwise, this becomes a problem of the Arabic lexicon, which has to be resolved by internal diachronic analysis suited to its own semantics. Whatever the case, the data provided and interpreted by Bohas are there and an explanation has to be found.

Lastly, the solution that G. Bohas proposes for the origin of the Arabic phoneme /jim/ (/ǧ/), as belonging to a double articulatory class (velar/voiced occlusive uvular) remains difficult to justify, not only from the aspect of phonetics (a voiced uvular /q/, pharyngalized or glottalized?[54]), but from the aspect of his theory of "features." The split of the phoneme /q/, which gives rise to various matrices, is opposed to the Semitic system; as a voiced uvular articulation would be derived or secondary in Arabic,[55] it would not be reflected in the matrices that, one assumes, are original and as such Proto-Semitic, but in the etyma. Should we accept a deeper "pre-matrix" level in this case or a stage of creation of matrices peculiar to Arabic? Once again, comparative proof is required.

Bohas' approach, nevertheless, has the great merit of suggesting that at the basis of the phonological system of a language there is no an "alphabet" that functions like a system of elementary decomposition into relevant discrete phonemes (this is an approximate and late operation based on specific, phonologically well-defined languages), but rather a "resonance," a synthesis of continuous sound "features." In the same way that at the base of semantics there is no a NSC system but "a similarity of functionality": what the setting means for me, not what it "is" in itself. It is with this that systematic and consolidated semantic theories are normally concerned even now, driven by a concern to "define meaning," the characteristic or categorical features of the referent (Greek logic). For etymological or genetic semantics, which is concerned with the origin of the phonological sign, the referent has as its denominator a "functional" importance fixed symbolically by the phonological features. It is from this that one must define the "basic seme" of the lexeme.

Excursus
A NEW DIAGRAM OF SEMITIC PHONOLOGY

For a long time the existence has been acknowledged, within the set of Semitic phonemes, of parallel series of different modulations or phonetic features with the same base of articulation. This is the case of the famous "triads" (voiced / voiceless / emphatic) that are often included, in the chapter on phonology, in textbooks on comparative Semitics and in the grammars of the various languages. This clear symmetry, even if partial, is based on the nature and functional limits of the apparatus for producing vocal sounds, which inevitably leads to the expression of phonemes composed on the basis of pairs of phonetic features. This binary distribution presupposes a striking economy in the production process of the various phonological signs and irretrievably creates a system of symmetrical combination that is completely predictable.

In fact, there have been many attempts to organize the diagram of the phonological system of Common Semitic starting from comparison of its historical forms in the various languages. Here can be mentioned the diagrams supplied by Cantineau and Moscati that are reproduced above (see pp. 32, 34). Instead, Weil corrects and improves them, creating a representation in space of inverted symmetry of biblical Hebrew consonants. But the obsession with "triads" as a determinative element deforms the final result. In fact, all these diagrams have a common structure, a triangular projection based on the recognition of the triads of phonetic modulation cited, that correspond to three different points of articulation. They become irreparably asymmetrical by leaving other points of articulation outside the triangle of phonemes and they only reproduce mechanically the binary tabulation with two-dimensional coordinates: point of articulation // modular articulation. Of course, outside this arrangement remain various phonemes that do not exhibit a clear correlation. However, this presentation has the advantage, over a simple tabular distribution, of depicting more clearly the symmetries of the system.

Below is Weil's diagram:

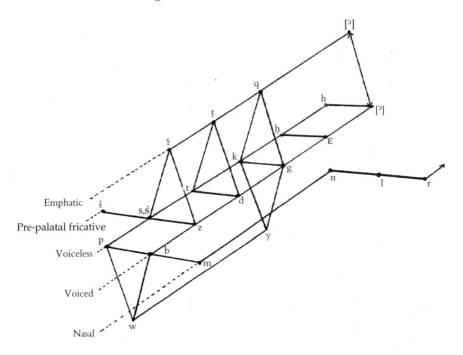

I propose (see below p. 51) a plan diagram of the (Proto-)Semitic phonological system that in my opinion has three advantages:

1. It incorporates organically into the binary distribution the features "lateral" and "sonant," which do not appear in the diagrams mentioned or in many of the usual distribution tables. On the other hand, a mere different arrangement of the articulation points would not highlight these symmetries of modulation, although a table with a distribution following a different order could include them all.

2. This diagram emphasizes a greater degree of phonetic symmetries: we have not only four triads of occlusive consonants but the ternary distribution appears also in a fifth articulation point (bilabials; see p 32 above [Cantineau]), once the existence of a Proto-Semitic phoneme / p̂ / is acknowledged (see p. 36 [Militarev-Kogan]) and required by the demands of the system. At the same time the existence of three parallel series of four realizations (sonorant, voiceless, glottalized and lateral) also becomes clear.[56] The position of the articulation point reduces the possi-

ble modulations of back articulations. This is why uvulars and pharyngeals are realized only as sonorants and voiceless, whereas the laryngeals
(/ʾ/ /h/), in principle considered voiceless, prove to be very inexact in
this regard, given the overlap of their articulation point with the very
origin of sonority.

3. Lastly, this diagram unifies in a single articulation-modulation system,
   the series of consonant, sonant, semi-vocalic, and vocalic phonemes,
   which no other diagram has succeeded in doing.

From the aspect of phonetic description, I have opted for the most objective
terminology possible, avoiding, on the one hand, "impressionistic" terms ('emphatics," "sibilants," "liquids" …) and, on the other, terms that are too analytical or not yet
common.

First I have arranged the axis of the coordinates according to articulation/
modulation, in line with classic phonetics, while giving the first the character of principal phonological feature and the second the character of co-articulation.[57] With
respect to determining the points of articulation, I have retained a discreetly classical
and supple terminology, one that allows, on the one hand, juxtaposing phonemes that
are close as regards articulation, sometimes not well-defined, and, on the other, justi-
fying the various characterizations provided by phoneticians.[58]

This difference of terminology is the simple reflex of an elementary fact: the
apparatus for producing vocal sounds (from the glottis up to the lips) forms a phys-
iological continuum in which the determination of separate "zones" becomes inexact.
This gives rise to differing "divisions" in each phonological system, generating articulations and modulations that are not pertinent for all.

With respect to the unification of the consonantal and vocalic systems (see
above p. 24 n. 20) one can say that although the consonantal phoneme can still be
analyzed as an alternating phoneme, either free or in vocalic distribution (/ba, bi, bu,
ka, ki, ku …/), it cannot be realized unless concomitant with a vocalic modulation.
This means that the true object of phonology is the syllable, while advocating the unity
of the system (consonant-vowel). The vowels, therefore, avoid being strictly described
according to point of articulation and are arranged according to the area of resonance
in which they are modulated (front, central, back / high, medium, low). The unifying
element between the two systems is the feature "sonant," which, while it retains
among its realizations a correlation of articulation more defined than those of the
vocalic system—in fact "sonants" are "con-sonants'—generates a phonetic subsystem
halfway, by its function, between consonants and vowels.

The horizontal axes mark the point of articulation—the inherent features of
occlusion, fricativeness, etc. are presumed implicit—while the vertical/slanting axes
(thick line) indicate the modulation of the phonation. In this respect glottal articulation implies in turn non-sonority (see above p. 34 [Moscati]), at the same time that the
feature sonant includes nasality and vibration (thus reaching the six phonemes
described as sonants). Other symmetries can be recognized following the secondary
vertical axes (dotted lines) that relate phonemes to different articulation points, but
retain special alternations all along the diachrony of certain languages. On one side,
/ġ/ and /ṯ/ in Ugaritic, and on the other, /q/ and /ᶜ/ in Aramaic, as reflexes of /ḏ:ḍ/,

with allowances made for the defective alphabetic notation. If one folds the diagram along its central axis, there is a complete symmetrical overlap of the sonorant-voiceless "gutturals" (/h/-/ʾ/, /ḫ/-/ġ/, /ḥ/-/ᶜ/), as well as the series of three or four modulations cited above. The system postulates /ʾ/ as being voiceless and the existence of a glottalized ("emphatic") phoneme / ṗ/.

With respect to the lateral feature of the four phonemes characterized as lateral, I refer to the studies, summarized above, of Cantineau, Cohen, Martinet, and especially of Steiner and Voigt. In this connection, we must take into account the double role played by the phoneme/grapheme /š/ as a lateral and as an palato-alveolar voiceless fricative, which makes it close to the Arabic voiced phoneme /g:ǧ/, as reflected in the diagram, putting them on the same axis of articulation.[59] In addition, it is a very fluctuating phoneme/grapheme in Semitic, as shown by the twofold diachronic convergence with /ś/, on the one hand, and with /ṯ/, on the other, in certain Semitic languages.

Lastly, in the sub-system of the feature sonant, /l/, the lateral by definition, forms a specific group with the nasals (/m/ and /n/) and the trill (/r/) due to their twofold function of consonant-vowel, in perfect correlation with the semi-vowels, which in turn amount to being homorganic with vowels. From the aspect of articulation, the bilabial character of /m/ and /w/ is certain, a correlate of the rounded feature of the vowel /u/. The alveolar-dental articulation of /n/ is clear; the semi-vowel /y/, however, has a rather (pre-)palatal articulation, in agreement with the very character of the homorganic vowel /i/. As for /l/ and /r/, they are clearly alveolar.

In connection to this, the system requires the glottal /ʾ/ (and even /h/), due to its function as a glide, to be grouped with the semivowels, as homorganic with the vowel /a/ (see above pp. 33, 44f.) and more generally as a precondition of the realization of the three vowels. (See the triple vocalization of /ʾ/ in Ugaritic and Akkadian.) In this way this "(pre-)phoneme" is the "keystone" of the two sub-systems, one of consonants and one of sonants.

The following diagram illustrates the multiple correlation of Semitic phonemes within the set of general phonetics. It also highlights the symmetrical nature of their realization that is at the basis of later transformations, both normative and exceptional, within each of the specific linguistic systems. This diagram can be set out as a table with binary and ternary coordinates, but I believe that the representation adopted here gives a better picture of the symmetry of the system.[60]

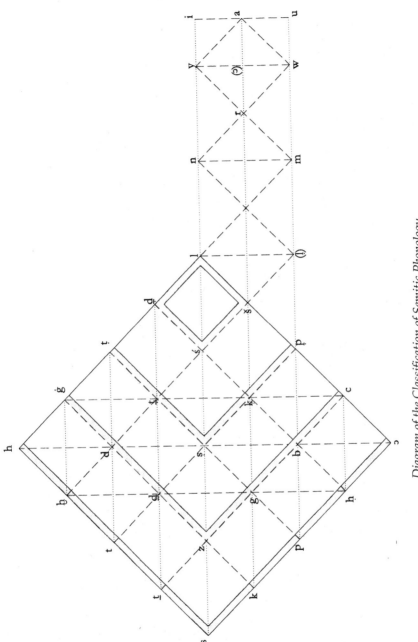

Diagram of the Classification of Semitic Phonology

Articulation	Modulation								
	Consonant				Sonant				
	voice-less	voiced	glottal	lateral	lateral	nasal	vibrant	semi-vowel	semi-vowel
glottal-laryngeal	h								
uvular-velars	ḫ	ġ							
dental	t	d	ṭ						
inter-dental	ṯ	ḏ	ṯ̣	ḏ̣					
alveolar-palatal	s	z	ṣ	ś	l	n		y	i
palato-velars	k	g	ḳ	š			r	(ʔ)	a
bilabial	p	b	ṗ			m		w	u
pharyngeal	ḥ	ʿ							
glotto-laryngeal	ʾ								

IV

THE PROBLEM OF
BI/TRILITERALISM

The presence of biconsonantal (biliteral) or binary articulatory lexemes in Semitic is quite obvious and has been studied for some time. In the semantic fields of family relationships and of parts of the body these lexemes refer to the oldest layers of Common Semitic. The issue is the extent to which the biconsonantal series is at the origin of the development of the Semitic lexicon by means of various patterns of expansion, especially in the case of verbal roots. The debate concerning biliterality/triliterality (biconsonantalism/triconsonantalism) has a long history and, even today, it is possible to find completely contradictory opinions on the matter, going from complete triradicalism (Voigt) to absolute biradicalism (Bohas), which to a large extent depends on the point of view of each scholar concerning the components of the "root," which I have already discussed. Here, I present a survey of the most well-founded opinions, followed by a discussion of the two most radical opinions, which I consider untenable, and then a reasonable synthesis. This is based on a complete and direct analysis of the Semitic biconsonantal lexicon of what we call the first two degrees of expansion/ intensification (see the following).

1. The History of Research

1.1. As regards the highly debated question of biliterality / triliterality as expressing the structure of the root in Semitic, it seems convenient to begin with the book by S. T. Hurwitz (1913),[1] even though it lies outside our time-frame. It provides a good summary from the point of view of "classical" scholars of the nineteenth century and, above all, presents the problem in all its complexity, exactly as it is still being discussed today.

After a detailed study of the problem, Hurwitz formulates his own hypothesis: "the Semitic triliteral is developed from a biliteral stem by means of a root-determinative" (p. 74). And after providing a large number of examples, he restates this in more general terms: "It is evident… that the Semitic root was originally biliteral…" (p. 107). In this way he summarizes and uses again, in a slightly shorter form, an old tradition developed throughout the nineteenth century (which he calls "the old biliteral school") and defended, either completely or in part, by the great Semitists of the time[2] as against another group, not so large but no less powerful, comprising such scholars as J. Barth (1887), F. Schulthess (1900), W. Wright (1896–98), C. Brockelmann (1908/ 1927). The theory derives from: (1) the formation, supposedly parallel, of quadriliteral roots with their determinatives; (2) biliteral forms of weak verbs (evidently geminated and hollow verbs); and (3) synonymous triliteral verbs, sharing a biliteral group—all facts that are interpreted differently by those who defend the contrary opinion. In the years following Brockelmann's *magnum opus*, the biliteral thesis was relegated to the status of an unproven hypothesis, indeed, even one that was unprovable and rejected out of hand, both in textbooks of comparative Semitics and in the grammars of individual languages. Such grammars usually start from the triliteral function of the root as a synchronic system operative in those languages, explaining, in agreement with that system, the few anomalies that could occur, especially in the treatment of so-called weak verbs. It was not until the 1930s that *GLECS* reopened the debate on the matter[3] on the bases established by Hurwitz.

1.2. Although it goes back to the 1920s, the study by H. B. Jušmanov (1929/1998)[4] is worthy of note for its influence on later Russian oriental studies (Majzel', Gazov-Gins-berg, Djakonoff). Its recent reprinting testifies to its relevance today.

Jušmanov was mainly an Arabic scholar and as such he refers to Arabic material. For him the Semitic "root" is composed only of consonants, normally three. Everything can be reduced to this triconsonantalism. However, this triconsonantalism is too complex and cannot correspond to the original situation. The root has a fixed element that he calls a "cell" (*jačeika*), composed of two consonants that, in certain cases, can form biconsonantal roots, but very few; normally it has "variations." One of these variations affects the radical consonants and another supposes the enlargement of the "cell." This expansion poses several questions: What is the meaning of the augmenting consonant? What is the normal position of this augmenting consonant (prefix, suffix, infix)? What is the role of weak consonants in this process? How can we label the variations of homorganic consonants of the actual "cell"? And, more generally, how does one arrive at the structure of the triconsonantal model as the basis of Semitic grammar? We are thus faced with a classic problem, outlined since the nineteenth century and already summarized by Hurwitz (see above). Jušmanov provides also a short historical survey (extension by prefixes, suffixes, both prefixes and suffixes, reduplication with dissimilation, combination of roots or words).

He tries to answer these questions, first collecting certain external influences that could have contributed to the formation of particular roots (loans, onomatopoeia, other homonyms, metathesis, rhyme, some expressive phonemes) and then studying the processes that he believes to be really productive. In this process he ascribes a particular role to "phonetic symbolism" (*Lautsymbolismus*), but above all he is concerned with the analysis of Semitic consonantalism as the basis of the process of root variation. The effects attested today are, in fact, a development of original "diffuse sounds" as shown by their interchangeability, the primary source of root variation. Even though this thesis, as a whole, is questionable, his attention to the "lateral" phonemes and to the semi-vowels as possible fossilized markers of certain verbal "stems" is quite extraordinary.

From this analysis of Semitic consonantalism, Jušmanov produces his understanding of roots: their basic (tri-)consonantal composition, their compatibility, the distinction between verbal and nominal roots, and the possible reduction of certain triconsonantal roots to biconsonantal ones. As to the type with a triconsonantal base, one cannot presuppose a single path of development from biconsonantalism to triconsonantalism. For him the main possibilities are consonantal repetition, the combination of roots, and morphemic extension. Thus he analyzes the types of differentiation that suppose repetition, as well as the nature of augmenting morphemes (prefixes, fossilized suffixes) and bases his proof on examples of tri- and polyconsonantal roots derived from biconsonantal "cells." This leads him to collect the various lists of "cells" proposed by his predecessors (Dietrich, Philippi, Cazet, von Gabelentz).

The final paragraphs of his study deal with a question that has had some resonance among Russian Semitists: the semantic value of nominal (and verbal) markers (third consonant) as defining semantic categories. In spite of the amount of material collected, it seems difficult to follow this path.

Be that as it may, Jušmanov's work remains an account of the problem that is still the concern of comparative and etymological Semitics and some of its proposals have been taken up by other scholars. He accepts triconsonantalism as the "normal" form of the Semitic root, but to explain it he has to leave it up to a proto-biconsonantalism that would be at the origin of the root through certain mechanisms of derivation.

1.3. After the 1940s, the topic was taken up again explicitly and systematically and in a general Semitic perspective. The first to do so was S. Moscati (1947),[5] with a study in which he begins by making a very relevant distinction: he does not speak of biliteralism but of biconsonantalism (the vowels are also "letters"). First, he collects witnesses who speak for and sometimes against the idea of biconsonantalism, from the Arab Middle Ages (Al-Bayḍāwī) to the end of the 1930s, including also the first witnesses of the seventeenth century (Simon) and the eighteenth century (Michaelis), as well as the substantial contributions of the nineteenth[6] and the beginning of the twentieth centuries,[7] ending with scholars from the second quarter of that century. In this connection he notes that, apart from the *Comptes rendus* of *GLECS* (Colin, Cerulli, Dhorme, Cohen), already mentioned, and a somewhat uncritical work by A.-S. Marmarğī (1937),[8] which tries to resolve Arabic roots into semantically varied biliteral groups, for this whole period, since Brockelmann's work, there is no important treatise on the matter. The following studies lie in the extra-Semitic comparative perspective: H. Möller (Semitic and European), C. J. Ball (Semitic and Sumerian), and C. Meinhof (Hamito-Semitic). To these should be added Baron Carra de Vaux, a defender of strict biliteralism and Semitic-Aryan comparisons, whose work *Tableau des racines sémitiques* (1919) was reprinted in Paris in 1944. Otherwise, the bibliographical horizon, especially with respect to the works of the great Semitists of the close of the nineteenth century, is as in the work by Hurwitz that Moscati claims he was unable to consult (p. 126 n. 2).

This is a pity as it is the most complete and most systematic work on the subject, both in relation to the origin of triliteralism and in relation to its nature, its function, and the number of determinatives that generate it, according to him. If Moscati had seen it, many repetitions would have been avoided; he would have been obliged to extend his field of study and, on the other hand, he would have been able to contribute important corrections and criticism to Hurwitz's thesis. As a whole, Hurwitz's study is not only more complete and systematic, but bolder and riskier, since he found himself attached to a thesis *a priori*. Moscati's work contributes nothing new or substantial, but defines the topic within more accurate and more reliable limits, less wide-ranging than those of Hurwitz. Suddenly, after noting that "in later times almost no Semitist has shown interest in the problem of biconsonantalism" (p. 122), he collects the basic data that establish the biconsonantal thesis: "It is not possible to question the existence of biconsonantal bases as making up the conceptual essence of many groups of Semitic roots" ("logical biconsonantalism" p. 123). Besides, "biconsonantal elements exist also in the historical phase of the Semitic languages," which can be proved in the primary nouns, in the forms of the weak verbs (basically hollow and geminated),[9] in the biconsonantal groups shared by triconsonantal roots in the strict sense, and in quadriliteral roots with reduplication /doubling, all generally roots with primary semantic meaning ("historical biconsonantalism," pp. 123f.). "Summing up: the biconsonantal roots in the Semitic languages are not an hypothesis but an historical fact" (p. 125); a biconsonantalism that must be understood as "partial-historical" in the present state of our knowledge (p. 126).

In the third section of his article, Moscati tries to illustrate the nature and function of the third element, called a determinative, assumed by triconsonantal roots that have the same biconsonantal group. It is analyzed in its various positions within the root, essentially based on biblical Hebrew, with the result: "according to this selection, all the consonants seem to be possible determinatives of third radical. The determinatives of first and second radicals seem to come from weak consonants or from grammatical forms" (p. 129).

With regard to the origin and function of these determinatives, after listing and evaluating the hypotheses put forward on the subject ("prepositional theory," determinatives of this kind in first position; "radical theory," resulting from the fusion of two roots; "grammatical theory," determinatives with the function of conjugation; "phonetic theory," produced by difference in sound with a semantic nuance), he concludes: "In the present situation of the Semitic languages the determinatives do not reveal specific functions in a decisive manner" (p. 131). This skepticism is opposed to the firm position of Hurwitz in favor of the grammatical theory, previously proposed by Lagarde, who reduced the determinatives in a significant way to a maximum of fifteen, with some secondary variants.

On the other hand, one should not forget that the binary radical groups or biconsonantal roots have been subject to general phonetic laws, especially exchange, phonetic transformation within its own articulatory category, and metathesis of position within the lexeme, as well as to analogy of sound (more or less articulatory) that tends to create semantically related binary groups. All this considerably complicates the study of the actual biconsonantal group. As proof, Moscati presents four biconsonantal groups taken from biblical Hebrew (/dk/, /hb/, /kp/, /pr/) and their different combinatory variations.

The chief merit of Moscati's article is that it once again posed the question that had emerged from the concerns of Semitists, and that it defined its terms clearly:

    a. the existence of biconsonantal nominal and verbal roots (bases);

    b. their expansion by determinatives;

 c. the possible semantic value of the determinatives.

However, both Moscati and Hurwitz before him, as well as the scholars cited by him, defined the Semitic "root" exclusively as a biconsonantal cluster, without paying attention to the lexical function of an original, radical vocalization.

1.4.   A few years later, this opinion was taken up again by G. J. Botterweck (1952)[10] in an analysis of the roots /gl/, /kl/ /ql/ in the various classes of weak verbs (*lamed-he* and others, hollow and geminated), as well as in the extensions produced by the determinatives /S, h, ʾ/ (causative), /n, m, t/ (reflexive-passive). Albeit the reduplicated forms and forms with lengthened vowels are semantically very close and probably form the commonest extension of the biliteral root, "weak" roots develop ("causative" aspect) their basic seme as modalities of an "onomatopoeic basic meaning" (*lautmalende Grundbedeutung*), referring to the various types of action. By following this "phono-symbolic" path, he looks for a semantic differentiation in each of the three phonetic modalities of the roots studied: sonant, voiceless, emphatic. These conclusions were already known and would reappear in our own time. Heller labels them as *apologias* for biliteralism and sees them as the product of bias. He thinks that for the moment it is not possible either to uphold and to prove this thesis or to refute it. The main objection lies in "the great semasiological variability of the presumed biliteral original roots" (p. 681). Since access to the initial situation was precluded, future research in this field has to be limited to the analysis of specific biconsonantal groups with related meaning. "In the case of triconsonantal roots is difficult to arrive at clear results with the present current methods" (p. 682).

1.5.   In a small brochure published the same year, L. Roussel (1952)[11] took part in a passionate defense of the biconsonantalism of the Semitic root. This is certainly hypothetical, but, at the same time, real and common to a whole family of languages. Its origin is unknown, "for us it is only a starting-point: one sees what comes from it, but not from where it comes" (p. 11). Contrary to common opinion, the root is not necessarily verbal. His basic thesis is that "the Semitic root, exactly like the Indo-European root, is essentially composed of two consonants or sonants" (p. 12); at all events, the term "triliteral" must be rejected. Between these two consonants in principle there is assumed to be a vowel, namely, Indo-European /e/. On the other hand, biconsonantalism has always been recognized by Hebraists and Semitists but without their drawing the consequences. It entails certain incompatibilities, such as the sequence of two identical phonemes and probably, no doubt, the impossibility of having roots that begin with /ʾ [alef]/, given its character of vocalic attack. From the aspect of semantics, he pleads for a specific original meaning of the root, not for an "average" of all the meanings, as is usually supposed.

 Now this biconsonantal root has been "padded out" by means of three procedures: reduplication, antefixes, and augments / extensions. The meaning of reduplication is completely clear. The antefix (first position), as against the subsequent prefix, is very old, welded to the root; a speaker is unaware of it as such. Instead, augmentation (third position) is a consonant added to the root, changing its meaning; the origin of augmentation is unknown.

The work is then devoted to giving examples of the three procedures in all their combinations. Almost all the consonants can function as an antefix and especially as an augment; a statistical analysis can illustrate their semantic meaning. On these bases, the language develops an inevitable tendency toward triconsonantalism, which becomes the commonest form of the "root" in Semitic. A statistical analysis of the frequency of augments in the first position "weakens the hypothesis according to which the augments are of wasted roots of which only the beginning has survived" (p. 47). By analyzing antefixes and augments, 250 (biconsonantal) roots are obtained, which form approximately 1000 (triconsonantal) roots. Logic leads the scholar to draw this astonishing conclusion: "It is possible that one day, by dint of extracting from the root all accidental excrescences, one will be led to define it as ONE consonant + ONE vowel" (p. 62).

The resemblance to the Indo-European root is obvious. These are views that will emerge again in our own time (see below pp. 79, 82 [on Bohas]).

1.6.   As for the system of biradical verbal roots (excluding geminated verbs) in Akkadian, B. Kienast (1962)[12] provides a significant study that can be extrapolated to "recent Semitic." He creates a different system of triliterality with anomalies in vocalization and consonantal doubling. By applying the general laws of phonology and by a moderated use of analogy and of *Systemzwang*, he distinguishes the following groups, depending on the position of the root vowel: *ASP (>ʾASP), hypothetical and left to one side, PIS (< /w:n-C-C/), PSI (< /C-C-w:y/) and PÛS (< /C-Û-C/). He then dwells on an analysis of their morphology and apophony (*Ablaut*), which are not our concern here. In this way he discovers the original biliteral forms that appeared in the pure state in the imperative. The force of the system will make them fit triconsonantal patterns. He acknowledges also the existence of monoliteral roots that occur as PSI and PIS types at the same time, due to double augmentation (/n:w-C-y/) (!). As a result, we can state that there is a series of Semitic verbs with roots that have fewer than three consonants.

1.7.   Starting from the well-known existence of triliteral roots with a common biliteral root and the third consonant free, and accepting the five incompatibility laws formulated by J. H. Greenberg, J. MacDonald (1963–65)[13] wonders "whether that third consonant really provides a variant to a (hypothetical?) biliteral theme formed by the first two consonants, or may it be that a third consonant, subject to strict rules, as described by Greenberg, developed within a once general tendency to add a third consonant with a specific or determinative connotation?" (p. 84). Leaving the second hypothesis aside as yet to be explained, he defends the derivation of the triliteral verbal morpheme from an original Proto-Semitic, possibly pre-Proto-Semitic biliteral morpheme, even if it is not a universal solution. The argument is based on the existence of verbal roots with a common semantic load, on the similar development process of multiliteral roots, and on the primitive function of the first radical (prefix) or of the biliteral element in the verbal derivation. The starting-point is evidently Arabic. Ten or so monolingual and plurilingual tables are set up, depending on the phonetic nature of the components of the biliteral group and of the third consonants. In this way it is possible to verify Greenberg's laws and explain the semantic nuance of the variation. It is attested to by series of verbal root patterns providing four types of doubling. Lastly, verbal derivation is analyzed, with the focus on the biliteral element and considering the D-form as an expansion of the same kind as doubling that affects the action and not its subject, as is the case in the other derivations (Gt, L, Lt, C, Ct, N). Perhaps this D morpheme, which affects the second consonant, represents the first derived verbal form.

MacDonald's position then is clearly in favor of Semitic radical biliteralism, but I think that neither his arguments nor his examples prove that they are really original biliteral "roots" and not variants of an original triliteral group.

1.8.   In Akkadian, W. von Soden (1968)[14] analyzes the morpheme /n/ as a prefixed augment to biconsonantal roots, with a form attested, for example, in the imperative of several Semitic languages (Akk., Syr., Heb.). It would be a specific case of triliteral roots produced by a determinative with a special semantic meaning. Whatever the case, the distribution proposed previously seems inadequate.[15] For this purpose he analyzes several examples in various languages, as well as special verbs that have the alternation between /n:l/ and /n:w/ in first position, or equivalent patterns of /n-X-Y/ and /X-Y-Y/ (Aramaic "nasalization") and more sporadically equivalents with the hollow roots (/n-X-Y/ // /X-v-Y/) in a single paradigm where alternative "roots" are developed.

1.9.   M. Fraenkel (1970)[16] published his studies on the phonetic weakness (*Laut-schwächung*) of root consonants, based on the theory of the weakening of gutturals in third position, which he had written a few years earlier (1962). The direction of his work is clearly defined in the subtitle: *Gleichzeitig ein Beitrag zur semitisch-indo-germa-nischen Sprachverwandtschaft* (*Along with a contribution to linguistic Semitic-Indo-Germanic kinship*). Even if these studies belong to a viewpoint that could be called "Nostratic," they provide suggestions, no doubt questionable, that in certain cases can help us to understand variations in the Semitic triconsonantal "roots." They also contain a very complete historical survey of these questions.

The study begins by analyzing the weakening and softening of the first and second root consonants in many examples chosen from the Indo-European and Semitic languages (especially Hebrew) either peculiar to each family or common to both. Here "Nostratic" is playing with all the stops pulled out. It is impossible to formulate a law governing these variations, but in general it is possible to state that the strong forms are the oldest (p. 18); weakening must be considered a "carelessness of speech," seen especially in the pronunciation of the gutturals. The problem of roots with final /h:j/ must be considered in this perspective. It is only a difference of degree (it can also disappear completely). Thus this final /h/ (with or without *mappiq*) is not merely "graphical" but rather refers to an ancient consonant and does not suppose a "vocalic" root, as the grammarians would wish (see above [Botterweck]). In addition, the distinction between IIIh and IIIy roots has no importance: "then both forms go back to an older form with either /k/ or /g/ final sound. The *lamed-he* forms show phonetic weakening, the *lamed-yodh* forms phonetic drawing back" (p. 22). There are no IIIw roots; they are labialized forms of original gutturals.[17] Even the apparent bilit-eral forms /ʾab/ and /ʾaḫ / refer to triconsonantal roots (see below [Voigt]).

He acknowledges that Indo-European lexicography (Pokorny) has the opposite opinion and considers forms with laryngeals as extended forms, whereas other Semitists admit the origin of /h/ in certain cases to be /ḥ/, but consider both as additions or endings (*Anhängung, Endung*). A detailed "History of an error" (pp. 31ff.) gives the present "state of the question." In this respect, the theory of the (biconsonantal) root, whether prefixed or (especially) suffixed (with a third complementary consonant), is to be considered erroneous and contradictory, in spite of the popularity of this theory, incorrectly based on the Indo-European model. In certain cases one can admit the presence of a prefix (for example /ʔ-/, /n-/, /b-/), but with no prepositional meaning (see also p. 57).

His appraisal of the nature of the phonetic laws in Semitic becomes very interesting. It is not as rigid as claimed, especially in a comparison that goes beyond the field of Semitics. A greater variability must be acknowledged in its various applications: they are not the laws of physics. He acknowledges that: "My basic attitude to Semitic phonetic laws is then unorthodox" (p. 54). He accepts H. Wirth's theory[18] according to which the (Indo-European) roots are not composed of consonants with defined articulation but of a series of consonants: "There is originally no k-, ch-(h-) or g-stem, but a series of guttural (palatal) k-, ch-(h-), g consonant stems" (p. 55; see below [Bohas]). The various phonetic "features" (voiceless, voiced, …) can alternate without difficulty.

The process includes about 200 roots that must be verified empirically, even though intuition can lead the way. Fraenkel sets out to explain them (about 250 roots, in fact) in the following pages, in no specific sequence and in a perspective that often goes beyond the Semitic (Indo-European) horizon. A few final pages try to correct what the scholar calls "false formations and erroneous derivations" (pp. 311–16). I do not think that his theory has convinced followers of "Nostratic" comparativism (for example Bomhard-Kerns), and even less are the Semitists ready to accept his explanation of the weakened origin of roots with a final /h/. Even so, there are interesting "intuitions" in his work.[19]

1.10. D. Cohen (1972)[20] formulated a series of reservations concerning Djakonoff's hypothesis on the structure of the Semitic root, as set out in the 1965 edition of his book on the Afro-Asiatic languages (see above). According to Cohen, in Proto-Semitic there was a combined presence of biconsonantal and triconsonantal roots, with the latter predominant (the situation is different in other languages of the Afro-Asiatic group), while at that time Djakonoff tended to consider triconsonantal roots as so many expansions of biconsonantal roots (an old theory that, as we will see, constantly reappears), on the basis of complements with their own semantic or grammatical meaning.

1.11. Then, commenting on and summarizing the ideas of J. Kuryłowicz (1961),[21] G. Jucquois (1973)[22] reviews the situation concerning the structure of the root and its expansion, both in Indo-European and Semitic. It becomes evident that in this field derivation is principally apophonic ("few prefixes and few suffixes are clearly attested"). The problem, well known since Gesenius, is that verbal roots form etymologically close biconsonantal groups, with a random third consonant. So it is not possible to determine either the nature of affixes of these complements or their semantic function "so that this thesis cannot strictly speaking and making use of present methods be either rejected or confirmed" (p. 492; see above: Heller on Botterweck). In the case of the first consonant, given the more restricted number of augmenting prefixes in question (š/s, ʾ, h, t, w), the thesis "finds itself that much strengthened."

With Kuryłowicz the author proposes a theory of derivation in three stages: "1. Basic verb → 2. deverbalized noun → 3. denominative verb." Finally, in the case of roots with a long vowel or second reduplicated consonant, the biliteral origin is clearer and can be proved by the morpho-semantic alternating of verbal roots (for example, forms with infixed or suffixed /y, w/ or quadriliterals formed through doubling). This proposal of deriving triliteral and quadriliteral verbs (by prefixes, infixes, suffixes or doubling/reduplication) must be placed within a set of incompatibility of phonemes due to their "distinctive features," similar to the set proposed by Greenberg. Kuryłowicz fixes in this connection the rules in force in Hebrew and Arabic. It would be desirable, according to Jucquois, to reach a clear mathematical formulation of the results on this subject and at the same time to extend the analysis of features to the whole of the lexical stock of each language, which would allow the phonological/semantic relationship to be determined (for example, the rate of homophony).

1.12. In a short note, J. Lecerf (1978)[23] "tries to establish in the Arabic and of course Semitic, even Hamito-Semitic vocabulary, the existence of privileged structures all linked to the concrete notion of "split, displace, separate' ... The most interesting is characterized by the initial consonant /F/ followed by a liquid and a palato-velar final consonant." Nevertheless, other groups are also analyzed: "For a set of 242 roots a number of approximately 63 and 8 dubious cases are recorded." We do not know the results of this research project, organized according to P. Guiraud's hypothesis on "the structures of articulated onomatopoeias." Although focused on a particular case of roots, the project sets a perspective that could have repercussions in the future.

1.13. The treatment of the Semitic root proposed by W. Eilers (1978)[24] is interesting, programmatic, and up to date. In line with the Indo-European model, he analyzes the Semitic root from biradicalism, considering triradicalism as an expansion, which can itself be extended both qualitatively and quantitatively (quadriliteral verbs). The expansion can follow various patterns, both in Indo-European and in Semitic: prefixed, suffixed (from the aspect of phonology, all the articulations come into play: plosives, gutturals, dentals, labials, sonorants, sibilants...), reduplicated (even apocopated reduplication[25]), patterns that prove to be equivalent. Many examples from the two families are cited as proof. Nevertheless, this approach is considered as clearly speculative, even if the results contributed by Indo-European confirm studies done in this way. Semasiology should check possible excesses. In fact, there are fewer roots than those supposed by the triradical approach. In the two families, the list of primary roots, from which the others derive, is reduced.[26]

To complement this study, which is interesting for its comparison to Indo-European, but somewhat elementary, one can consult the more detailed discussion of the various categories of biliteral roots.[27] The Indo-European example should help overcome the perplexity produced by the derivative ambiguity presented by many Semitic roots.

1.14. An interesting article by Z. Frajzyngier (1979)[28] analyzes, in agreement with the opinions of Kuryłowicz, the geminated or intensive Semitic root (Heb.-Ar.), of the type $R_1R_2R_2$, as the basis of later doubling (pi^{c}el) and first derivation; it is not the primary form, which can never be attested. The arguments are repeated from synchronic analysis and Semitic reconstruction, as well as from Afro-Asiatic comparison. In spite of the laws formulated by Greenberg (and, one could add, in spite of the OCP), forms of the type /X-Y-Y/ do exist, which means that incompatibility between homorganics does not operate in the case of derived bases. The difficulty appears especially in geminate verbs in Egyptian (witnessing not simple intensification but double articulation) that can then be considered as derived. Given that the category exists in all the Afro-Asiatic families, it can be considered as proto-Afro-Asiatic, even if its semantic value escapes us.

1.15. A general and up-to-date discussion of the structure of the Semitic root, directed toward analysis of biliteralism/triliteralism, has been completed by G. Conti (1980),[29] and it can reasonably serve as a survey up to 1980. It belongs to a perspective comparing Egyptian and Semitic, and so goes beyond my own approach and envisages an extremely important pre-Proto-Semitic (Afro-Asiatic) horizon from ancient lexical material that, at the same time, is contemporary for both languages. He starts with the existence of biconsonantal groups with a third free consonant, but with more erudition than rigor, in my opinion. These groups have long been known (see above, for example, Hurwitz and Moscati) and their existence has been brought up-to-date by unsatisfactory reference to the Indo-European parallel, the problem of the value of the third consonant always remaining without a satisfactory solution. Thus Conti proves that this idea has had its opponents, decided defenders of a strict triliteralism, which conditioned the recognition of the former (he ends his summary with Moscati). Later there was noticeably more interest and a more positive approach to the topic, with much more precision in determining the biliteral root (Botterweck, MacDonald, Kuryłowizc, Zaborsky, Djakonoff, Cohen).

Conti arranges the well-known "evidence" (for example, see Moscati) in favor of the biliteral thesis: primary nouns, alternative weak verbs, and biliteral or reduplicated groups with identical semantics (even though these do not occur separately). He then sketches a phonological and semantic analysis and especially a treatment of the problem of the third consonant of the groups mentioned ("radical integration"), rehearsing the various theories (prepositional, etc.), apparently without reaching a clear solution. Yet, account must be taken of the various functions of extension: in third position any consonant can appear, in first position, eight (morphemes already noted by Hurwitz) and in second position, only weak consonants. The first series, judged inexplicable, is not considered (with Kuryłowicz); Conti retains the second series, with prefixes, which becomes verifiable by the formation of quadriliterals, as well by the reduplicated series, both allowing a functional explanation of "radical integration." In the case of weak and geminated roots this becomes more difficult, but the alternation, mentioned with the reduplicated roots, guarantees the thesis that originally they were biliteral. Their "triliteration" would be the result of a process of "structural absorption" (analogy) due to their special lengthened vowel that becomes a consonant. But shared lexical clusters remain without explanation (triliterals); on this he remembers the criteria of expressiveness and homorganic oscillation (for example, the binomial voiced / voiceless, p. 32). Thus it is not possible to verify a general biliteralism. The triliteralism that co-exists at the Semitic level would have produced a process of analogy (simply out of lexical necessity...). But it is at the Afro-Asiatic level that the situation is confirmed. The situation in Berber and in Egyptian is very close to Semitic, with a predominance of triliteral roots, either attested or reconstructed. In Cushitic, however, there is an equilibrium or a slight predominance of biliterals, some that can be reconstructed also as triconsonantal roots. In Chadic, triconsonantal roots clearly predominate. The two types co-exist. Whatever the case, according to Conti, this aspect of Afro-Asiatic comparison has not been emphasized enough. It is from this perspective that he programs his own research, limited to Egyptian and Semitic, to tell the truth a little against his own earlier point of view, which reproached his predecessors for not referring to Afro-Asiatic in general, given the difficulty supposed by the other families that are linguistically more diffuse.

By means of the analysis of a structure that suggests inclusion of a radical (/n/) peculiar to Egyptian and Ethiopic, a group of biliteral roots that are common from the aspects of phonology and semantics should be revealed, opening in this manner the way to other revelations, which apparently did not happen. For Conti, such an analysis confirms the biliteral theory, as well as the independence of the structural procedure that develops that theory.

1.16.   In 1983, A. J. Militarev, after his own previous studies on the topic (1973, 1978, 1978),[30] which developed the ideas of his teacher and grandfather, S. S. Majzel', edited his work posthumously (1983).[31] In the introduction he writes a summary and adopts a rather critical position toward its basic thesis: the diversification of Semitic roots by means of "allothesis" as an explanation for their phonetic and semantic alternations.

After several general chapters (on semasiology and the position of Arabic within the Semitic languages) Majzel makes some comments on the root in Semitic. The root is consonantal by nature, the vowels only have an auxiliary role to assist the pronunciation of the consonants. Its firm triconsonantal form attests to this. Thus the Semitic root becomes an "abstract," in some way, from the phonetic point of view, but semantically it is no less real and concrete than the Indo-European root. Majzel' is opposed to theories of the "biconsonantal cell" (especially Jušmanov's) as the basis of the Semitic root and defends its radical triconsonantalism, whose phonological frame he discusses at both the Afro-Asiatic and the Semitic levels.

Militarev examines all the criteria suggested by Majzel' to explain the main topic of his book, which is the variation of root consonants, and he assesses its importance: chance concurrence, fictitious or dialectal origin of the variation, particular phonetic transformation and its borrowing within the Semitic family, theory of an Afro-Asiatic or other substrate, the possibility of proto-phonemes as yet unrecognized, conditioned change within the consonantal chain or due to vocalic influence, addition of a third consonant that is or is not morphemic (affixes). These criteria are valid to some extent, especially those involving dialectical borrowing and an Afro-Asiatic substrate, but it is not possible to accept them as a sufficient global explanation of root variation, which is not a late process. Root variation is ancient and universal in the Semitic and Afro-Asiatic languages, not only in the Arabic lexicon, which is found in all stages of their development and which, according to Militarev, is deeply connected to contamination from contact among them. This produces a variation with a possibility that largely depends on compatibility of phonemes. Its moment of flowering must be set in the period immediately after the decline of the common Afro-Asiatic language phase.

It is at this moment that Majzel' puts the process, without semantic change, of "consonantal alternation" produced by the interdialectal contacts among the Afro-Asiatic groups that begin to separate from the proto-language and whose *Urheimat* must be located in the Levant. We are in the remotest phase of "diffuse phonemes" and, at this stage, contamination becomes a spontaneous process of "formation of roots." In support of this, Majzel' uses many examples to show the possible alternation among the four established consonantal groups (labials, buccals, liquids, and gutturals). Opposed to this spontaneous alternation is "allothesis" as a conscious way of creating new "nouns/roots" with a change of meaning. Again, Majzel' provides examples taken from Arabic and other languages in support of the central point of his concept of root variation in Semitic. In addition to this opposition, "consonantal alternation" // "allothesis," Majzel' proposes another as a way of expanding roots in Semitic: "transposition" // "metathesis." Transposition, in parallel with consonant alternation although later, is also the result of contact between ethnic groups and does not entail semantic change. On the other hand, it already supposes (in)compatibility of consonantal sequences and, therefore, most often produces lexical external loans. But in this connection Majzel' is radically opposed to accepting consonants as markers of nominal classes (see above Hurwitz and Jušmanov). He then elaborates a set of conditions favoring this transposition depending on whether the root consonants belong to different articulatory strong groups or one of them is a liquid, weak (/w, y/) or sibilant. Many examples are given in this respect. Metathesis instead, like allothesis, means an alteration with a change of meaning and is, for the scholar, not an unconscious / unintended phonological accident but a very important means of forming roots proved by many examples.

It is here, for him, that the question is posed of augmenting biconsonantal roots as a denominative process. It is an automatic transformation conditioned by the position of the phonemes, whereas allothesis is not conditioned. Written transmission has been able to collaborate in taking on forms from other dialects in which the various laws of consonantal incompatibility impose variations. Again they would be variations by contamination. But in certain cases, such variations also prove to be very old and original.

These systems of phonological variation/derivation have a proof from the semantic aspect in the "semantic chains" (see below pp. 87, 89f., 96f., 103) to be found in various languages. From there one can trace a set of lexico-semantic transformations in the Semitic languages: polarization of meaning, functional semantics, metonymy of part for whole and *vice versa*, association of similarity, metonymy of object for action; one can even make conscious use of these mechanisms of variation as a stylistic device.

Allothesis and metathesis, then, are for Majzel' two "phonosemantic" means for the formation of roots, original and earlier than "morphology by affixation," typical of historical languages. This thesis seems very unlikely given that Afro-Asiatic morphology proves to be already very fixed in this respect and similar to classical

Semitic morphology. One should rather assume, with Militarev, that the "phono-semantics" of Majzel' coexisted with other means of derivation by affixation and internal inflection, not very numerous in Semitics certainly.

Thus Majzel' does not discuss the problem of bi/triliterality at the etymological level. His starting-point is the triconsonantal root. And in this perspective, he is interested only in the old problem of triliteral roots with variations in one of their consonants. To explain it, instead of turning to the theory of complements or determinatives that are more or less free and aleatory, he creates a system of derivation by semasiological intent. His "allotheses" are not simple phonematic variations among the various Semitic languages; they also create semantic variants, just like the "metatheses," but in this instance as the result of variation within each language. All these variations can become independent roots of their original etymon with their own semantic meaning, independent of the generative process (phonological, morphological, or phono-morphological) that has led to their formation from a particular etymon. This lexicalization will then follow the paths of morphological and semantic transformations peculiar to each language. But the problem, as has already been noted above, is that the morphological process (affixation and even inflection) invoked by Majzel' as a secondary principle for the variation of roots proves to be very ancient in the Semitic languages and goes back to a common Afro-Asiatic stage. Saturation of the lexical stock is then achieved and other mechanisms of morphological derivation come into play. If this is accepted, it would be through Majzel's semasiological process of allothesis-metathesis that the radical "isosemantic" series would be generated, while the "bisemantic" would be derived by means of normal morphological mechanisms and the processes of polysemy and homonymy. Revised in this way, his thesis is a very interesting contribution to comparative Semitics and the reconstruction of Proto-Semitic. In spite of its limitations, the rich material provided will always be of great use and has to be taken into account.

In his 1973 thesis, A. J. Militarev develops and partly corrects Majzel's ideas. He insists on the distinction between phonetically motivated "alternation," very rare and subject to the incompatibilities proper to each language, and "variation," not phonetically motivated and unpredictable, frequent in the Semitic languages, especially in Arabic. The thesis wishes to study the latter, the history of which it traces, and establish as far as possible the correlation between variation and consonantal compatibility. In this way one could determine the different criteria governing possible combinations. It would even be necessary to re-examine from this point of view the nature of certain consonants, beyond the classic description.

The starting-point is the Semitic "root" as an objective reality, even if the question of its original triconsonantal nature or its derivation from a biconsonantal base remains open. Militarev is interested only in the study of its variation, considered as paradigmatic, as opposed to its compatibility, which would be syntagmatic. The first chapter reviews 500 examples of radical variation in Arabic and about 200 in other languages, as well as a number of examples that involve several languages. It is the most complete study of the phenomenon today.[32] From this material Militarev tries to classify the phonemes according to their ability to create variations, a capacity closely linked to their phonetic features: variation and compatibility are related in inverse proportion to their phonetic proximity. In fact, the degree of radical variability basically coincides with Greenberg's compatibility groups (see above). It is interesting to note the importance that all the phonetic features have in this process, not only articulation, as well as the limitations imposed sometimes by semantics.

From these findings he formulates some precise rules on consonantal assimilation imposed by incompatibility. At the same time, the hypothesis of a lateral feature of certain phonemes is confirmed, traces of which are shown by root variation. This provides the opportunity for also reconstructing certain Proto-Semitic phonemes not accepted by traditional Semitic phonology.

The conclusions to be drawn are as follows: the root variation of consonants is very common in the Semitic languages; normally it occurs when there are identical consonants or consonants with similar distinctive features; a high level of variation normally corresponds to a low level of root compatibility; groups so defined carry out the incompatibility laws; the variations can be useful to better determine the nature of certain phonemes and even to postulate others; root variation is shown to be very ancient in the Semitic family, but is also operative in diachronic historical development over time, even perhaps in modern dialectology.

Posed in this way, the fundamental problem of Proto-Semitic or etymological lexicography, namely the existence of triconsonantal groups and groups with a variable third consonant and a similar semantic load, is reduced to a purely phonetic process of chance, like a process of lexical display, in no way conditioned by the semantic value of the "complements" or variable elements. I think it is a thesis that has to be accepted, even if often one cannot agree on the details. There is still one outstanding gap to fill: What is the lexical value of the stable group of variable triconsonantal roots? Are they really biconsonantal roots "augmented" by a third consonant or are they rather originally triconsonantal roots with several variations in a specific position? The problem then is to know what the original triconsonantal form is, if there was one or whether the triconsonantal root is originally pluriform from the aspect of phonetic articulation (see below pp. 84, 119).

1.17. A few years later, K. Petráček (1985)[33] returned to the problem once more, commenting on the work by S. S. Majzel', edited by A. J. Militarev, whose ideas had already been proposed by V. P. Starinin.[34] He also comments on the contributions of several other Russian scholars (Djakonoff, Porchomovsky, Mel'čuk, Maslov, Melkinov, Gabučan, Lekiašvili, Dolgopolsky), beside his own (from 1953–54) with regard to pharyngeals in Semitic and Hamito-Semitic (see his 1983 summary). He thinks that his ideas have been ignored, even though they complement the theories of Majzel'. Acknowledging that his own target is the triconsonantal root and its alternative forms, he comments: "of considerable importance in the study by S. S. Majzel' is the thesis that the variations (alternations) in radical consonantalism have been exploited at the semantic level making it an important tool for the formation of words (a phonosemantic process alongside the process of the morphology of affixes) and for enriching the radical stock of Semitic languages. The symbolism of sounds is a special kind of phonosemantics, exhibited for example in the alternations of emphatic/non-emphatic phonemes in expressive words. The influence of expressionism (emotionality) on the formation of pharyngeals / postvelars is an important point of our thesis"

(p. 173). On the other hand, Petráček accepts the editor's rejection of Majzel's theory on "allothesis," based on glottogony and ethno-phonetics, to explain phonetic and semantic alternations.

1.18. Contrary to the opinions expressed until then since Moscati's article, H. B. Rosén (1987)[35] adopts a restrictive position (following Kuryłowicz) with respect to biliteralism in the specific case of the groups that I have just been speaking about, which are unlikely in Indo-European (p. 538). Properly so-called biliterals occur in the semantic field of nouns connected to life and the family, primal objects, numbers and pronouns. Verbal roots, instead, are subject to expansion by inflection, which can alternate with degree zero in final position (for example, IIIy verbs) (p. 540); in medial position an extension or a repetition can occur; expansions are also found in Indo-European. Expansion in initial position, typical of Semitic, best reflects its secondary character, given the different alternation in the various languages. There is also a morphological expansion, which he notes in certain monoradical nouns (*p-*, *m-*), that would be present also in the morphology of biliteral roots (dialectal Ar. /jāba/ < /jā + b-/ as well as in the formation of normalized triliteral roots (for example with the prefixes /t-/ and /s-/), in the same way as in Indo-European. This is a defense of moderate, original, and expansive (morphematic) biliteralism to the exclusion of the combinatory type (biliteral groups with a third free consonant).

1.19. The work of R. M. Voigt (1988)[36] represents the most tenacious and best organized defense, from Arabic, of total triliteralism as against so-called biliteralism. He also takes account, even though to a lesser extent, of Common Semitic, especially Akkadian, in line with Brockelmann's position, and he is aware of the Indo-European model. His attention is focused on two problems: the classification of the verb in Semitic and biradicalism. On biradicalism he states: "The problem of biradical roots in Semitic belongs to formulations of the question that can be solved from within Semitic.… Whether triradicalism, which is typical of all the Semitic languages, represents an innovation of Semitic can be resolved only with reference to the other branches of Hamito-Semitic. The new can be recognized only against the background of the old" (p. 12).

For this he proposes a sensible transcription, which thus heralds his later phono-morphological interpretation (p. 13), taking account of long morphemes, consonants, and vowels, which he considers as double or bi-phonematic (p. 14), excluding the opposition /i::y/, /u::w/ (= /i/, /u/),[37] even though sometimes /w/ and /y/ can have their own secondary consonantal value. Originally there are two types of vocalic-consonantal length: primary or morphological and secondary or by elision/contraction. "It is hardly possible to raise objections to this concept and its relevance in Arabic, more likely perhaps to isolated applications…" (p. 15). In this way he believes he is able to resolve the problem of biliteralism, while "each generation appears to discover afresh the root variations in Hebrew and other cognate languages and explain them in terms of biradicalism" (p. 16).

In following this approach, Voigt analyzes Arabic morphology according to a theory and a linguistic terminology that are very complex (pp. 17–19, 22–24), the result of combining various metalinguistic formalizations (Kruszewski, Koch, Pike, etc.). He himself distinguishes various levels of phonetic effect: the effect of surface phonology (at word level, which besides is not an autonomous level) and the effect of deep phonology (level of the morpheme), which explains the change of "weak roots" (IIIy) according to general assimilation patterns (p. 22). "Radicals" are at the deeper level of the moneme (p. 23). Next there begins a morphological analysis of Arabic, which allows weak roots to be explained as triradical, that is, as "strong" roots (p. 27) by "morphemization" (deep level) and generalization/derivation (surface level). On the other hand, "monemization" is peculiar to the Semitic languages and is applied to the segmentation into "root" and "pattern" (p. 36), which corresponds to an analytical bearing deeper in principle than the one derivation can achieve. From the radical moneme one can keep score of the processes of derivation (from moneme to morpheme) according to various modules imposed by semantic transformations that intersect each other (pp. 39ff.) A special case is the derivative process of the "verbal stems" (pp. 44–46).

Immediately afterward, special attention is paid to the specific problem of biradicalism, to which Voigt responds with a twin battery of arguments. Clearly he discards symbolic phonetics as his base. His argument is well conducted but is rather summary; onomatopoeia cannot be excluded generically. Today, this point of view is enjoying a new boom.

Otherwise, and it would seem correctly, he rejects reference to "determinatives" in parallel with the system that operates in the Indo-European root, one reason being that the requisite semantic precision is missing from Semitic. Just as invalid, in his view, is to resort to a supposed "Hamitic" biradicalism, rather reductionist in nature, given that reduction is preferable to expansion as an explanation of derivation. Besides, Hamitic belongs to a debased linguistic layer that is not useful for speculation on original forms (p. 56), in spite of what he said earlier on the need for reference to Hamito-Semitic/Afro-Asiatic. This rejection seems rather hasty: "Proofs for a biradical origin cannot be derived from these languages in this way" (p. 56). Moreover, the presence in this field of triliteral roots common to several languages strengthens the argument. But the argument does not hold if it is a question of partial biradicalism.

The argumentation used with respect to the so-called weak verbs is closer to our own problem. Voigt sees no reason to deny that the semi-vowels (/w/, /y/) are consonants, in spite of their tendency to disappear, as this also happens in Greek. By analogy, it would explain the morphology of the apocopated forms of weak verbs, whereas in the case of long forms, one has to reckon with a "long" radical vowel that would put them on an equal footing with the strong verbs. The result would then be the four positions (/y-ktub/) peculiar to the strong verbs, given the bi-phonematic value attributed to the vowel.

However, for a correct application of "monemization" (root level) by the root/ pattern scheme, according to the classic version, the solution is found in the development of the long vowel of "weak" verbs into two short vowels (!) (p. 60). In this way, the similarity between weak and strong vowels is complete /iaktubu/ = /iaquumu/: "In any case the idea of the vocalic radical offers the advantage of the phonetic transparency and effectiveness of the phonetic laws" (p. 60). Further triconsonantal analogical equalization by means of the phonemes /w/ and /y/ confirms the vowel as a radical element (!).

However, he admits as valid the biliterality of primary nouns comprising two consonants and he tries to include it in his overall triliteral conception in three ways:

a. by assimilation by monemization (root / pattern) to the pattern /facl/, assuming loss of the third radical;

b. by rejection of monemization ("a noun *iad* would accordingly belong to the small class of nuclear morphemes that cannot undergo monemization" [p. 62]);

c. by recognition of a biradical monemization pattern.

But this would mean that originally there were biliteral and triliteral (bi-/triconsonantal) nouns, total biliteralism (and even triliteralism) being difficult to defend. Scholars give different values to the original nature of each of these nominal morphemes and their etymology. Voigt suggests that some of these nouns come from triradical roots (which means that, ultimately, he accepts the first possibility). In turn, triradical morphemes develop by expansion, especially IIIy forms.

On the other hand, one must separate from this group not only the biradical nouns derived from triradical forms (as just pointed out), but also the long, hollow forms with four positions. The famous "six nouns" (ʔab, ʔaḥ ...) merit separate consideration; they are reduced to triradical roots due to their special suffixes. This would be another case of an (indeterminate!) vowel as a radical (in fourth position, [facl] pattern), with no connection to the case-ending of which it is supposed to be a relic, according to Brockelmann and later grammarians. It has, therefore, been suggested that these forms can be explained to be the result of final stress due to the inherent pronominal suffix, but Voigt prefers to consider them as roots with a third vowel, evidently rather than to see here analogical lengthenings to fit the triradical four-position pattern.[38]

On the other hand, the problem of "root variation" (biliteral groups with a varying third radical) is dismissed with some disdain. In this regard Voigt presumes three positions. First is extreme biradicalism (all roots are biliteral with augmentation possible in any position) at the Nostratic or Afro-Asiatic level. His critique is both pitiless and faultless, showing it to be simple and the legacy of the nineteenth century, while acknowledging the opinion to be current today. Second is moderate biradicalism / triradicalism, as accepted by Voigt himself, which starts from the form of the imperfect (not the imperative, as Brockelmann preferred) and explains uniformly weak and strong roots according to the triliteral (four-position) pattern, both in the imperfect and the perfect, beyond the apparent biliteralism of many other forms.

A summary of his theory, repeated several times in the course of his book, is the following paragraph: "Also the middle weak form *i=aquum=u* can in no way be called biradical, as a comparison with the strong form *i=aqtul=u* shows. The difference between both forms only lies in the fact that in one case the second radical is a vowel or semi-vowel merged together with the distinctive vowel and in the other case it is a consonant. We find the same difference in the nominal domain with the nouns *bait* 'house' and *kalb* 'dog,' both formed according to the nominal pattern *facl*. Here, too it would make no sense to speak of a biradical root with a diphthongal distinctive vowel with respect to *bait*. In Arabic it is true that all phonemes can function as radicals of a root in the same way!" (p. 76). This position ends, like Brockelmann's, in a strict triliteralism to explain Arabic morphology, a theory that Voigt tries to support. He rejects the so-called lack of importance of one of the radicals and denies the supposed biradicalism (in fact, biconsonantalism, as we have noted) attributed to Brockelmann, with a new explanation of hollow verbs, clarifying the distinction between synchronic and diachronic reconstruction.

Finally, he rejects the third position, i.e., extreme or radical triradicalism (triconsonantalism) as an explanation of the weak verbs. He calls extreme triradicalism the position that wishes to reduce the weak verbs to the strong ones by accepting an original semi-consonant. According to Voigt, no one actually holds this view but, in fact, it is in the classical Semitic grammars. For him, the weak radical is originally a vowel, not a consonant. Similarly, against the view, then, which claims development from biliteralism toward triliteralism (from their initial co-existence, as Humboldt had already suggested) he opposes the lack of a pattern or a law able to explain such a derivation. It is a simple generalization based on the triradical pattern.

He repeats it yet again: there are no variable biliteral roots (groups that can be expanded) nor is there a "grammatical law" that governs their shift to being triliteral. The only exception may be the form of the geminated root, type $/C_1C_2C_2/$. But expansion of the root by "suffixation" is methodologically incorrect; the concept of suffix is missing. Determinatives do not have a clear and specific function and there are too many of them (all the consonants, in fact, could have this role!). Furthermore, extended biliteral roots do not occur independently, as separate from triliteral roots. With these determinatives we enter the field of Hamito-Semitics and pure speculation (even though earlier he had acknowledged resorting to this field, as we have seen!), which allows unlikely games (for example, recovery of the "root" /lb/ from /ḥ-lb/ "milk" and /lb-n/ "white").[39] By their nature suffixes postulate real, actual surface forms.

He cites various reasons to explain this new approach to the inevitable existence of root variation: chance in a wide semantic field (with German examples *ad absurdum*, p. 80), *Reimwortbildung* ("word formation based on rhyme") and assimilation/attraction/contamination of phonetically and semantically close roots. Only Semitists resort to prefixation/suffixation to explain root variation. In any event, we cannot explain everything by *Reimwurzelbildung*. The Semitic triconsonantal root has been subjected to a very tight net of associative transformations, "but that escapes our searching eye, which cannot—even by all the methods—penetrate into the language history in a discretional way" (p. 83).

However, there are certain forms that could make one think of biradical roots: first, the doubled quadriliteral verbs, many of which become triliteral by dropping the weak consonant, and the verbs alternatively with middle vowels and second geminated consonant, although the alternative forms are not so frequent as is claimed, which as a result requires the assumption of biradical roots. In this way their formation by morphological contamination can be explained, while their semantic difference often requires different roots (geminated and weak) to be assumed (p. 86).

With regard to the supposed biradical roots augmented by an /n-/, Voigt criticizes their claimed semantic, onomatopoeic, and directive function as proposed by Von Soden, based on Akkadian; this function is not clear and the morphological explanation proves adequate yet again. This type of increase has not been extensively studied and the alternations are few in number. To explain these cases, it is enough to refer to analogy, rhyme, and morphological exchange, as mentioned. Other possible ways of new formations or changes of root would be: assimilation, dissimilation, conjunction of functional morphemes both for nominal and verbal forms. These are clear features of modern languages and very likely of Proto-Semitic. The ideological transformation of the root can also have an influence. All these phenomena were developed and systematized later by Zaborski (see below).

Finally, Voigt once again summarizes his argument against the biradicality of weak verbs, from a theoretical point of view and with specific examples, and he concludes as follows: in Semitic there is no model of derivation by prefix, infix, or suffix; many of the weak roots have very different meanings and cannot be reduced to each other; they are then multiple and in every case can be explained by *Verbaltypenwechsel* ("change of verbal type"); the affixation of weak roots in any position at all is not permitted. The mistake of the biradicalists is to suppose that there are no original weak roots (with vowels), in other words, "vowels in the positions of radicals" (p. 90).

In the case of root variation with equivalent or similar meaning, one could imagine a biradical root spread by synchronic but not diachronic "generalization (etymology)." In fact, such a root never existed. In this case, *Grundtyp* ("basic type") is confused with *Urtyp* ("original type"), *Grundbedeutung* ("basic meaning") with *Urbedeutung* ("original meaning"), although the two levels follow a similar development process. The root variations come from a triliteral root that contains the *Grundtyp*, not from a biliteral root (the so-called *Grundtyp*) and are generated by multiple "analogy" (von Gabelenz) and phonosemantic parallelism (Güntert). This leads to multiple popular etymologies, by analogical bias, which is, in fact, a fundamental process in the development of language. Another element of development is contributed by "sound symbolism" (p. 96), which will be discussed below in connection to the theory of Bohas. To summarize: "generalizations lead to the reshaping of roots" (p. 97).

The class of *mediae vocalis* verbs is treated by assuming that their vowel is a radical (with the value of a consonant); as a result, the apophonies and conditionings in the inflection of the various semantic classes (state and action) are interpreted on the basis of the phonological principles sketched out by Brockelmann (with predominance of the /a/ sonority, above all). The analysis is extended to the Akkadian present and to the passive and derived conjugations, as well as to the secondary derivations (denominatives and deverbatives), but all this remains outside this discussion. As a colophon, the question of a possible biliteral interpretation of these verbs is introduced. Once again, Voigt is certain that his analysis is the only one to justify the fact of the structural parallel of biliteral and triliteral verbs, following a pattern of four positions, the position of the second consonant being assumed by the vowel /u/ (which is short, of course), which together with the thematic vowel produces the long vowels /ū/, /ī/, /ā/ (p. 162). The explanations by "analogy" are not valid for Voigt. What we have here is a "phonetic law" that can be verified in Arabic. "The form *iaṭVulu* is exactly as

triradical as *iakburu;* the difference lies only in the character of the middle radical..."
(p. 162), a character that, for him, is clearly reflected in forms such as *ṭul-ta, ṭib-ta,*
which otherwise cannot be explained by the triliteral pattern. The long vowel does not
refer to a primitive vowel, as the biradical explanation would wish (Müller, Wellhausen, et al.) by analogy with the triliteral system, but is the result of the fusion of the
radical and thematic vowels.

Even so, there is a class of verbs that cannot be explained in this way and are
genuinely original biliterals. This is the class of initial /u:w-/ verbs. In fact, they occur
throughout Afro-Asiatic. One can no longer speak of augmentation in this case, only
of the alternation of verbal types. Synchronically, as in the other cases, one could speak
of biliteralism with respect to the *Durchschnitt* ("average") actual forms of the root; but
to speak of them at the diachronic (etymological) level one must refer to the pre-Afro-
Asiatic layer, which is very uncertain (pp. 164f.).

He ends his analysis with a concession that nuances his apparently slightly
radical position: "If we disregard the possibly primary biradical nouns of the type
dam, (ʔ)*sm,* the assumption of a biradical origin appears meaningful only for *mediae
geminatae*-type roots. The evidence for such a development in other types as well lies
only in the postulate—unquestioned by many—of an original biradicality of all types
of root" (pp. 209f.). It is a "postulate" that awaits proof by its defenders. In his turn,
Voigt thinks that he has provided an explanation for the morphology of all these types
based on the triradical pattern.

1.20.   C. Ehret (1989)[40] proposes a completely opposite explanation of the phenomenon of triconsonantalism, as the result of a process of lengthening the simpler roots.
This feature is found also in other Afro-Asiatic languages, even though to a lesser
extent and with "extenders" that are suffixes or complements, with a clearly defined
semantic value. Internal reconstruction of Arabic reveals the existence of this known
phenomenon that has been mentioned several times: a series of triconsonantal roots
with a different third consonant and related meaning. "When the verb members of
such sets are grouped according to their third consonant, there emerge recurrent
correlations between the presence of particular consonants in C_3 (third) position and
the presence of particular varieties of meaning modification in the roots containing
those C_3" (p. 110). This suggests that at the pre-Proto-Semitic stage, these consonants
in third position operate as "suffixed verbal extensions" according to their own
semantic models, sometimes also "as noun or modifier suffixes." Here the eternal
problem and even the solutions sketched out long ago (see above Hurwitz, Moscati,
Majzel', and others) come to the surface and they will continue to be proposed (see
below on Bohas). The original aspect in this case is found in its radical and global treatment of the problem, always limited to Arabic, "the best-attested Semitic language"
(p. 110).

Ehret distinguishes 37 semantic modifications due to Semitic phonemes (all
taken into consideration), since some of them represent the combination of different
proto-Afro-Asiatic phonemes (especially velars, labials, and sibilants) with their own
modifying function. At this level we are dealing with the analysis of a productive
process that then becomes lexicalized. He justifies the value of each of these extensions
and gives a list of triconsonantal roots that have the same extension and a related

meaning, before comparing them to others in which the extension varies, in order to prove in this way the semantic variation. Next, he introduces the list of (112) roots with their first two consonants identical and the third different, to make evident the semantic variation induced by each extender, as well as the resulting polysemy. This is explained by the coalescence of Afro-Asiatic vocalic variants (possibly 20) and consonantal variants in the same biconsonantal root (/CvC/). As a result: "Cognizance of the polyphyletic origins of most Semitic root shapes is essential in the comparative reconstruction of Semitic" (p. 186).

Among the extenders, some have a morphematic character (suffixes), even belonging to the nominal class. The functional doubling derives perhaps from laws of incompatibility, which favor or impede their appearance. Furthermore, it is appropriate to take note of their semantic development from Afro-Asiatic and the convergence of phonemes and, therefore, of functions originally distinct, as it is possible to note in other proto-Afro-Asiatic (Cushitic) languages. Extension by a third radical with its own semantic value was particularly productive in Semitic (less so in Berber and Egyptian, and even less in Chadic and Cushitic) and led to its own triconsonantal structure. Even biconsonantal roots have been adapted to this pattern by means of gemination.

The first criticism that this theory provokes comes from the presupposition of a model of proto-Afro-Asiatic with complex phonology (consonantal and vocalic) and simple morphology (biconsonantal roots) based on the Chadic and Cushitic languages, and as such has been rejected, correctly (see above on Voigt). He does not take enough account of the innovative character of these families and wishes to reconstruct a proto-language as the sum total of all the features of the languages of the phylum (on this see below p. 99 [Garbini]). Furthermore, his explanation of a supposed undifferentiation and multifunctionalism of the extenders proves too hypothetical and requires mental gymnastics as important as the other possible explanation by semantic derivation do (p. 186). On the other hand, the starting-point of his analysis, the Arabic dictionary of Steinglass [1884] (p. 111), proves to be suspect and requires in turn a previous exercise in historical semantics (see below pp. 120ff.). Hurwitz had already correctly refuted (see above) the semantic precision of root "complements" and I do not think that Ehret's theory will provoke a change of opinion.

1.21. The problem continues to be discussed and E. Lipiński (1991)[41] proposes first of all that we should speak rather of "monosyllabic" (biconsonantal) roots, considering also the bearing of the vocalic phoneme. Taking into account its quality and length, as well as those of the second consonant, their combination can produce nine variations, apart from free compensating variations. The meaning of the qualified vowel already appears in the triliteral verbal system, but it is better preserved in the group of monosyllabic nouns, even though it can also be verified in verbs from the imperative. The various possible combinations would give a total number of 7,569 roots ($29^2 \times 9$), which would be enough to form a completely developed language in terms of the lexicon. But this supposes that the length of the vowels is an original phenomenon and takes no account of the laws of incompatibility that would substantially reduce this imaginary figure. On the other hand, the secondary character of morphemic elements in the triconsonantal roots is absolutely clear, once their alternation (for example /y:n-/) in the various languages has been considered. In addition, the process of forming triconosonantal verbs (hollow or second geminated) from monosyllabic biconsonantal roots becomes operative even in triliteral forms by its turning into diphthongs in Syriac and Arabic or by doubling one of the consonants.

At all events, a clarification is required with respect to terminology. If the biliteral/ biradical/biconsonantal root (and even the compensating module /C-v-CC/: second geminate consonant) can be defined as monosyllabic, why not the triconsonantal root of type /C-v-C-C/: /faːiːuᶜl/ nominal types). The impression given is that this is a rather elementary treatment of the question.

1.22. The important survey proposed by A. Zaborski (1991)[42] begins by clearly demarcating the two topics: original biliteral roots and triliteral roots with a variant third consonant, excluding an original universal biliteralism. It must be supposed that certain "weak" roots, and obviously other "strong" roots, are original triliteral roots that sometimes co-exist with biliterals and sometimes are produced by expansion of biliterals or contraction of quadriliterals (which in turn come from biliteral or triliteral roots). It is even possible that there are quadriliteral roots with what are called affixation phonemes (/n:s:w:y/…), which do not always need to have this character and can also be radical phonemes in origin. Account must also be taken of other processes to explain the origin of triliterality: phonetic, morphological, and semantic similarity, neutralizing opposition, etc. In conclusion: "It can be taken for granted that a majority, although perhaps not a very big majority, of verbal roots was triconsonantal" (p. 1677). Next, successive processes of expansion by affixation/suffixation are listed, first of all derivation (deverbative # denominative) by affixation, especially of morphematic prefixes (/š:s-, h-, ᵓ-, t-/…), but also suffixes, at the same time evaluating and criticizing exaggerations in this respect, such as those caused by the interpretation of "root determinatives" (Ehret). Other expansion processes include infixation, vocalic lengthening reduction, consonantal doubling, as well as expansions at the margins: reinterpretation of the article, of the case-ending, of prepositions, postpositions and particles as radical elements. There are also processes of contraction of triliteral or quadriliteral roots, already mentioned, and processes of elision, of contraction of compounds, of phonological assimilation ("rhyme"), of pseudo-correction, of euphemistic substitution, of metanalysis or reinterpretation of expressions and of popular etymology.

All these processes are really secondary and operate during the later period of Arabic or South Semitic, from which new roots emerge that are apparently biliteral or triliteral. "Most of the methods mentioned above were either spontaneous or due to manipulations by poets and grammarians so that some roots could be, as a matter of fact, never really used outside a particular text, or in other words, they could be artificial in a sense" (p. 1683). Also mistakes by scribes, in writing or due to hearing, differences in dialect (also verifiable in Arabic) and other types of assimilation, according to the laws of incompatibility, can provide an explanation of etymologically equal roots with the variation of one consonant, ("Assimilation has been responsible for the appearance of a considerable number of pairs of roots differing only in one consonant" [p. 1685]). The situation can be aggravated by diglossia favored by the corresponding substrate languages and the different evolutionary origin of the documentary sources that have been used as a basis for compiling the Arabic lexicon. It has undergone a very marked secondary semantic differentiation.

All this, like the assimilation already mentioned, could have generated geminated radicals of triliteral origin, and given that all consonants can originally be doubled, all can appear in principle as "root determinatives." Other processes, such as sandhi, spirantization, original abnormal phonetic changes(/š:ṭ/, /š:ḍ/, /ḍ+t:š/, /ṭ:t/), metathesis, pausal forms, loans with various phonological forms, mistaken pronunciation, expressive phonological symbolism, mere coincidence or semantic neutralization, etc., can generate roots with a variable component without the need to resort to "root determinatives." Their phonological or semantic relationship can be apparent or imaginary and has to be checked from actual cases. On the other hand, possible variation due to vocalic influence must be taken into account. Semantic development can induce new oppositions between roots with common phonological elements, but with no etymological relationship. In this respect, the limited number of phonemes in a language and their reduced combinatory field must be taken into account. Furthermore, some of these processes can take place conjointly. Therefore, it is by a particularly exact analysis that one can track each of them, separating what makes up the original root and what is the effect of a transformation. Renewed analysis of the cluster /p-r-Cx/ shows how complex the matter is.

Zaborski's contribution is thus shown to be illuminating with respect to the correct evaluation of triliteral roots with a variable consonant without resorting to "root determinatives." This still remains the fundamental datum of the problem concerning the biconsonantal or triconsonantal structure of the original Semitic root. It is then an argument that Voigt's somewhat hasty and *a priori* critique has left hanging.

1.23. G. Bohas then begins (1991, 1993)[43] a series of contributions that, as we have already seen with respect to the "structure of the root" in Semitic, have particular and innovative importance with respect to the problem we are dealing with, due to the application of his principles to the matter. (We leave to one side the transformation of the phoneme /ḍ/ in Syriac.) It offers the scholar the chance to propose another solution to the extension of reduced roots due to the OCP, namely the well-known one of the epenthesis of the glide (hollow roots), which supposes a widening of the linear system of association from left to right (which does not allow expansion of the root from right to left and, therefore, does not permit the forms /$C_1C_1C_2$/ [p. 11]).

"In the plurilinear frame … for *madad*, the consonantal melody, i.e., the root, is biliteral, distributed over a three-position skeleton, as we have just seen. In other words, the fact that the roots are bi- or triconsonantal does not clash with the triconsonantalism of the verbal pattern in Semitic. In yet other terms, as the consonantal melody has been made independent, there is a better chance of discovering the principles governing its composition" (p. 11). This serves to give an explanation of the existence of "doublets"—/C_1C_2-y/::/C_1-w:y-C_2/—with identical semantic load, as can be verified in Syriac and Arabic. On the other hand, the equivalences of the patterns /$C_1C_2C_2$/ and /C_1C_2-w:y/ favor the left-right association, while such an equivalence cannot be explained from association of the margins, which leads us to think that association and epenthesis are free, as strategies for expanding the roots that each language uses as it wishes.

This enables us to take account of the alternation $/w{:}y\text{-}C_1C_2/{::}/C_1C_2C_2/$, which also occurs in Arabic. In turn, the gradation $/C_1C_2C_2/{::}/C_1C_2\text{-}w{:}y/$ is itself the subject of study, as are its semantic relationships through 120 biconsonantal Arabic roots (with special attention to the extension $/\text{-}(C_3)y/$, which explains many semantic alternations) without specifying, however, the type of semantic relationship, weak or strong (SSR/WSR) between them, which is a lack of accuracy. The possibility of epenthesis in the guttural roots (in positions C_1 and C_3) and in the sonants is also examined, the latter not yet having been studied. All this leads him to study alternations by expansion or glide/shift in the light of the articulatory groups, in the direction proposed by Lecerf. For example, {occlusive/velar obstruant + dental occlusive} gives the meaning "to cut." Subsequently, Bohas has refined this approach thanks to his new theory of "matrices." This hypothesis seems to be confirmed in other Semitic languages (Syriac, Neo-Aramaic). He then repeats his article from the *Fs. Tsereteli* on actual forms of doubled biliteral roots (types $/C_1C_2C_1C_2/$ and $/C_1C_2C_1/$, which alternate with $/C_1C_2C_2/$), which require a new process of free association in which only the original root is subject to the OCP.

What I can say, at the moment, is that it is a praiseworthy effort to find "laws," general formulations that allow phonological and semantic features, which have always been known, to be systematized and to formulate a theory of radical derivation on the basis of certain principles of claimed universal validity, like the OCP. Up to what point this is valid and accepted, and above all functional and useful, remains to be seen. The same scholar, however, had invited us to go beyond this approach to the problem of biradicalism and its expansions by later, more systematic and complete works.

In fact, in two books published recently (1997/2000),[44] which I have already mentioned and discussed together, since they complete each other, G. Bohas develops his theory of what can be called the "universal biconsonantalism of the Semitic root." One could think that this is nothing new or surprising. Indeed, we have seen this thesis defined more or less explicitly since the nineteenth century. It is true that Bohas makes the theory quite radical and never better expressed, as it never had been until then. It is biliteralist brinkmanship in which even the concept of "root" becomes superfluous.[45]

For Bohas, the structure of the Semitic root is universally "biconsonantal," organized on "etymons" with a binary structure. His etymons have two projections. One is forward, giving "triliteral / triconsonantal roots." These are traditionally considered as the constituent roots of the lexicon and of the morphology of Common Semitic, but, in fact, they are only expansions of genuine biliteral roots, which he calls etymons. Even apparently irreducible triconsonantal roots can (or will be able to) be explained from biliteral etymons (see 1997, pp. 49/52), an operation in which all kinds of complements or determinatives, morphematic and not (even if one cannot determine their semantic function in every case) take part irrespective of position. Besides this process of expansion (prefixation, diffusion, and epenthesis) there are others (increment, shift, augmentation by one consonant, and doubling). So far nothing spectacularly new; it is once again the biliteral theory just as developed by Hurwitz (1913).

But there is also projection backward. All these etymons are grouped under a number of "matrices" that, at first, were considered to be binary combinations of "articulation zones" numbering six to seven (1997, pp. 9, 81), but later were understood to be binary combinations of "phonological features," and not only of articulation points/zones (2000, pp. 17ff.; but see already 1997, p. 90). All the forms that have come from this matrix have a "family resemblance" that binds them to each other. Once again, as we pointed out formerly (above p. 46), he extrapolates to phonology Wittgenstein's well-known semantic theory (1997, pp. 73f.; 2000, pp. 71f.). It is an approach that is remarkably new, even if already set in train in several isolated studies (see for example above p. 61 [Lecerf], p. 54 [Jušmanov's "resonance"], p. 58, [MacDonald's articulatory groups]); it is also a more thorough approach to the radical lexeme in Semitic. His appeal to the combination of "features" extends the proportion of possible matrices that ran the risk of being too restricted if only zones of articulation are taken into account (2000, pp. 20f., 60ff.). But, in spite of everything, this approach presents nothing unheard of. We shall come back to it later to evaluate its bases. For the moment, it should be noted that there are many other phonemes having the same pairs of "features" but that cannot be taken into account. In fact, "pairs of features" function only in each zone of articulation, making preferable the first pattern of "matrices" to others based on a different pair of features. The formation of "matrices" by "features" becomes too generic and vague (see below).

In addition, the theory of Bohas offers another, newer contribution, one could even call it spectacular, unprecedented apart from the almost always exceptional and sporadic form of "metathesis" (see for example Majzel's theory, p. 63), either free or conditioned, the results of which can seem much more debatable. It is the "reversibility of matrices" and, therefore, of the etymons, neither of which is sequenced (2000: pp. 20f., 30). This means, first of all, reducing their number by half, which is of less importance. More serious is the claim that the matrix is "mimophonic" (1997, p. 197; 2000, pp. 26; 84, 149, 156ff.), thus recovering the well-known theory of the expressive nature of language as an explanation of its origin or of part of its lexicon. One cannot say that the theory of G. Bohas lacks originality, as a whole, and once again we have to admit that its orchestration is massive and impressive. We shall come back to this later.

1.24. The problem of biliteralism/triliteralism is broached also, even if very briefly, by A. R. Bomhard and J. C. Kerns (1994),[46] who quote and summarize the views of Djakonoff and Ehret. Finally, D. Baggioni and P. Larcher (2000)[47] maintain that biliteralism is very likely from the diachronic aspect even if from the viewpoint of derivation of specific languages it is not important, given that derivation develops according to the triliteral pattern without usually going beyond quadriliteralism. Taking into account the existence of primary biliteral nouns and since quadriliteral roots derive from augmented triliteral roots, "one is tempted to see in the famous 'triliteral root' the *result* of the derivational process. It does not emerge as a starting-point, but as a point of arrival" (p. 128).

1.25. G. Goldenberg (2005) has dwelt also upon the subject of bi-/triradicalism.[48] After pointing out the inadequacy of the division consonant/vowel in the treatment of root reconstruction and after analyzing the sense of this concept, he sets out the

distinction between "root" and "unmotivated word," and among "root" (derivational entity), "etymon" (proto-root), and "stem" (see above pp. 8ff., 13ff., 26). Triradicalism relates to root as a lexical derivational morpheme. Unmotivated biliteral
nouns are and have no "root." To become so they must be augmented by a third
component. Actual triliteral roots are "*a-posteriori* roots" extracted form actual forms
at any time. Into this three-slot pattern short or larger roots have to fit. This situation
is made clear by examples taken from the derivational morphology of different
Semitic languages. The process involves recognizing the following terms: root-
morpheme, augmented stem-root, tense-scheme, and base-morpheme.

As for biliteralism, there are biliteral words, but no biliteral roots. "A renewed
discussion of Semitic biradicalism is, therefore, unnecessary" (p. 17), as proved by
Voigt's study (see above pp. 67ff.). The so called biliteral "cells" are not roots. The
alternance of weak verbs is due not to different consonantal complementation but to
the re-analysis of a polymorphous paradigm, to assimilation or other fluctuations.
"As we all know, there are no biradical roots in Semitic, and no one can imagine forms
derived from such roots" (p. 19). Criticizing interdigitation as a base-formation, both
the syllabic structure (CV tier) and the OCP (obligatory contour principle) (see above
pp. 42f.) are rejected in Semitic derivational morphology, in its original version
(McCarthy's) or in its new reformulation (Bohas).

Finally in connection with semantically related roots with two radicals in
common, rather than taking them as real roots, the phenomenon could be explained
by "meaningful assonance, rhyme or alliteration ... and association of sounds and
meanings" (21) (see above pp. 74f. [Zaborski]). The whole problem of bi-/triradical-
ism is thus very incisively revised. The author's stance in favor of a pure triradicalism
is patent, but I think his argumentation relies too much on the force in word-formation
of the secondary analogy induced by *Systemzwang* (triradicalism) and, in general, to
the morphological derivational level. The answers to the problem are already known
and remain somehow imprecise. In any case, if the "basically ternary structure of
Semitic roots is then marked both by completing the deficient and by compressing the
overflowing," which must be accepted, then the existence of the "deficient" is
presumed.

2. Appraisal

Some years ago (1998) I wrote[49]: "Lexicographically, it is possible that the monoconsonantal series represents the most primitive stratum of the Semitic languages and
takes us back to a stage of linguistic indifferentiation in relation to other families" (p.
38). And I concluded: "At the end of this inquiry we can point out some facts that seem
relevant in relation to the monoconsonantal series in Semitic. First the absence of the
'characteristic' Semitic phonemes: not one velarized, velar fricative or laryngeal
phoneme is productive in this lexical series. And since for many reasons this series
seems to be primary, one could deduce that these phonemes (just quoted) and in
general the 'Semitic' linguistic layer is a peculiar (alien to almost all other linguistic
families) and later development constructed on a non-Semitic base. Secondly, there
are no monoconsonantal lexemes of the denotative (nouns; the apparent two or three
exceptions can easily be ruled out) nor of the predicative (verbs) series. This fact

points to the biconsonantal combination as a basic phonological structure of the Semitic languages. And finally, the monoconsonantal lexemes correspond only to the functorial series (leaving out the morphemic series that does not form a lexematic series) and they go back to a layer of primary mainly deictic lexemes that appear as lexical and semantic Universals, some of them of onomatopoeic phonological origin. It is evident that this layer represents a pre-Semitic substratum in which simple artic-ulations had lexematic value. Perhaps the morphemic series also goes back to this substratum, too, but its limited and multifunctional character points instead to a mere random phonetical value in the progressive grammatical articulation of the language. The impression given by these facts is that the Semitic family, as a peculiar and distinc-tive linguistic entity, is the result of a somewhat late and perhaps highly analogical process of evolution" (pp. 71f.). Here I ended my own proposals on the possible expansion of monoconsonantal elements without claiming to have gone beyond the level of what can be proved empirically in the research of a hypothetical reconstruc-tion of an inaccessible Proto-Semitic.[50]

The analysis of this monoconsonantal series has been useful, however, in defin-ing the limit of etymological research in Semitic, a limit that should not be overstepped in spite of the many inducements in that direction.

In fact, these monoconsonantal lexematic *nuclei* are not independent elements of the lexicon. Nor are most of the claimed biconsonantal roots concealed behind semantically related strong triconsonantal roots with a different third consonant. Only a systematic, exhaustive empirical analysis involving in its comparison the vari-ous classical and modern Semitic languages can help to define in the etymological domain the meaning of this lexematic formation—and this before formulating theo-ries on the biconsonantal character of the Semitic root. This analysis should refer to what we may call the "original biconsonantal series" and its "intensive expansions," both of the second consonant ($/Cv\underline{C}$-/) and of the vocalic-syllabic modulation ($/C\underline{v}C$-/), resulting either in doubling ($/CvCC/$) or in (pre-)lengthening or epenthesis/glide ($/C\underline{v}C$-/$::/C^{w:y}C$-/) (se above p. 3). One cannot yet speak properly of short/long vowels. These are due to a prosodic opposition/contrast within the grammatical pattern oppositional distribution that may be considered "original" or Proto-Semitic but not at the lexical level. Instead, at this level it is a matter of vowels constrained by whether or not the second consonant is intensified. Nor is this intensification/gemi-nation yet a derived double articulatory formation. It does not imply a double conso-nant and has no connection to the OCP. It is also different from morphological doubling, which belongs to the inflectional system, even if both intensification and doubling can have a certain identical semantic motivation. Exceptionally, due to its frequent semantic alternation with the foregoing, one could include in this inquiry also morphemic (non-vocalic) expansion by /w/ and /y/ in third position ($/-C_3w:y/$), this morphemic expansions taking us already into the stage of the triconsonantal lexicon (see above pp. 2f.).

As a result of this tendency to phonemic intensification, the biconsonantal "root" proves to be unstable and tends to appear as intensive ($/CvC$-/ → $/C\underline{v}C$-/$::/$ $Cv\underline{C}$-/). These two intensifications are, then, alternatives in the same language or in another language, and are differentiated only by semantic contrastive nuances; at the same time, they both reproduce and express the meaning of the simple biliteral base. The expansion ($/C_1C_2(C_3)$-w:y), sometimes an alternative form of the preceding, normally tends to have an "effective" meaning (terminative; when the bases are "objective" or active), rather than "stative" (this is the usual value in the case of bases called "immanent" or "intransitive"), as has often been said. Whereas, the morphemo-semantic function of other determinatives remains to be established, assuming that they do have one and are not random complements.[51]

Any other expansion by affix, infix, or suffix, whether structural or analogical, must be considered as secondary and needs to be compared to the original series to verify the existence of possible clusters or biconsonantal groups with a random third consonants that are semantically close.

In principle, biliteral roots that are phonetically identical and semantically different or even opposed should not be assumed. Here we touch on the problem of "determinatives," "complements," or modifiers, always present in this discussion and whose function and nature have to be submitted to an empirical and systematic analysis. This would also allow us to define the relevance of the biconsonantal clusters implied with respect to their independent existence as well as the function and semantic value of the complementary phonemes. To do this, we must consider the monoconsonantal "functorial" series as a basic starting-point. At all events, we must take into account the fact that these "determinatives" can also be radical phonemes; we should not be swept off our feet by reductionist zeal. This means that all roots that are apparently augmented do not necessarily go back to biliteral roots but can be more or less free assonantal variants of a triliteral whose *Grundform* (as against the *Urform*; cf. p. 71 [Voigt]) becomes a biliteral reflex considered to be sufficient to ensure its meaning.

However, we note that, independently of this analysis, theories have been formulated for some time and they must be evaluated. Its starting-point is the two series of facts, to some extent conflicting, that we have seen discussed by the scholars mentioned above. Arguments in favor of biconsonantalism are: primary nouns, "weak" roots with multiple biconsonantal forms and semantically related triconsonantal roots with different third consonants, a phenomenon, however, the Arabic grammarians already labelled *ibdāl al-ḥurūf*, which does not suppose necessarily an independent biconsonantal cluster. In favor of triconsonantalism: primary nouns, a morphologically universal triconsonantal system that is expandable and analogical, irreducible triconsonantal roots. Against this situation three theories have been formulated according to the well-known dialectics: universal triconsonantalism (or perhaps it would be better to say triradicalism), radical biconsonantalism, and bi/triconsonantalism with a shared base.

We think that it is the third position, as is often the case, that gives the best account of the facts. Today it is held by many first-rank Semitists and comparativists. But above all, this choice is based on decisive objections with which the other two views clash, illustrated in the works of two Arabic scholars, R. M. Voigt and G. Bohas, and to which we must pay attention. These two points of view are unaware of each other—in Voigt's case due to the date of publication—and furthermore, both ignore, to a very large extent, the opinions of Slav scholars.

After reading Voigt's writings, one might say: *actum est de biconsonantalismo.* Nevertheless, his theory has not gained general acceptance among Semitists.[52] Indeed, most of them, including some Arabists who have dealt with the problem, have ignored it, possibly due to the fact that his book is quite difficult to read. However, this is not the most suitable way to respond to his thesis. As we have seen, his concept of the "root" can be summarized in three points:

    a. every root is triradical;

    b. the radical can be either a consonant or a vowel (short, of course) (p. 15);

    c. the radical vowel can occur in any of the three positions.[53]

One could accept Voigt's analysis, simply assuming that in the "weak" and apparently "biliteral" roots, the vowel has a special function with a tendency to intensification, to become quadripositional. But this does not make them "triradicals," still less "triconsonantals," unless one wishes to assume a confusion of meaning.[54] In the triconsonantal roots, the vowel, at least according to the concept of root/base presented above, is also "radical." For Voigt, "biconsonantal" (or "biliteral," if one takes "consonant" as *littera*, in linear alphabetic notation) roots are at the same time "triradical" (!), but triconsonantals are not, therefore, quadriradical. This gives a paradoxical result: a "root" such as /k-t-b/ also supposes a "radical" vowel, just as /q[u]m/ does. Why is the vowel radical in the second example but not in the first? Why cannot the vowel /a/ be "radical" like the vowels /u/ and /i/? (pp. 15, 19). Why must a root have two contiguous vowels, one radical and the other thematic? Are they not sequentially incompatible, as Semitic phonology demands? According to Semitic phonology, a form such as /qauama/ is impossible, as even auto-segmental phonology admits (McCarthy). It is an *a priori*, as is the biphonematic value of long vowels, required by the constraints of the system selected. In fact, "triradicalism" does not contradict "biconsonantalism," which can be called also "triradical" if one likes. But the question is posed with respect to the opposition biconsonantalism/triconsonantalism.

By his alleged double function of vowels in the organization of the radical lexeme, Voigt erases or dilutes the phonetic opposition consonant/vowel (on this topic see above pp. 67ff.) and misconstrues the function of /w, y/ as glides, always in combination with a vowel, not instead of one; the equivalence /u:w/, /i:y/ defended by Voigt is unacceptable. We are not dealing obviously with original semi-vowels /w:y/; this would be triconsonantalism pure and simple; as such, they represent a late analogical reconstruction. In this sense, the use of these phonemes, therefore, can well be a reflex of Indo-European phonetics, no one denies that. But not content with mistreating the phonological distinction consonant/vowel, this equivalence annuls or deforms the validity, accepted by Voigt himself, of the system "(consonantal) root / (morphemic-vocalic) pattern." Of course, vowels function also as "radicals," but they certainly do not usurp the function of consonants. In any case, this "positional" function of the vowel amounts to recognizing the difference of structure between weak and strong roots by means of different phonematic elements. Thus, there is a double system of "roots" in Semitic although from the aspect of morphology they can be harmonized. In this sense, Voigt's work is a remarkable and successful attempt to

formalize the evidence. One could say that his system is valid, to use his own terminology, at the "functional"/"synchronic" level but not at the "etymological"/"historical" level (p. 164), in other words, at the surface but not at a deep level (p. 23).

The unremitting reiteration of his own thesis throughout the whole book
suggests that he is not satisfied with his own argumentation, which at bottom is only
an emphatic assertion of the impossibility of the opposing thesis and a denial of the
validity of reference to Afro-Asiatic: "Seen from here all the reflections on the origin
of the triradical root are…pure mental juggling (*reine Gedankenspielereien*)" (p. 79). On
the one hand, he shows an excessive and insistent confidence in the scientific nature
of his own analysis of triradicalism of the Semitic root according to "laws" of general
application without exceptions. But, as we have seen, he ends by accepting the possibility of biradical roots (pp. 209–10) in the case of geminates and even in some cases
the possibility of the alternation of weak roots with the same semantic meaning.

I find his critique of the variation of triliteral roots (*Wurzelvariation*) as a proof
of biradicalism to be successful and well founded. His argumentation coincides
largely with Zaborski's, made several years later (1991). It must be taken into account
when it is a question of studying triliteral groups with a third variable consonant.
Similarly, his critique of symbolic or semantic phonetics (*Lautbedeutsamkeit*) as the
source of root variation is very well structured (pp. 48–50). Generally speaking, I find
that Voigt is more successful in criticizing the excesses of others than in establishing
his own theory.

At the opposite extreme to R. M. Voigt's theory is the theory of G. Bohas, which
I have outlined above. It is a defense of a strict and global biliteralism/biconsonan-
talism of the root in Semitic, and the difficulties of this thesis have already been noted.

First of all, ignoring for the moment the difficulty posed in principle by a
defense of universal biliteralism based on biliteral etymons, their "matrix" level, by its
very nature and "depth," takes us back to a pre-Proto-Semitic, namely Afro-Asiatic
stage. As a result, if this theory is valid for Arabic, it should be valid also for all other
Semitic languages. They are Semitic "matrices" at the basis of etymology. In principle
there is nothing surprising about this thesis, as I have said. We only await proof, by
means of an empirical study, from common and comparative Semitics.

His theory of the reversibility or "non-sequentiality" of matrices is something
completely different. It is rooted in the glottogonic level of language and its mechanisms, transforming the whole radical lexematic system of Afro-Asiatic into a, shall
we say, "palindromic" system that is very difficult to accept. Is such a glottogonic
mechanism acceptable from the aspect of the structure of the linguistic sign? Above
all, is it semasiologically acceptable in principle? What is its *raison d'être*, its motivation? What meaning does it have from the aspect of the economy of signs? What are
its advantages? Can it be verified in other families of languages at this glottogonic
level, not only at the secondary or derived level? Here, even more than in the case of
the matrices, a phonological-semantic proof at the Afro-Asiatic level is required. If
this mechanism proves to be impossible or merely debatable, the data in its favor
provided by Bohas, which at first glance are impressive, would remain an internal
matter for Arabic lexicography that would have to be explained by a critical analysis
of its own semantic development (Zaborski). In fact, Bohas acknowledges (1997, p.

195) that reversibility is more frequent in Arabic, which means that it is probably peculiar to that language and thus not originally Semitic. It is not etymological but derived. If, indeed, it is a structural component of the Semitic root, it should occur in all the languages that have these roots. In fact, the only two examples given of reversibility in Hebrew do not appear to be acceptable (2000, pp. 106f., 120f.). Those taken from dialectal Arabic are scarcely valid either, since the dialects evolved from or formed part of the Old Epigraphic Arabic cluster that is already established as triconsonantal.

But it is particularly with his theory of the mimophony of "matrices" that we touch the foundation of the theory; Arabic becomes the original language or at least its direct reflex. In other words, all the other languages, not only Semitic languages, must also reflect, more or less, the same system of "matrices," the mimetic basis being the same for all. As Carra de Vaux would say: "the biliteral root is the phonetic element to which the human instinct attaches a meaning." All these questions await a response.[55]

This argumentation (organization by matrices, reversibility or non-sequentiality, mimophony) leads logically to the monoconsonantal root, to the simple phoneme as the pre-matrix or nucleus, to a reduced number of articulations/modulations (features)[56] as original phonological and semantic elements, as suggested for example by Nowak-Krakauer's mathematical model, which I have spoken about above (see p. 2); a model proposed some time ago (see Voigt's critique), used again in our time (Lecerf), and briefly sketched by Bohas himself, who sometimes speaks of monoconsonantal verbal (1997, pp. 76, 158) or nominal matrix/root (1997, p. 69 n. 50). This would also explain the lack of ordering of the matrices, each monophoneme becoming independent from the aspect of semantics. But, curiously, there are no or hardly any monophonemes in the Semitic lexicon (see above). We are now in the purest glottogony from which we would do well to distance ourselves, if we wish to carry out research that is probable.

Nonetheless, a specific reply must be given to the amount of data collected and arranged by Bohas. We cannot simply refuse on principle. For the moment I have examined the series /k-*/, using the dictionary of Ullman-Spitaler, and have realized that: (1) the supposed reversibility does not occur in other Semitic languages; (2) not even in Arabic, among the "primary" meanings of the alleged matrices; (3) it occurs only between primary and "derived" meanings. All this means that it is an inner development of Arabic semantics and not a structural "feature" of the Semitic root. It is a mirage. The first thing to do is to put some order into the semantics of the Arabic lexicon following "metaphorical" and "metonymical" transformations that are more or less lexicalized, an operation to which the patterns of semantic derivation proposed by Bohas himself can contribute greatly, completed of course by the patterns of "poetic" transformation, in the wide sense, essential in any semantic analysis. Semantic derivations must be made from the basic concrete seme, usually obtained as a result of the contrastive confrontation of these realizations in the various languages.

In this respect, in Bohas there is no wish to classify the meanings of an etymon and set them in a hierarchy. Whatever the case, every semantic variation is presented as primary, all at the same synchronic level. Here there is a discrepancy between the phonological diachronism, the deep etymological level of Semitic, according to Voigt, and the semantic synchronism of Arabic.[57] Unfortunately, the mirage of Arabic as a self-sufficient and self-explanatory language is experienced as completely normal in the Arabic-speaking world (see below pp. 114ff.).

At first glance, by its very nature, this etymological "palindrome" ("mirror image") seems phonologically unnatural; it raises the arbitrary nature of the sign to its extreme and establishes semasiological ambivalence, which is completely contrary to the particular and univocal function of the sign. The Egyptian pictographic palindrome is, in fact, not a real inversion. It is the direction that changes, as happens in writing, not the internal sequence of its components. As in the case of Voigt, though in the reverse sense, this is a very well-constructed formalization but valid, at the very most, for Arabic. Here, for the moment, I think it is better to return to the level of the well-defined etymon or phonetic articulation rather than to the level of the inexact magma of matrix features (on the concept of "resonance," see below p. 118). To use it in order to arrange the Arabic lexicon, as Bohas suggests, would at present entail a large degree of subjectivity.

Faced with such a wide range of opinions, it seems preferable to stick to the facts and adopt a more nuanced and less systematic stance. Almost everyone today agrees (even triliteralists such as Voigt, as we have seen) in accepting a biliteral base in the Semitic lexicon that, in turn, exhibits a dynamic of expansion in the direction of triliterality as its asymptote. One is also prepared to accept an original triliteral stock, the structural and derivation system of which becomes determinative in the whole Semitic domain (for the coexistence of the two systems, see Cohen, Kuryłowicz, Zaborski, Djakonoff, Conti and others, whose views we have summarized above). This prevalence of a double base must have a primary origin, attested even at the Afro-Asiatic level. It now remains to determine the relationship between the two lexical systems and to know the extent to which the triliteral cluster is independent and original and the extent to which it derives from the biliteral cluster. Reconstructing the biliteral level of Semitic leads us inevitably to the stage of common Afro-Asiatic. But this in itself does not presuppose a primary biliteral level, universal and unique. On the contrary, it co-exists with a triliteral level even before the scattering of the families of the phylum (Egyptian, Berber, Chadic…). The requirement of biliteralism as a unique original system of proto-Hamito-Semitic cannot be proved, as Voigt states, especially if one considers the degenerate nature of certain Afro-Asiatic families that are predominantly biliteral.

It is a question that only empirical analysis of the Semitic lexicon can settle by counter-proof, from the complete list of primary biliteral bases with a first degree of intensification, about which I spoke earlier. On this basis it will be possible to determine whether or not triliteral bases with a different third consonant and identical semantic load, have an expansive and derived nature, which always remains the key problem of the two analytical approaches of Semitic lexematics. At the same time, objective statistical data will be acquired to determine whether alternating phonemes are morphemic in character.

In this respect the view put forward by Kuryłowicz, Voigt, and Zaborski to account for "root variation" seems to be the most reasonable. It provides a list of linguistic features with universal value, which can explain the origin of this variation in a large number of cases, in contrast to the view that refers to a weakly motivated random mechanism.

In any case, faced with the dilemma of biliteralism/triliteralism, what remains to be explained is not only the original form of actual lexemes, but the origin and purpose of triliterality as a "structural" system of a whole super-family of languages, even if one can also find it somewhere else in an unsystematic way. As for biliteralism, it is more universal in character. There is an element of originality in it that operates at the deepest level of Proto-Semitic, involving the other levels. One should not say that triliteralism derives from biliteralism by expansion but rather that biliteralism is absorbed and transformed by triliteralism. It is the problem concealed beneath the concept of "radical integration" (p. 62 [Conti]) mentioned occasionally. It is not possible to establish a chronological sequence of priority between them, but a "teleology" of development according to which the tendency to a more complex particular sign has operated since the dawn of language even if it is the last to be achieved.

In this sense, even the use of glides (/w:y:ʔ/) must be taken as due to this impulse toward the triliterality of the Semitic base (moved perhaps by its verbal morphological development). As a result, this use of glides appears as a complementary and spontaneous "articulation," in other words originally these glides were or tended to be consonantal, even if they are not true consonants. Their further reduction to monophthongs is derived and results from an opposite tendency, a tendency to phonic economy, while still retaining their consonantal character when morphology allows (against Voigt, who considers the use of glides as later). Vowel intensity is their starting-point (here Voigt is correct, in my opinion), to become open to the use of glides: intensification > development of glides > diphthong > reduction to monophthong. The universal intensified realization of biliteral bases makes intensification, both consonantal and vocalic (parallel or isomorphic), appear as triconsonantal: the dilemma of bi/triconsonantalism has no meaning. In this sense, Voigt's thesis is valid: /dvf-/ > /dvf̱-/ > /dvfvf-/ // /dvf-/ > /f̱v̱f-/ > /dvv(:v)f-/, with doubling of the phoneme in both cases.[58]

It could be said that the biliteral shape of the linguistic sign is completely normal and self-explanatory, starting for example with the definition of the root given by Kuryłowicz and Indo-European scholars and applied to Semitic. It is the universal minimal phonological base (/Cv[C]/). In Semitic, this base tends to be surpassed (for the moment we do not know whether this is spontaneous or under the influence of a triliterality that is already developed), only operating on elements susceptible to intensification. It is even possible to establish the expansion levels of biliterality/biradicalism in this way:

a. primary, simple biradicalism (very few examples) + triradicalism;

b. intensified biradicalism (first degree of [internal] expansion by intensification [lengthening and doubling] of its positions 2 [vowel] or 3 [/C_2/] or by *glide*);

c. bi/triradicalism by expansion (second degree of [external] expansion by affixed determinatives in the three positions);

    d.   reduplication, total or assimilated, doubling, total or assimilated tri-/ quadriradicalism (third degree of expansion);

    e.   crossed tri-/quadriradicalism (fourth degree of expansion).

The question is how to establish the shift from one to the other of these degrees of expansion and to explain how triliteralism has become the normative system of the language. Why does this "expansion" occur? One could think of the necessary expansion of the lexicon. But that is not very convincing, since the possibilities of a biliteral lexicon have not been exhausted and many of its expansions are homonymous or almost so. I think that we must look for the reason in the pressure or constraints exerted by inflection, especially internal inflection (Djakonoff), which has imposed itself as a structuring system in the Afro-Asiatic(-Semitic) languages and has found its lexical "prototype" in becoming "triliteral" asymptotically. In this sense, it is necessary to go beyond the biliteralism/triliteralism opposition and consider them to be two functions of the same basic dynamic of Semitic lexematics: in a general way we can say that triliteralism depends largely on biliteralism and was born from it, which in its turn appears unstable and requires to be surpassed, to become triliteral. The primary character of the biliteral noun lexicon can be ascertained in the semantic fields that in turn can be called "primary": "parts of the body," "family relationships," "simple movements." But even within these semantic fields there is "original" triliteral expansion by intensification and original triliteral bases.

Other problems, such as the mimophonic origin of roots, belong to the level of lexicography and etymology. This is what we are going to consider next.

V   COMPARATIVE AND ETYMOLOGICAL SEMITIC LEXICOGRAPHY

The aim of comparative and etymological lexicography and semantics is to reply to a series of questions that to some extent Semitists attempt to resolve by trying to bridge the gap separating their achievements in these domains from the work of their Indo-European colleagues (see above p. 1). And what is most striking is the different perspective that these colleagues have. Whereas many modern textbooks on lexicography/semantics deal with living languages and refer to those speaking them as the final criterion for verifying meaning, Semitists work largely with material from the past "that does not speak." In fact, neither phonological nor semantic verification for these dead languages has an external point of reference, the living languages of the family often being subjected to a long secondary process of contacts and contamination by various adstrates and substrates.

As a result, many of the solutions and suggestions proposed in general textbooks of modern lexicography/semantics are valid only to a limited extent for Semitics.[1] Many aspects of this problem have already been tackled in the previous chapters. Here, we are only going to survey a few theoretical discussions of semantics and the comparative method proposed by Semitists, leaving to the end of the chapter my own point of view. In fact, there are not many such discussions. Most obvious is a great lack of interest for lexicography and semantics in grammars of comparative Semitics[2] or in manuals of sector-based philology, such as the one by Fleisch for Arabic.[3]

1. Aspects of Theory and Method
(etymology, comparative study, reconstruction)

1.1. In a posthumous work, the Semitist J. P. Palache (1959)[4] developed a very interesting system of arranging/classifying Semitic lexemes/"roots" based on parallelisms of "semantic chains" provided by various languages (even of different *phyla*).[5] They are patterns of shift or development, semantic and not lexical, the coincidence of which would prove the validity and enable certain meanings, apparently conflicting, to be grouped under a single basic lexeme/seme. The process is not developed in his posthumous notes in a systematic way as the original manuscript has been lost.

This theory, which had already been formulated by Russian Semitists (see above p. 63 [Majzel']), has been revived and used in our time by M. Masson (see below pp. 102f.) in the analysis of a specific seme and, more generally, by Eilers (see below pp. 96f.). It is also confirmed by the "interdialectal distribution" of semantic equivalents set out by Held-Cohen: "corresponding idiomatic phrases even when such correspondences involve only semantic and non-etymological equivalents" (p. 13).[6] This theory, in all its various forms, could belong under the more general theory of "linguistic universals" as a case of "universal derived semantemes," although they are not primal universals.[7]

1.2. A general survey of the problem of comparative Semitics is provided by E. Ullendorff (1961)[8] (see above pp. 5f.). Once again, he outlines the history of research that we have already found given by other scholars. Like him, we should remember actual applications of the comparative method to studies of grammar that are historical (for example of Hebrew by H. Bauer and P. Leander) and even descriptive (for example, of Amharic by M. Cohen, of Ugaritic by C. H. Gordon and of Akkadian by W. von Soden). Even so, I think that he allows himself to be carried away by his enthusiasm for certain successes and by his simplified evaluation of the results (for example, see his opinion on the significance of the Ethiopic languages for comparative Semitics and their dependence on *Ge'ez*, pp. 21f.).

Nevertheless, with H. Birkeland[9] he notes the failure to appreciate general linguistics that Semitists often display. Yet, comparative linguistics proves to be indispensable for a correct and in-depth explanation of the grammar of a specific language: "no Semitic language, not even Arabic (and probably no single language ever) can by itself provide such explanatory data...and historical and comparative investigation answers a deep-seated human urge of inquiry" (p. 25). In this case, because usually there is no "mother" language available, one must refer to Proto-Semitic, but only as a working hypothesis, without claiming actually to reconstruct that language. This must be envisaged as "a set of inferential data that assist us in explaining parallels as well as divergences" (p. 26). The task of general and comparative Semitic linguistics, of which Birkeland deplores the almost complete abandon in his time (the 1950s), must first of all be to determine the linguistic type and its characters, for example the function of the vowels, triliterality (with the possibility of having one of the three consonants as a semantic modifier, cf. *supra* Ch. IV), and structural compatibilities of the root. The statistical method, applied, for example, to the analysis of vocabulary, classified by semantic fields, can provide very useful information for comparative studies. Here, whatever the case, linguistic contacts must be taken into account to define diachronically the relationship and classification of each language. The future remains open for the work of generalist Semitists.

1.3. A more systematic treatment of the semantic question in Semitic, even if only from the perspective of biblical Hebrew and its own specific problems, is by J. Barr in two surveys. Even though the perspective is historically and culturally specific (with regard to the gap between different linguistic and ideological systems and their out-of-date character), in the first of these surveys (1961/1969)[10] there are certain developments that open up general problems of semantics and etymology that may be interesting to retain. For example, he considers that it is not possible to separate lexicography from grammar, while at the same time he places nouns and verbs in a close relationship in any linguistic system, criticizing the views of Boman and others, who would like to establish an opposition of the type "dynamic *versus* static" between these two categories. From the viewpoint of original semantics, Barr declares himself to be against "the root fallacy" or "the root meaning," although "that...can confidently be taken to be part of the actual semantic value of any word or form which can be assigned to an identifiable root" (p. 100; see also p. 290). At the practical level and in the framework of morphemic grammatical variations, he thinks this is acceptable, but it should always be acknowledged that the "root" is a "consonantal" abstraction that can give rise to derived forms with seemingly unrelated semantic values: "the significance of the root is historical and is not a guide in itself to the sense of the words" (p. 102). In other words, semantics has its own history.

Here he brings to light the basic problem of the distinction between "etymological semantics" and "historical semantics" (which we will discuss later) and to which he pays great attention, on the one hand, through several examples from Hebrew lexicography and, on the other, insisting on incorrect use of the "etymologizing interpretation" as an explanation of the actual or real meaning of words ("Etymologies and Related Arguments"). However, he recognizes the importance of comparative etymology for determining the meaning of badly documented words as long as it is used together with the context (p. 158). It can also be useful for the recognition of homonyms, "but it cannot impose a sense authoritatively upon known usage" (p. 158). In any case, the author's specific preoccupation with fighting a particular ideological or "theological" method of interpretation of texts sets his book somewhat outside our own field of interest.

In general, with respect to his mistrust of etymology as a semantic method, it can be objected that here, in my opinion, there is a lack of attention to metaphorical or metonymic shifts, historically very important, in meaning and the lexicalization that ensues from it. Against his "root fallacy" ("etymologizing," p. 103) one could set a "lexicalization fallacy" that pays attention only to the distinction due to evolution and not at all to the common origin of lexemes (and of morphemes, for example, of the *hif̒il*) in the various languages (in fact, the comparative perspective is almost completely missing from his book). The two perspectives should not be confused, but one should not deny or abolish one or the other just because of bad usage and the conclusions/extrapolated fantasies (etymologizing) that have been extracted due to preconceived ideas (Boman, Pedersen). At all events, some semantic value has to be recognized in etymology (p. 108).

His second work (1968)[11] intends to establish the foundations of the "philological" method, that is to say, based on "comparative linguistics" (the "dictionary") as a suitable procedure to approach an ancient text, obscure and badly documented, as against the "textual" method, which starts from the corruption of the text (the "critical apparatus") (pp. 6f.).

Within this aim, he deals with specific problems of linguistics that affect us closely. Among them can be noted: the retrieval of many neutralized homonyms (*passim*, p. 349, index), words the meaning of which had been lost (pp. 25f.), operations for which the method of comparative philology becomes useful (pp. 35f.). This method is described and discussed extensively. For Barr it supposes a certain reconstruction of the proto-language: "the existence of such an entity was and is one of the assumptions in method made by comparative philology" (p. 79), even though very hypothetical, incomplete, and not directly verifiable. But "the reconstruction serves as a basis from which the extant languages can be described historically as the product of fairly consistent changes" (p. 79). The phonetic and semantic changes and correspondences are, in fact, the fixed points on which this method pivots, which support each other, and whose rigor, especially of phonetic changes, must be maintained. More uncertain remains determination of the regularity of semantic changes compared to the regularity of phonology and morphology: "one may say that semantics formed the Achilles' heel of comparative philology…In contrast to forms, meanings are rather slippery to handle" (p. 88). Its field of variation is found within each language and in spite of the usefulness of the comparative method, "the meaning of a word is its meaning in its own language, not its meaning in some other" (p. 90). (This means that determination of meaning results from two coordinates: etymology and context, where context takes precedence; this is a problem that appears specifically when interpreting languages without speakers.) The flexible use of "chains of semantic analogy," which occur in various languages (see above p. 87 [Palache] and below pp. 96f. [Eilers] and 102f. [Masson]), can help to determine the meaning of lexemes (pp. 90f.).[12] This comparative procedure becomes indispensable in deciphering new languages, but must be used with some care, always respecting phonological and semantic correspondences as a whole. Immediately after this, Barr sets out the implications of this method in the interpretation of texts, especially in Hebrew.

One question to emerge from this philological or comparative treatment of texts that is of great interest to us from the aspect of etymological semantics, even though Barr considers it in principle only at the morpholexical level, is the problem of "homonyms" (pp. 125ff.). These need to be organized and can, for example, be phonetic (homographs-homophones by the convergence of phonemes in the various languages) or rather apparent homographs (non-homophones) radical/original (partial or complete). Their differentiation can be noted from their different usage in the "stems" (p. 133), as well as from their different formation ("word formation") to which little attention is paid and where vocalization is important. They can be distinguished also by their position in a syntagm and in a semantic field. The problem of communication supposed by homonymy is evidently more acute in the case of primary bases or sources of meaning. It is here that homonymy seems rather to be pure polysemy (pp. 142ff.) and not derived or convergent polysemy, even if for the speaker and modern lexicography this distinction is meaningless (p. 143).

Be that as it may, I think that complete "radical" homonymy (in all the phonetic complexity of the base, both consonantal and vocalic), with the exception of onomatopoeia, is unacceptable. Homonymy is diachronic, derived or borrowed. In fact, many cases of onomatopoeia prove to be late and etymologically secondary. But in the case of "primary" onomatopoeia, its conditioned non-arbitrary sound glottogony makes possible the coincidence with non-conditioned phonological clusters.[13] The unacceptability of pure radical homonymy is imposed by the univocal nature of the linguistic sign and its own semantic value. It is an elementary principle of semiotics.[14] The ambiguity of a sign is contradictory; it would annul it as a signifying element: if a traffic signal is ambivalent, a crash is inevitable. In the case of language, only context can help to resolve the historically developed polysemy.

Lastly, a final point of interest to us here. Barr is concerned about the distribution and overlap of the lexicon among the Semitic languages, from the aspect of form (phonology) and meaning (semantics) (pp. 156ff.), which can diverge. Even if his main concern remains the interpretation of the Hebrew text (sometimes badly attested), his suggestions for the organization of an etymological dictionary of the Semitic languages must be taken into account: "such a work should not only register the existence of a word in a certain language, but also negatively its nonexistence…likewise, where it exists only in one or two particular fixed forms, and is no longer free or productive" (p. 299). Within this problem, the biliteral theory that supposes "roots" with two fixed consonants and one that is free has its role. In this sense his conclusion is interesting and at the same time surprising: "conceivably there were two sectors in Semitic vocabulary. The first was already in a fairly fixed form in the proto-Semitic period…. In the second sector, however, the root sequences were still not firm in the proto-Semitic period, and various branches developed their words independently later, through expansion of a vague common base" (p. 169). In turn, the organization or simple bundle of semantic fields proves very different in each language for the same lexemes, which make lexicography even more difficult. The forms can be predicted but not their meaning (pp. 172f.): "because…it is dependent on interrelation with still other words, which interrelations are not predictable at all" (p. 173).

A very special case is internal or external enantiosemy (*aḍdād*), the origin of which is to be explained. Perhaps syntagmatic change has to be taken into account, that is, the position in the sentence of the "object" of reference, such as happens with prepositions in many languages (p. 176). Finally, the data of glottochronology provide a glimpse of a large gap in the historical formation of the lexicon of each related language. Other matters of textual treatment considered by Barr are not of interest to us here. In the final pages, problems such as onomatopoeia (pp. 273ff.) and cultural semantic derivation are tackled. He correctly notes the presence of onomatopoeia in the Semitic languages, but is opposed to its use as a principle generating words (p. 275): "the elements commonly called onomatopoeic may perhaps be better expressed as motivated terms, motivated 'as stylizations of acoustic impressions'" (p. 275), which, in fact, are different in each language. In other words: lexemes do not imitate natural sounds, so defining their "basic meaning," and phonemes have no semantic meaning connected to their sound (see above p. 61 [Lecerf]) as "sound symbolism" would have it. Onomatopoeia is of minor importance in semantic change. The arbitrary nature of language, as the most orthodox structuralism states, proves dominant also in Semitic. To close, the validity of the philological axiom according to which the original meanings are always "concrete" (p. 276) is questioned.

Even though he is concerned with the philological treatment of Hebrew texts, his comments are very balanced and always valid for historical and comparative semantics in general (pp. 290ff.), even etymological semantics. For example, for him semantic derivation does not start from a basic idea or a basic meaning common to various linguistic forms as a whole, but the semantic relationship can derive from various aspects of existing forms: "Meanings are not derived from one basic idea, or directly from a class of referents, but from the meaning of forms already found" (p. 291), through a process of transfer of meaning defined by linguistic usages that can be tangential to the "basic meaning" supposed. In the same sense, a distinction must be made between "meaning" (reference) and "applications" (information) that can be used in the various languages and as such are simply not transferable (p. 292). Yet again he reiterates that words have their own meaning in "their" language and not in another (p. 292). And in each language, the meaning of words results from their inter-relationships within their own linguistic system (oppositions, positions, context, which can be determined from outside; pp. 293ff.), although the meaning of the root in that language is always determinative (p. 295).

But etymological semantics does not claim to define the meaning of words in each language nor to transfer it from one to another. It starts from the meanings that the words have in each language and tries to retrace the transfer process without claiming to give them another meaning. As in the case of the philological treatment of uncertain texts, this process has to be approximate and it is the context that makes it more precise. The whole problem depends on the type of language in question: Is it spoken or not? Where no speakers are available, checking is possible only from context. In my opinion, Barr does not pay enough attention to this and sometimes mixes the requirements of the two forms of semantics (p. 293).

In the wake of J. Barr, various scholars have applied the principles of semantic theory to the analysis of the Hebrew lexicon. Of these, J. F. A. Sawyer (1972)[15] merits particular mention. His work has become a good example of a description and at the same time a concrete application of this method. Contextualization, the associative field of a term, as well as synchronic and historical description of that term, helps in a decisive way to define its meaning and specify it with respect to its correlatives within the same semantic field. In a few final pages, he summarizes these basic principles, which have to be taken into account in the analysis of biblical Hebrew. Language has to be examined from the general principles of structural semantics, valid for all languages (relations of meaning, componential analysis, etc.). Noteworthy is the predominance he accords to monolingual analysis (the only type usually considered by modern semantic theory, but impossible in the case of languages without speakers and even risky in the case of languages with differing diachronic levels), as well as to contextual analysis over etymology, as insistently preached by Barr.

J. C. Greenfield (1993)[16] also discusses and applies the various types of semantic etymology proposed by J. Barr in his 1974 study,[17] which followed the works just discussed. These types or levels of etymological analysis are: (1) prehistoric reconstruction; (2) historical research within an observable context; (3) the discovery of loans from other languages; (4) the analysis of words in their morphemic composition and semantic shifts; (5) the use of a cognate language to discover the meaning of Hebrew; (6) simple comparison of institutions named in a similar way.

1.4.   Before his series of studies on common Semitic lexicography (see below p. 108), P. Fronzaroli (1964)[18] proposed some reflections on "the aim and method of comparative research" that are worth remembering. For him, the task to be accomplished is the reconstruction of the common Proto-Semitic lexicon, which enables its historical development in the individual languages to be followed. This leads immediately to the question of general semantics, especially structural semantics, the development of which he outlines. But the focus of his interest is comparative semantics, which leads to "linguistic palaeontology" from the observation of this lexicon common to the Semitic languages, for which Indo-European scholars have provided models since the nineteenth century. He surveys the ideas of some of these scholars (Pisani, Pagliaro, Devoto), who are concerned with seeing languages in relation to peoples and their movements. The concept of "iso-idea" alongside the concept of "isogloss" emphasizes the importance of the *signifié* in semantics as against the more formal treatment of the lexeme. On the other hand, the signifying content is useful to determine the patrimony that is common and specific to the peoples in question. The common Semitic lexicon enables us to suppose "the existence of peoples of Semitic language, more or less mutually differentiated, in the phase immediately preceding the historical period" (p. 6) and fully differentiated from other Afro-Asiatic populations. He specifies the criteria he used to define which word belongs, or can be considered to belong, to the common Semitic lexicon: it must appear in one of the dialects of the three branches of Semitic: East, Northwest, Southwest, clearly a criterion that is too restricted. In addition, the strictest phonetic rigor, which sometimes is excessive, governs his lexematic choice based on the classical literary languages. But it is particularly the semantic level (word, semantic field, expressiveness, and other levels of use) that will concern him in the search for cultural implications: "it is possible to acknowledge that the study of the Semitic lexicon is able to provide first-hand information on the culture and life of the Semites" (p. 14). In what follows, the specific determination of the common lexicon and its large semantic fields, as a system of organization constructed on this basis, as well as the hypotheses on the dialectal or innovative origin of lexemes, are for the moment outside our interest.

In a later study (1974),[19] Fronzaroli returns once more to some of these ideas, accepting the validity of linguistic palaeontology as a historical source for knowing the cultural structure of ancient societies. For this he insists on the importance of semantics (associative fields and lexico-semantics) to discover the cultural universe, in spite of the fragmentary state of the lexicon and the difficulty in moving from archi-lexemes to specific lexemes that prevents relevant oppositions being established: "the *signifié* of a lexeme is formed by the sum of its own distinctive features (or semes), within the lexical field to which it belongs" (p. 175). In fact, these oppositions are the only ones that enable the determination of the level at which each word functions as an archi-lexeme or else in binary opposition within a special type of language, for example, the language of the cult. This reconstruction of the Common Semitic lexicon refers back to a real phase of the language, shortly before the historical period. Instead, its relationship to the "Hamitic" lexicon does not allow the reconstruction of an organic common Hamito-Semitic/Afro-Asiatic lexicon. In any case,[20] Common Semitic must be considered a historical reality "referring back" to a continuous dialectal area, in the phase immediately preceding the historical period (p. 177). One fact to be taken into account is, of course, the involvement of Afro-Asiatic in the process of fixing Common Semitic. But the two systems prove to be quite different.

In the framework of his project of compiling a dictionary of comparative Semitic, which as yet has not been completed, P. Fronzaroli (1973)[21] raises questions concerning the reconstruction of forms. In any case, he favors not going beyond the stage of Common Semitic in a strict synchronism. To go further, that is, to the Afro-

Asiatic phase, is allowed only when one finds Common Semitic proof, which has to be applied in a special way to the biconsonantal hypothesis and to its mechanism of derivation, which can, in fact, be followed, to a large extent, in the Common Semitic stage (on Djakonoff's opinion on this matter see above pp. 17, 27, 30), as well as in roots of onomatopoeic origin, whether lexicalized or not. Particular care must be taken about the claimed "expressive" changes to avoid subjectivity. This point of view is seen to be backed up by wise reflections on etymology, analysis, and semantic arrangement from specific lexemes and their precise context in each of the linguistic slots. For example: "therefore a direct comparison of all the attested forms that in the different Semitic languages may belong to a root BWR, would be scarcely significant. On the contrary, our task is to try to ascertain the area of diffusion and the antiquity of every root recorded in the different historical languages" (p. 13). Comparative study alone is not enough; historical reconstruction is necessary. It is clear that the reference to Afro-Asiatic can explain and confirm the form and the semantics of some bases and roots, but one should not fall into the excess of glottogony, in the claim to be able to have access to the origin of the language. He then gives a sample of an etymological dictionary of Semitic (the "root" BBR and its cognates).

Fronzaroli returned once more to the problem (1975)[22] in a programmatic article in which he explains and develops the results that have guided him in the preparation of his studies on the Common Semitic lexicon. He accepts as belonging to the proto-language, or Common Semitic, about 500 lexemes, not derived and occurring in at least one language of each of the three great families (Eastern, Northwestern, and Western) as against the 156 of G. Bergsträsser[23] (attested in the five classic families) and the 306 of D. Cohen[24] (based on statistical criteria and semantic continuity) plus the numerals, certain particles, and the personal pronouns. By 1969, of these 500 words Fronzaroli had studied only 275, belonging to five different (associative) semantic fields (see below), of interest for the study of the cultural and ecological conditions of the speakers. And it is precisely on these conditions and the significance of the proto-lexicon that he concentrates. In this respect he analyzes the various associated fields. But for the moment this is not our concern.

A few years later, P. Fronzaroli in collaboration with G. Garbini (1977), returned to the same topics. Garbini himself had already formulated his ideas, collected together later here.

1.5.   Two contributions by C. T. Hodge must be taken into account. The first (1970)[25] discusses the likelihood of the cyclic sequence of linguistic types predominantly morphological (inflection) or syntactic (grammar). Without wishing to separate them, as I also suggested above with regard to the proto-grammar (see p. 15), analysis of the stages of various languages, especially of Egyptian, suggests that "proto-Afro-Asiatic was a period of flexibility, that is, a predominantly syntactic stage that would give rise to the variant morphologies to be found in the daughter branches" (p. 5). If this cyclic thesis proves to be correct, one must think of an inversion of the process of etymological derivation while accepting its complexity as a starting-point. Instead of a dictionary of the proto-language, it would be necessary to establish the proto-syntax, first, since "the morphology is frozen syntax, sooner or later doomed to be replaced. There is, however, a syntactic component that remains and that creates new morphology" (p. 6). In any case, one must always pay attention to the presence of a possible pre-inflectional stage of Semitic where, for example, the distinction between noun and verb (see above pp. 27f.) was not operative, in agreement with Hirt's opinion, cited by Hodge (p. 3). It remains, however, to determine at what stage of the cycle (Proto-)Semitic must be placed. From equivalence with ancient Egyptian, one would think of a prevalently morphological stage (sM in the author's notation), for which lexical reconstruction would be decisive.

The second contribution by C. T. Hodge (1975)[26] formulates, following Bloomfield, a series of 23 postulates, with brief commentary, that must govern change and linguistic relations. Change is presented as a linguistic universal, permanent at all levels. Each postulate reflects an aspect of this, empirically verifiable from the aspect of the structure of the language and of socio-linguistics. Of course, many of these postulates are extremely obvious first-class proofs. Even so, this axiomatic panorama is a good point of reference for attacking semantic analysis of historical lexematics in which change is a fact the speed of which can be verified (p. 211). Commenting on the effects of change, Hodge states "that lexical items (i.e., vocabulary) and isolable morphological units are the best source of evidence for remote relationships" (p. 212), at the same time that he affirms the existence of focal points of the community of speakers who catalyze the "areal" development of dialectal changes, which then became the languages and the groups of different languages, defined by the common innovations. These languages, however, retain their genetic relationship, openly defended, and refer to a common source or "proto-language," considered as "spoken." "Languages which derive from a common source may retain sufficient structured material for their relationship to be determined," namely a sufficient amount of "shared innovations." According to Hodge, "this postulate is the basis for comparative linguistics" and the surest guide (and even for the moment the only one able to be used for this purpose [p. 215]) is phonetic correspondence (p. 213). Time marks the difference and, therefore, the distance of the relationship, but does not erase it. In other words, change or innovation need not be an obstacle to comparative research, the semantic element being more inaccurate in this respect. But semantics is the subject in which universals appear most clearly, so creating a great linguistic continuity.

A close reading of this picture of the data would save much useless discussion. These postulates can serve as a *vade-mecum* of comparative study.

1.6. The problem is considered again by D. Cohen (1973)[27] from the viewpoint of the history of Semitic comparative studies, starting with the Amoraim and continuing through the Jewish Middle Ages, the Renaissance, the Enlightenment, and the modern period. He analyzes the continuity and discontinuity between the various periods of research, their methods and results, their successes and failures. Making Arabic instead of Hebrew the basic language for comparison is a first step toward respecting "regular correspondences" by distinguishing them from phonetic analogy (*'ibdāl*). He shows the importance of the exegetical role both of traditional biliteralism and of enantiosemy that continues to our day in Semitic lexicography. Modern research is directed toward the study of semantic fields—even though there is much of it that has not been explored—and to the study of sociolinguistic palaeontology, linked to identifying the original homeland of the Semites and the classification and glottochronology of these languages. In this perspective he concludes: "since statistics have a bearing on the whole lexicon, it is undoubtedly necessary to consider the degree of connections among the lexica of the various languages as a measure of the intensity of relationships and exchanges in the course of history, rather than as an indication of a particular genetic connection" (p. 201).

But a comparative Semitic dictionary always remains a project. He notes the various attempts at this (especially his own; see below), as well as the difficulties surrounding them: a lack of solid studies on many Semitic languages and a lack of suitable semantic distribution, just like the problem posed by the apparent biliteralism of many roots with a variable third consonant and still with a large number of possible permutations; the role of the third consonant still needs to be defined. The process of triliterality would have been different in each language. The problem of the relationships between biliteral and triliteral roots remains to be explained, since there is a majority of triliteral roots with two biliteral groups, one of primitive nouns and the other of expressive nouns. The certainly inevitable Afro-Asiatic perspective only complicates matters given its own deficiencies. In summary, "today, comparative Semitics, in spite of all its antiquity, is faced with more problems than it has resolved and the very progress of our research opens up deeply unsettling perspectives" (p. 208).

Some years later (1978),[28] D. Cohen returned to the question with respect to his own comparative dictionary, which he had presented in the previous article. Since then he has tried several times to present and justify its structure (see below).

1.7.   At about the same time, W. Eilers (1974)[29] set out a long and enthusiastic account, at once theoretical and practical, of the comparative method in oriental studies. The comparative method as such has been extended to several disciplines following its success in linguistics. In spite of possibly incorrect use in some cases, it is clear that "comparison really constitutes the essence of discerning scientific work" (p. 6). In all the cultural and natural sciences, external observation provides the best perspective. In our case, it is a "semasiological" method, that is a study of meaning, which has not been developed systematically in our linguistic studies. The semantic field of the parts of the body is a good example; they all mirror a verbal seme, both in Indo-European and in Semitic. The same applies to toponymy, which offers a mine of semantic information and brings to light the existence of a sort of common semantics: "common fundamental features are inherent in language as such wherever people speak" (p. 10), whereas the phonetic sign presents great diversity even in the same linguistic family. Form and content (morphology and semantics) are in opposition in this respect. This basic structure, common to all languages, makes translation possible and guarantees semantic comparison, even between different languages, allowing to understand "from which fundamental ideas the construction of their outward appearance was reached" (p. 11). But to get there one must know etymology, which provides us with comparative morphology. The examples quoted are excellent proof of the "semantic chains," discussed above (see p. 87 [Palache]) and appear to be tendencies rather than laws of the same kind as phonetic laws.

Of course, loanwords and semantic calques are not considered here, while natural and cultural conditions sometimes restrict the common existence of certain semantic chains. But, even if each language can have its own phonetic framework and, therefore, a different acoustic perception of the world (acoustic symbolism), Eilers resolutely sticks to the opinion of the ethnologist Adolf Bastian (1826–1905) "that under the same or similar conditions everywhere in the world, the same or similar representations arose in mankind, without them necessarily having been borrowed from each other, so that mankind, purely from inner predisposition and development and in the same external circumstances, arrived at the same trains of thought" (pp. 19–20). Linguistic research can help to discover primitive concepts. It can be noted, first of all, that everywhere word-ideas, that is, the names of things, are formed independently on the basis of the same root-ideas. It is this identity between human physiology and psychology that guarantees this linguistic concurrence. But this also implies that the dominant element is the root-idea; there are no "primitive nouns" ("the so-called *nomina primitiva* of classic Semitics do not exist as a category" [p. 21]), nouns derive from verbal roots. "This is an effect of the principle of predominance of the abstract over the concrete" (p. 21).[30]

On the one hand, this semasiological method highlights the unity of humankind and, on the other, it assists research into etymology based on the same semantic development. In this way a new path can be traced both to confirm and to find answers to these questions. However, this kind of comparative method must be used with a great deal of skill, while leaving some decisive power to cumulative examination.

The rest of the book is devoted to a discussion of a series of semes, either general or specifically Semitic. No doubt this type of "long distance comparison" or "semantic Semitics" (*versus* phonological Semitics) can help greatly to organize basic homophones and in general the historical lexematics of languages, but, as the author stresses, it presupposes a good knowledge of the philology (phonology and morphology) of each language. However, in my opinion, his rejection of "primitive nouns" is not to be retained.

1.8. K. Petráček (1975)[31] poses the problem of the "(re)construction" of a proto-language as the first question to be considered and it must be understood as a meta-linguistic "construction," not as the recovery of a historical reality, in spite of the studies by Fronzaroli on the common Semitic lexicon and by Tylloch, Cohen, and others on the proto-lexicon. The difficulty of the enterprise derives from the heterogeneous nature of the data involved: the Semitic and the "Hamitic" languages. This in turn supposes the construction of a complex linguistic "proto-system," not a simple collection of isolated facts. Moreover, the starting-point must be the whole "group" of languages, a concept that becomes clear only for the Semitic languages, connected by genetic relationship. We could restrict ourselves to this group even though the questions raised remain unanswered.

Some years later, even though in a Afro-Asiatic perspective, K. Petráček (1984)[32] gave a very lucid account of the problem of the comparative method and the new perspectives and methods as well as the limitations and shortcomings. The methods concern especially the study of phonology and morphology. However, the rich bibliographical information, also useful for comparative lexicography and the classification of the Semitic languages, is noteworthy. Starting from the ideas of the Prague School, Petráček emphasizes scholars who have been concerned with linguistic methodology as applied to Semitic studies. For him the starting-point is the structuralism of the Prague School mentioned above, with its concept of language as a dynamic global system both at the synchronic and diachronic levels, developing continually. This system "functions as an instrument of *social communication*" (p. 425) and of its requirements, which, in turn, release new impulses. This complexity of the system makes it necessary to accept all methods and approaches, even if extra-linguistic, to complete the study. "This open perspective demands a profound contact between Hamito-Semitic studies and general linguistics" (p. 425) that results in overcoming the dominance of the Semitic perspective. New approaches to Afro-Asiatic comparative studies open out, taking into account the social implications already mentioned. In fact, there are different types of comparisons, of which he outlines the most important. For some scholars, typological analysis becomes determinative for the classification of languages, whereas others find it inadequate. This typology leads to the reconstruction of the internal history, not only of "ancient" forms but of the development of the whole system and in this way can provide the whole set of features that define the language type. These features must concern morphology and the system as a whole. In Semitics, morpho-phonological analysis and analysis of derivation and internal inflection are found at the basis of the study of the root and of the development of languages. In this connection, various studies on incompatibility and apophony are developed and "it is possible to reckon that the time has come to set up a *new unified theory of the Hamito-Semitic root*" (p. 430; see above pp. 23ff.). Another methodological approach is to discover a "linguistic cycle" (see above, pp. 94f., on Hodge) that affects the whole system of the language and can be found in the various groups or stages of the Afro-Asiatic languages. He finds this overall or systematic synchronic as well as diachronic perspective at work in specific studies on the system of prepositions or the sequential reconstruction of Akkadian. In any case, it is morphological analysis that takes precedence in all these studies and that, taken as a whole, can really help to "overcome gradually the atomistic conception of neo-grammarian comparativism and to introduce in this way the concept of system in comparative work" (p. 432). This perspective has, in turn, led to a new vision of the classification of the Afro-Asiatic, "areal" classification instead of "genetic" classification (see below p. 99, on Garbini). In fact, this is an old tradition in Semitic studies, a more "dynamic" concept that counts on the innovative thrust, in concrete terms of Amorite, which spreads out over a wide area and reaches languages considered "different" or apart, in line with the classical genealogical classification. Another model, which is dynamic also, uses quantitative methods (glottochronology) to define the relationships between the various phyla and "makes use of the drives of the *social reality* that in the last analysis represents the motive power of the linguistic development of the dynamic center of the Semitic languages" (p. 434). All these types of methodology lead us to ask the question of the development system of languages that "according to the postulates of the Prague school is itself systematic…and does not represent a game absolutely free of chance" (p. 434) as opposed to the structuralist theory of the Geneva School (system against structure). Its laws of development are also both the immanent laws of structure and the laws of social development. The dynamics of such a system make it necessary to visualize linguistic, phonological, and morphological features as the result of internal oppositions throughout the development of a language. Language proves to be a system that is always evolving, of which the decisive factor is the social and historical reality of peoples. This complicates linguistic analysis, given the amount of data (archaeological, anthropological, sociological, etc.) that must be incorporated, but it is indispensable. It is a matter of a future perspective in Afro-Asiatic studies.

There still remain other issues to resolve, such as defining the limits of the Afro-Asiatic languages, to be found more in temporal than in spatial terms, and taking into account that descriptive and statistical methods prove insufficient to deal with phases completed over the course of time. Other issues arise also, such as "coincidence," not only as a simple resemblance but, from the systematic aspect, as a structural tendency with divergent results in each language. Then there is the problem of "reconstruction" or "models of reality," in the historical dimension. The task to be completed is immense and must be completed with new methods, while still using the results of our predecessors.

1.9. In a summary article, G. Garbini (1977)[33] surveys the contributions and problems posed by comparative Semitics. He is particularly critical of the linguistic theories of the neo-grammarians, with their model of a "proto-language" and of a "genealogical tree" as a pattern for linguistic classification and with their inviolable "phonetic laws," but also of the structuralism and other theories based on scientific methods, applied unsuccessfully to linguistics, as for example, glottochronology. He declares himself in favor of a "historical" treatment of Semitic linguistics, the development of which Renan seems to have foreseen. He criticizes especially the position, born in the nineteenth century and dominant until the present, thanks to Brockelmann's authority, which sees Arabic and the reconstruction based on it as the authentic form of Proto-Semitic. For Garbini—and I think he is correct—Arabic represents an innovative stage in the development of Semitic. It is only recently that some voices have been raised against this perspective in favor of a new classification of the Semitic languages and the use of Afro-Asiatic comparison in this respect. Without rejecting "genealogical kinship" completely but rather its obligatory character, Garbini thinks that "the preliminary task of comparative Semitics, therefore, will be *to determine what type of kinship unites the Semitic languages to each other and to the Hamitic languages*" (p. 121). And he adds: "the purpose of comparative Semitics must be *to reconstruct progressively increasingly older historico-linguistic phases*, starting, of course, from the most recent as they are best known" (pp. 121–22) (author's italics). His position, then, is not as drastic as initial criticism would have us believe. In fact, his program of action seems eclectic enough: "comparative study of the Semitic languages must, therefore, proceed by steps: first of all it will try to reconstruct the historical development of the Semitic languages in relation to each other, in order to sketch out a picture of the linguistic data that characterize the oldest phase of Semitic (that is to say, the innovations produced in the historical period); next, the ancient Semitic identified in this way will be compared to the Hamitic languages, starting with Egyptian, which is the only Hamitic language attested at the same time as ancient Semitic" (p. 122). And to carry out this program, all contributions have to be used, even those of the "neo-grammarians." The reconstruction of lost linguistic phenomena on the basis of their variants is justified by genealogically related languages. However, one must reject the claim of wishing to see each of these variants, especially when the mother-tongue is no longer known historically, as the reflex or necessary correspondence of an original phenomenon. This is what prevails, especially in the case of consonantal reconstruction. Instead, it may be an innovation peculiar to a particular language. Garbini insists, I believe correctly, on this aspect of linguistic innovation, especially in languages that have reached us in what we call the "oral" stage.

There was already a systematic development of these ideas in his book on the Semitic languages (1972),[34] in which he opposed the Arabic model with his own "Amorite" model, for the comparison and derivation/classification of the Semitic languages, of which he analyzes the "trace." He constantly expresses distrust of "Proto-Semitic" and always argues in favor of a comparative study of languages ("ancient Semitic," p. 22) free of any ethnic or cultural implications, but which must also imply the Afro-Asiatic perspective especially in the case of the reconstruction of Semitic, if the correlation of the families called Hamito-Semitic is accepted. In this context, there is no sense in speaking of a "Proto-Semitic" (p. 14; it is rather a question of finding a "Proto-Hamito-Semitic" parallel to "Proto-Indo-European"; on this see below). But for the moment, the Hamito-Semitic/Afro-Asiatic correlation "which everyone admits, when set against the facts, proves to be so vague and elusive that in practice it is as if it did not exist" (p. 16). In fact, the Semitist is left to his own domain (!) (but remember, this is 1972). And with reason: the languages called "Hamito-Semitic" are, in fact, African languages with "Semitic" forms acquired by diffusion: "some African languages have become Hamitic when they were transformed by the action of a strong Semitic superstratum" (p. 20), after the Semitic population from Asia penetrated Africa. Here he follows Pisani's opinion,[35] an opinion that would be difficult to hold today. However that may be, Semitic comparison has to take account of their acquired Semitism: "precisely because in the Hamitic languages it is possible to find extremely ancient data, ancient Semitic based exclusively on Semitic will have to change" (p. 22). These ideas have been refined in later contributions, such as the one outlined above.[36] Otherwise, the book is devoted to specific Semitic languages and finally to the problem of their relationships and classification.

1.10. In a collective work on linguistic change and reconstruction, P. Baldi (1990)[37] provides a general description of the method of comparative reconstruction. This should be universally valid and able to be repeated, i.e., to give the same results for different researchers. Until recently, nineteenth-century Indo-European comparative study was the model to be followed for the genetic reconstruction of proto-languages. It based itself on the following concepts: (1) the significant number of original coincidences in the nuclear lexical fields; (2) the regularity of phonological change in the same conditions; (3) the regularity of systematic correspondences between at least two languages, which reveals the positional allophones of the mother language; here internal reconstruction can help to determine the correspondences while at the same time the principles of universal structural typology can check the validity of the phonological reconstruction; (4) the use of written documentation in agreement with the orthographic customs of each class of texts; (5) the evaluation of the analogy and of the various processes operative in phonological changes; and (6) the correlation of irregular morphemes between different languages. In addition, position and general analogy generate and at the same time neutralize many irregularities, creating from them a new norm. This method is basically phonological, even though other changes (morphological and syntactic) are possible without exhibiting the regularity of phonological changes. Such a method, however, is not without problems when it comes to reconstructing the proto-system and its intermediate forms (the old forms and the innovations or loans) and discerning the features that defined the genetic relationship. The coincidence of original linguistic features is not the result of accidental induction but supposes a common ancestor for the languages that document it. Usually, the starting-point is the vocabulary: the basic list where there are clearer and more certain phonetic correspondences (vertical level), absolutely clear in some cases and less so in others, due to the irregularities peculiar to each language. In this way Indo-European and other language families have been reconstructed.

But the method has been criticized in our time for its apparent circular and subjective nature. On the other hand, it has been suggested that changes operate originally at the level of word-classes, by a sort of lexical diffusion, and not at the level of phonemes. Also, there are languages in which the change operates not according to the Indo-European phonological correspondence model but by lexical replacement imposed by various social and ethnic conditions. The use of the comparative method to reconstruct a proto-language is also disputed, as well as the conditions and aims to be attained in that case. In this perspective, the reconstruction of Proto-Nostratic has been carried out in accordance with the principles of classical reconstruction. It is evident, in spite of its faults and limitations, that the comparative method works, and not only with the Indo-European languages. "Yet one must not stop trying, for the search into history should never be proscribed by our failure to find ways to do it" (p. 13).

To complement these reflections of Baldi, we can also take account of those by S. J. Lieberman (1990)[38] in the same collective work, this time with respect to the Afro-Asiatic languages. The mixed nature of the group of languages (literary and oral) can be both an advantage (a new and more varied perspective) and a disadvantage (different results to be gained and different methods to be used) for applying the comparative method and checking the appraisal of linguistic change. On the other hand, in studying the most important of these languages (Semitic and Egyptian), philological interest applied to understanding their ancient and sacred texts has dominated, while linguists have preferred to consider spoken languages. Both viewpoints must be combined in attempts to reconstruct the *phylum* and at the same time develop the study of the cultural resources and the contributions of these languages, the study of which has often been of benefit to general linguistics, New methodological approaches, such as the theory of the "linguistic circle" (see above p. 94, on Hodge) or the use of linguistic data for cultural reconstruction, have been completed recently by analysis of orthographic modalities, as a means of access to the original forms, and especially by the discovery of the combined evolution of morphological and syntactic structures. The time-lag that affects the *phylum* is seen very clearly in the difficulty of obtaining a coherent classification and a chronology for the various dialects. But it is in the field of reconstructing the lexicon ("roots" or radical proto-lexemes) that agreement is most tenuous and where new studies are needed. The Semitic family is best placed in this respect. The reconstruction of the phylum remains a task to be completed, as is reaching an agreement on the phonological and lexical bases that must govern this reconstruction.

In the same publication and with respect to the persistence and universal value of the comparative method, H. M. Hoenigswald[39] notes that we have to accept different degrees of results in applying this method to that reconstruction. However, this does not invalidate its universal value. The result, more or less felicitous, depends on the group of languages to be analyzed, of which Indo-European is the prototype. On the other hand, writing can assist this process, but does not define it: "neither the comparative method nor internal reconstruction depend on written records" (p. 379). It is precisely these two methods of reconstruction that are used in comparative studies. Often there is a clear difference between the two. But to have a productive reconstruction and not only a projection into time immemorial of completely simple changes, it is necessary to have "paradigms with a fair amount of allophony" (p. 380), which enable the framework of morpho-phonemic characteristics peculiar to related languages and to their proto-language to be established. He sets out four conclusions: (1) the comparative method is general, not limited to one family of languages; (2) if the languages are very similar (as their ancestor is very recent), reconstruction is not interesting (does this apply to the Semitic languages?); (3) reconstruction becomes more interesting if the languages have developed a different typology; and (4) reconstruction based on morphology and on conditioned phonetic changes proves to be more productive.

1.11. One of these questions, in particular, raised many times in the perspective of comparative lexicography, is treated very clearly by W. S. LaSor (1990)[40] in a short article. It is the matter of "proto-languages," in our case, Proto-Semitic, whether or not as a historical reality. In spite of all the objections raised against this concept and against the genealogical or genetic tree-diagram that represents it, he tries "to demonstrate the reasonability of an *Ursprache*, a common linguistic origin of the most basic elements of the Semitic languages" (p. 190), as shown by the famous grammatical and lexical isoglosses and as phonemic development enables us to glimpse. This is not a matter of excluding external influences that could have contributed to the formation of these languages. Leaving aside grammatical isoglosses, he proposes a list of about three hundred words belonging to eleven different semantic fields, common to seven ancient Semitic languages. The article is significant: "It is my opinion that the Semitic languages that have such an extensive basic vocabulary must have developed from a parent language, which for convenience we may call Proto-Semitic" (p. 192).

1.12. M. Masson (1991)[41] has provided a very interesting account of the organization of the lexicon, from the aspect of semantics, based on a specific seme, namely "to pour." He lists all the phonological forms of this seme (its lexemes and roots) and analyzes metaphorical expansions on the basis of semantic parallelism, that is, of the convergence in two lexemes of a binomial of different semantic features: central/afferent term [n. 6]. To do this he sketches a whole system of semantic analysis, which, in his opinion, is essential for a scientific lexicography that helps, for example, to go beyond concepts such as "strong semantic relationship" (SSR)/"weak semantic relationship" (WSR) (see above pp. 3, 76), an analysis that has still to be developed in a general and systematic way.[42] In my opinion, the move should be toward a system of patterns of semantic derivation, especially from metaphor as the basic linguistic device that is "poetic" in the proper sense, considering language as a process of creating meaning (see below).

1.13. A summary of the problem of the comparative method is provided by A. Faber (1992)[43] from a similar position. The first thing to be taken into account is the change that inevitably affects languages and causes their erosion. This generates the various language groups "all descended from a common ancestor" (p. 193). This unknown proto-language "must be inferred on the basis of the structures of their descendants, as well as on general linguistic principles" (p. 193). On the other hand, contact can induce a non-genetic similarity between languages. Comparative study, as a process of reconstruction, must, therefore, take account of both the differentiating change and the assimilating convergence. After a very clear graphic example of the relationship between languages, as both genetic (the "tree") and isoglossal (the "wave"), Faber analyzes its presuppositions and concludes in favor of a more complex model that combines both change and convergence. The issue is knowing how and when the change took place that is characteristic of a language or group of languages and makes it distinctive. Is it conservation or innovation with respect to other languages and the mother language? Of these possibilities "a final possibility is that two options existed in the parent language, each of which was preserved in one of the two languages in question" (p. 197). In other words, the proto-language is polymorphic or polysemic, a possibility that very often is not taken into account. In each case the nature of the phenomenon must be examined to determine its origin, accepting the fact that no single language is more conservative or representative than another to provide a principle of *a priori* explanation in this field, whether that language is literary (Akkadian) or modern (Bedouin Arabic). Establishing the old or conservative features of a language is the task of the comparative method (in this case, only the phonological level is considered), bearing in mind all the data of the language family and usually on the basis of regular and predictable change (neo-grammarians), but without excluding the existence of change produced by lexical diffusion. These are two possibilities that, again, do not exclude each other and can be encoded simultaneously in a diagram with different "nodes" (pp. 96, 205). This method operates on the basis of systematic correspondences in the same contexts, the multiplicity of which can produce different changes for the same proto-phoneme ("correspondence sets will often be in complementary distribution"; p. 200). The reconstruction of the series of original phonological correspondences must be concrete in order to define the nature of the relationship between the languages (innovation/conservation). In the case of different realizations in the related languages, one usually accepts only one of them as original on the basis of economy of explanation, but given the multiple constituent features of a phoneme, it can have numerous variants of which we do not know the original. Once the original series has been determined, establishing the innovations peculiar to each language, whether autonomous or by diffusion or convergence, brings out the historical grammar of each. The "tree" representation naturally favors presentation in the form of a diagram of the shared innovations, in groups. Clearly the method can be applied to other phonological levels and especially in morphology. At all events, comparative analysis of a linguistic element must always be completed within the whole system to which it belongs. This remark is seen to be particularly relevant and agrees with my own view of the global reconstruction of the proto-language (proto-grammar) not only of the lexical part ("roots").

1.14. In 1998 L. Edzard[44] published a book that fully affects our problem and its aim is summarized as follows by the author: "This study is concerned with two major problems: the question of an appropriate model for linguistic evolution, and the application of that method to Semitic and other sub-groups of Afro-Asiatic. In particular, as I will argue, the traditional 'family tree' model should be rejected; i.e., no hypothetical 'proto-language' is to be assumed from which sub-groups or branches (daughter languages) allegedly 'descend.' With respect to Afro-Asiatic, this study thus challenges 'monogenesis' as an appropriate account for the origin of language families" (p. 23). Any claim of reconstructing a proto-language (proto-Semitic) is excluded, because in the "beginning" there was diversity (polygenesis). R.M. Voigt[45] has provided an extensive review of this work, with which I am basically in agreement, which saves us going into detail here.

In order to fulfill his objective the author makes use of a model taken from modern scientific thought that presupposes an evolutionary process in three stages: primitive chaos, resulting convergence, final entropy, as the result of a process of convergence (p. 26; also pp. 62–63). One would have expected a thorough explanation of this model, but such an explanation never succeeds in getting under way. It is a model taken from the "sciences," as in the case of "family likeness" (cf. p. 77) or "information theory" (cf. p. 41) with respect to the phonological structure of the root in Semitic. After setting out the postulates of the "family tree and reconstruction theory," in a first attempt the author presents his own thesis in six lines, "assuming" how language originated (pp. 43–44) and the language families finally appeared. The perspective is "glottogonic" and curiously supposes some unity of human language, at least in each area in which it arises: "Just as human beings in contiguous areas look somewhat alike, they also can generally be assumed to speak somewhat alike" (!). From this point there begins a process of reduction/selection that ends up shaping the language families. I do not know whether "imagination" of this kind is enough to found a complete theory, but in any case it evidently involves much too large a jump between the two extremes of the process. On the other hand, it is not specified whether this reduction implies that diversity is abandoned once the family has been established, or whether it continues to function in the final stage, as, in fact, seems to be assumed. At all events, it is this stage of "family" homogeneity that classical reconstruction looks at, not the previous "chaotic" stage that is presupposed. This, instead, is from where the author normally argues in the presentation of his "corroborative examples," often elementary and worthless with respect to the problem of the reconstruction of the proto-language: "...the assumption of a 'chaos' of linguistic variation...will be considered ...the usual case" (p. 33).[46] Above all, possible loans (p. 34) and actual convergence ("accidental," as the author acknowledges)[47] can neither annul nor explain the global concurrence shown by the members of a language family, in this case, Semitic. It cannot be forgotten that the possibilities, both phonetic and morphosyntactic, of human language are physiologically and structurally limited and, therefore, coincide independently. Therefore, isolated phenomena are not relevant in a reconstruction. This will always be incomplete (Nöldeke), abstract (Bergsträsser), and proto-dialectal (Brockelmann), even idiolectal, in certain aspects (pp. 30–31), but no less valid, therefore, as a homogeneous global "image" of a whole language family. The arguments raised against the genetic model ("the family tree model"; pp. 39–43) prove to be inadequate (in particular, the argument that assumes the absolute value of "proto-," which must always be understood relatively, with respect to the family in question). The difficulty inherent in the classification of languages, e.g., Semitic languages, forces us, of course, to be cautious about the specific "family tree" that is drawn up (pp. 51–53 ; also pp. 79–80, 84–85, 86–94, 150). I prefer a combined model[48] of bifurcation/diachronic-synchronic development that takes into account and also tries to incorporate allogenic diffusion in the perspective of the historical movement of the speakers.

Instead, Edzard tends to elevate to the state of general linguistic model historico-cultural diffusion, of which medical terminology (p. 46) is an extreme case. It is possible to absorb the "wave-model" (pp. 54–59) completely into a genetic model, whereas the radical polygenetic models (pp. 60–61) provide an innate ambiguity that makes the original dialectal diversity co-exist with belonging to a single group of speakers. Where does this diversity spring from? Logically, from an earlier "unity," potentially idiolectal > dialectal.

In the second chapter a better explanation of the model is promised. In fact, this never materializes, but instead its counter-proof is presented through a series of considerations of problems that emerge in the Semitic languages and that the model of chaos-convergence-entropy would resolve more satisfactorily, according to the author, problems that are secondary in the perspective of reconstruction and, one could say, have perfectly valid classical solutions. Unquestionably, this chapter, which should have claimed preferential treatment in his program, turns out to be disappointing, repetitive, and not very convincing, and, in several cases, too elementary.

This is the trend maintained in the following chapters, with application to Afro-Asiatic, Semitic, and Arabic respectively, with the same way of discussing specific problems and their solution by the new model.[49] In fact, in several instances there is a simple rejection of the validity of the genetic solution, without a well-founded proof of the new model. Typical of this approach is his treatment of the Afro-Asiatic phoneme inventory (pp. 80–84; cf. also pp. 95–110).

In the case of Arabic, the new model is more consistent (pp. 136–68), given the peculiar system of the spread and establishment of its dialects: "The high mobility of Arab tribes in the early history of Arabic provides very strong *prima facie* support for the notion of linguistic convergence and entropy in the Arabian context" (p. 150). However, in many cases they are internal problems of Arabic grammar and largely irrelevant with respect to the reconstruction of early Semitic.

As for the question discussed in the final section, which is directly related to our own topic, the problem of bi-triradicality (pp. 169–76), the author's view is similar to the one favored in our own presentation, of the original co-existence of the bi- and triconsonantal models, apparently a "polygenetic" attitude, the meaning of which we explained above (pp. 84ff.). The same applies with respect to the topic of root expansion and determinatives, although in this case his attitude is less well defined. Even so, the discussion remains somewhat concise and elementary.

Edzard's book has the merit of a revulsive and strengthens the problematic nature presented by Semitics in its basic questions. However, I think that neither by its presentation nor by the development of its thesis does it succeed in proving its validity. It can even induce a false interpretation of the author's own intention. He states that he does not claim to oppose either classification itself (p. 62) or comparative linguistics (p. 24) and that he assumes the validity of phonetic laws (p. 95). He does oppose, and in no uncertain terms, the reconstruction of a proto-language, that is, ultimately etymology as the single explanation of linguistic phenomena/data that affect a whole family of languages and even more, a language phylum, even one that is documented over the centuries. The historical perspective remains very diminished.

In the historical perspective, with Edzard's book, we are within the purest linguistic tradition of fashionable Arabism. From this viewpoint we can conclude that Arabic (and, it goes without saying, this applies to any other language): (a) has no prehistory outside itself because it is a closed system; and (b) from the beginning it contains within itself its own variety. Or what amounts to the same thing: Arabic and its dialects are explained from Arabic, or rather: they need no explanation. "Primitive" Arabic, like Semitic or any other family or sub-family that wishes to be defined in its most "primitive" phase, already contains explicitly its later attested diversification. There is no internal historical development, only external processes of convergence between different language varieties. Exaggerating somewhat, we could say that languages have no history, only a series of accidents like "cosmetic surgery." These can change its appearance, even profoundly, but they are always exogenous.

With this summary of L. Edzard, we end this brief survey of the various viewpoints, selected from many studies published on the comparative method as a way to the phonemic and semantic reconstruction of Proto-Semitic.[50] In this regard, Faber's paper reflects in a preferential way the harmonizing, perhaps even eclectic, position that seems to be required these days.

2. Projects and Achievements

Even before materializing in a complete and satisfactory way in its own domain, etymological and comparative Semitic lexicography has been superseded in our days by versions that refer to it, or rather to its various branches and languages, in order to propose a wider frame of linguistic correlation. I refer to "long-distance" comparative studies, first "Afro-Asiatic," but also "Nostratic" (and there are other labels), essentially Indo-European // Afro-Asiatic.

2.1.   *The "Nostratic"/long-distance comparison Level*

Leaving aside the very imaginative work by Baron Carra de Vaux (1919/1944)[51] and the grand but incomplete project of Illič Svityč,[52] which often lacks a critical character, today we have two dictionaries, very different in their structure and academic approach, that try to establish an etymological correlation between the various families and super-families (or *phyla*) of languages. S. Levin (1995)[53] remains within the classical horizon, opened in the nineteenth century, of a "Nostratic" correlation (Indo-European and Semitic/Afro-Asiatic), while A. R. Bomhard and J. C. Kern (1994)[54] go well beyond it and include in their comparison and etymological relationship even the Kartvelian, Uralic, Dravidian, and Altaic families (601 common bases). These are interesting undertakings, but as yet somewhat premature, given that for many of these families there are no convenient tools for a semantic and etymological arrangement of their own lexicon. At all events, they lie outside our subject matter.

2.2.   *The Afro-Asiatic Level*

The "Afro-Asiatic"[55] horizon is closer to our own purposes and in this domain it is worthwhile emphasizing, first of all, M. Cohen's pioneering *Essai* (1947),[56] exemplary for its rigorous method, even if limited by the state of Afro-Asiatic studies at the time. After him, the baton of these studies was taken up by the Russian School created by I. M. Djakonoff. If we leave out some partial contributions, concerning both lexicography[57] and methodology,[58] the first important reconstruction of comparative Afro-Asiatic was put forward by Djakonoff and his students, first in Russian,[59] then, in revised form, in English.[60] Djakonoff himself presented the work on two occasions (1978/1984),[61] but it remained incomplete. The undertaking was completed some years later by two of his students and collaborators: V. E. Orel and O. V. Stolbova (1995).[62] The reception given this dictionary has been rather critical, beginning with I. M. Djakonoff himself, who in collaboration with L. Kogan, penned a very harsh review (1996).[63] At the same time, but with completely different structure and aim, C. Ehret (1995)[64] provided a common Afro-Asiatic lexicon with a strictly phonological base. The result is the reconstruction of 1,011 proto-Afro-Asiatic "roots" (with additional roots the number is 1024). In Appendix 1 of this collection there is a group of roots that can be considered "pre-Proto-Semitic," agreeing with the evidence from Arabic. Ehret's work has been received with reserve and has even been rejected by some specialists.[65] Finally, the first volumes of the excellent dictionary by G. Takács (1999),[66] even if limited to Egyptian, are extremely important for comparative Semitics, given the historical and documentary proximity of the two families that can be reflected at the level of etymology.

2.3.   *The Semitic Level*

Comparative Semitic lexicography goes back to the Jewish lexicographers and grammarians of the Middle Ages (Ibn Qurāyš, Al-Fāsī, Ibn Ǧanāḥ, Ibn Barūn...) and after the Renaissance was continued by the polyglot dictionaries (Castell, Schindler, Hottinger, Nicolaus, Ludolf, Buxtorff,...),[67] which were "cumulative" rather than "comparative." From the nineteenth century, some studies of ethnography (Guidi)[68] and comparative Semitic grammar (Bergsträsser)[69] incorporate lists of comparative lexicography, as is still the case today (Bennett).[70] But these are always attempts that cannot disguise the lack of a really complete tool of this type in comparative linguistics, in spite of partial essays such the one by Guillaume (1965).[71]

Throughout the twentieth century, various projects of this type have been announced and even started (Brockelmann, Segert, Fronzaroli).[72] Fronzaroli's project was not implemented but, as we saw earlier, it had already been preceded by a complete series of studies of the lexicon of Common Semitic (1964–71),[73] arranged in six "semantic fields." As we have noted, these studies on the lexicon of Common Semitic refer only to some four hundred lexemes and the focus of interest is semantic and socio-cultural, with the lexico-phonological component remaining in the background.

2.3.1. Following a request by the Oriental Institute of Prague to compile a comparative dictionary of the Northwest Semitic languages, S. Segert set out the broad lines of the project in an article (1960).[74] After a general survey of the history of grammar (Brockelmann, Zimmern, Gray) and a more extensive survey of comparative Semitic lexicography (Schindler, Hottinger, Castell), he acknowledged yet again the deficiency in Semitic studies. He notes the conditions required for such an undertaking: correct classification, suitable phonological and morphological correlations, and the availability of good dictionaries of the various languages. This was the chief obstacle at the time (1960). Segert takes stock: "for many years to come it will not be possible to compile a comparative lexicon embracing all Semitic languages..." (pp. 474, 479). The situation seems more favorable with respect to Northwest Semitic, given the large number of lexicographical studies on the various languages in that area (Ugaritic, Canaanite, Aramaic), of which he provides a list. As a result, a comparative dictionary of Northwest Semitic becomes feasible. Then, he describes the structure of such a work. It should also include reference to other Semitic languages, but only in support of Northwest Semitic material. Of course, the arrangement will be according to the classic system of "(tri-)consonantal roots" and "patterns," taking into account the original consonantal system of Proto-(Northwest-)Semitic, which at times can present difficulties. This minimal "reconstruction" will make the "comparative" dictionary into an "etymological" dictionary to some extent. The second part of the article is an attempt to find the most suitable system of transcription for each language (computers were not available yet!).

The project was never completed, even though it had been commented on and presented several times.[75] Since the last presentation, (1973),[76] the emphasis has been on the arrangement of words by subject-matter and the presentation of the relevant computer program.

2.3.2. At the same time, D. Cohen (1970-)[77] began the publication of his comparative Semitic dictionary, based on a comparative card-index prepared by J. Cantineau, which Cohen had presented several times.[78] In fascicle 3 (1993), F. Bron and A. Lonnet collaborated with Cohen. The most recent fascicle is dated 1999 and has reached the letter /z/ in the sequence of the Hebrew alphabet. It is fervently hoped that this undertaking will be completed.

It is not an "etymological" dictionary (like Pokorny's dictionary for Indo-European, which has no equivalent in the Semitic languages) but is "comparative," including not only related forms in at least two languages, but every "root" documented in any Semitic language, even in isolation, as well as loanwords and their "roots" or consonantal skeletons. One could ask how we know that such forms are related if we do not already know their etymology. They could be non-homophonic homographs. Circular reasoning is always a threat in comparative research. In any case, this "functional" concept of the "root," the significance of which Cohen explains, must function as the basis for arranging the lexicon, at the same time acknowledging the existence of specific primary lexemes that have that radical form. Moreover, to each entry are added various etymological proposals provided by scholars.

A number of questions arise on this subject. For example, must we distinguish two types of root: nominal and verbal? Apart from their different system of derivation, nothing guarantees the distinction at the "radical" level; "no proof can be afforded of the primary or secondary character of a lexeme, either noun or verb, that does not exhibit a derivation mark" (p. 95; and even less at the phonological level; see above pp. 28, 97). The hypothetical phonological distinction postulated by Greenberg based on incompatibility rules does not seem sufficient "to differentiate between nominal and verbal 'roots'" (p. 97). This does not mean to say that there are no primary nouns (on this subject the authors give relevant criticism of Djakonoff's position; see above pp. 18ff.), but only that they are not easy to determine. The question of bi- and triconsonantal roots is also posed. In classifying the lexicon, Cohen distinguishes between biconsonantal roots with a vocalic or consonantal extension (XY > XYXY, XYY, XwY, XYw) and roots with a different third consonant, difficult to explain, with a common semantic load, that are not all necessarily biconsonantal. The reference to the common segment is for information only. Lastly, the more important problem for organizing the lexicon is found in semantic precision: semantic chains or homophony of roots. Here a certain degree of subjectivity is unavoidable.

Cohen presented these ideas once again in two forewords to the dictionary (1970/1996). The first, which is very short, explains the origin of the idea and structure of the dictionary in keeping with Semitic lexicography at the time, where the conditions have, of course, changed considerably in the twenty-five years that separate the first fascicle from the latest one to be published. Everything makes us fear that this enterprise will also remain incomplete.

The second preface, with the title "À propos de racines," insists on the non-etymological and even strictly non-comparative character of his book. One could label it "globalizing"; it aims at collecting all the roots that are attested in all the Semitic languages of any type, even loans, as we said. Accordingly, it then takes time to specify the concept of "root," for which we already know the data (see above pp. 7ff.). Here let us recall only his conclusion that it was impossible to define "root" from semantics: "no really scientific possibility exists that would allow the limits of metaphorical usage to be set or to know *a priori* the semantic associations that each culture established" (p. IV). One must begin with the "consonantal pattern" (p. III), in the "functional" meaning of the term, as a principle for classifying the lexicon, which is also valid for loanwords. The etymological and even Afro-Asiatic aspect is presented in a second section of entries. Even so, there are words that provide no "bases for derivation" (p. VIII) and, therefore, cannot be reduced to one "root." On the other hand, he repeats, the distinction between "noun" and "verb," which is itself very difficult to sustain, has no relevance from the point of view of "root." As for biconsonantalism, once again it is noted that there are very few original biconsonantal forms, if one excludes the secondary derivations that can easily be explained and the group of triconsonantal roots with a different third consonant and the same semantic load. This does not always correspond to a biconsonantal "root," given the complexity of the process by which they are formed, as has been pointed out many times. On the other hand, attention must be paid to the correlations among these groups by reason of homorganic phonemes. All these lexematic variations pose the question of their semantic differences in a concrete language, as in other languages. Cohen thinks that "semantic chains" and "semantic parallels" (see above 87f. on Palache and 102f. on Masson) can assist in finding a solution to the problem, but often they are not available. The real solution, perhaps, is found in the "position" or syntagmatic and "social" use of the language, but that is verifiable only in a lexical system with living speakers. While taking these limitations into account, it provides Semitists with a valid tool for lexicographical comparison of which they feel the need.

After Segert's first study, cited above, a good account of the problems posed by compiling an etymological dictionary of the Semitic languages, which is also an incisive critique of D. Cohen's *Dictionnaire*, is provided by W. von Soden (1973).[79] He retraces the origin of this dictionary and describes its content. While acknowledging the need for such a tool, he concludes that to compile a dictionary with these features is an impossible undertaking today (1973). There are no reliable dictionaries for the various Semitic languages. But above all, he sets out a solid lexicographical theory based on the structure of the Semitic root that takes its various categories into account: nouns, (active and stative) verbs, exceptions, new formations and loans, as well as their vocalism. From the aspect of semantics, attention must be paid to their *Grundbedeutung*, even though in many cases it is difficult to establish; perhaps it may not even exist. In any case, it is useful to obtain this meaning from the lexematic classes mentioned. Of course, such a work would have to be collective, the work of a team, if one wishes to avoid the many mistakes to be found in Cohen's *Dictionnaire*. At all events, anything doubtful or uncertain must be left out and the list of sources (dictionaries) from which the data are derived must be given.

2.3.3. Recently A. Militarev and L. Kogan (2000)[80] have begun an etymological dictionary of the Semitic languages, with the publication of the first two volumes out of a total of eight (plus an additional volume for the index and bibliography). It is organized on the basis of wide categories, not all completely clear but sufficient: anatomy, fauna, basic lexicon, flora, intellectual culture and society, material culture, ecology and landscape, verbal and nominal roots. In the prologue to the first volume, they explain their vision of the current status of comparative Semitics, developing their own opinions and positions on etymology in general and on Semitics in particular, and comment on the structure of the dictionary and its individual entries. The sections of the introduction on phonology and morphology include detailed analyses and present new hypotheses of the authors on this subject (p. VII). In the prologue to the second volume all those aspects are adequately complemented. Particular reference must be made to the section on "Phonology" (pp. LVII–LXV). This dictionary, then, follows the path traced by Fronzaroli (see above p. 108) in his organization by "semantic field," which, at the comparative level, allows access to the oldest stratum of the whole Semitic family. However, an alphabetic arrangement is not excluded in future volumes. In their introductions, all the questions implied by Semitic comparative study are surveyed and form the basis of the task undertaken by these scholars. In this way, they become a sort of general introduction to this problem. Thus, the scholars' own points of view on the classification of the Semitic languages, the problem of etymology and the reconstruction of proto-forms are set out, as well as their view on the root and its derivational models. Particular attention is paid to semantics and to related matters, such as loanwords, contaminations, and the Afro-Asiatic horizon. The problem of "root variation," which was the subject of A. Militarev's doctoral thesis, deserves special mention (see above pp. 63ff.). Nevertheless the differences of opinion on this and other subjects that divide the authors are made manifest.

As might have been expected, two long paragraph are devoted to the phonology of the Semitic languages as the basis for all lexicographical research, which has been discussed above (Chapter III, pp. 36ff.). Finally comes a list of nominal morphological patterns that are attested in the reconstructed proto-forms. Below we shall return to many of these questions and to the points of view of these scholars.

3. Appraisal

3.1. *Reconstruction and Proto-language*

As is well known, lexicography implies two inseparable questions, presupposed by "the double articulation": the form of the linguistic sign (phonetics) and its referential value (phonology/semantics). In our case, it is a matter of etymological lexicography, which also supposes the "reconstruction" of a proto-language, in effect, Proto-Semitic, the "historical" character of which has to be determined.[81]

When one wishes to reconstruct a "proto-language," is his intention a reconstruction of a separate proto-vocabulary or discontinuous system or else a continuous proto-system of communication? This would suppose a syntagmatic interaction that places the lexemes in relationship to each other, that is to say, a proto-grammar (see above p. 15). Thus, when one speaks of an "inflected language" it denotes a "proto-characterization" of the linguistic system that implies a whole system of inflectional resources from its very beginning that must, therefore, appear in the reconstruction of it as a system.

First of all, this "reconstructive" character distinguishes etymological Proto-Semitic from Common Semitic, which is "comparative" in nature; the reconstruction supposes comparison but at the same time goes beyond it.[82] Common Semitic is the result of checking the source of the corresponding forms or phenotypes (for example, Common Semitic /kalb-u/). The comparison collects all the corresponding morphemes in the various languages, relates them to each other, and can even find in them one that seems the most original, but stops at ranking them according to a model of derivation that explains their formation diachronically.

Proto-Semitic, in its turn, is a hypothetical reconstruction based on a model that includes common and specific data. In this way, etymology and proto-language coincide, both appealing to reconstruction. The basic problem is its historical reality. This is sometimes resolved when both Common Semitic and etymological Semitic coincide, as in our example, but often this is not the case. However, in spite of everything, whether the proto-morpheme is empirical or only hypothetical, the opposition between comparison and reconstruction becomes unreal. Every comparison reveals a correlation of data that implies a ranking of developments and refers to a common element, that is to say, it imposes an inevitable reconstruction, unless one wishes to live in a permanent linguistic inhibition. As well as being a system, language is also a process; synchronism always includes diachronism, the present includes the past.[83]

It is possible to ask what the historical value of such a reconstruction might be. Did such a proto-language actually ever exist? How unified was it? These questions are linked to the diffusion model of the group speaking that language. If, as is customary, we accept the model of transmigration or displacement of populations, this supposes the dislocation of the group and its scattering in various places, a situation that entails a greater or lesser difference of dialects and allows little room for a single historical primitive proto-language. In this context, the reconstruction of "one" proto-language, which, in fact, is polymorphic, becomes, in turn, a hypothetical model that is very difficult to pin down in time.

Furthermore, given that today we accept Semitic as belonging to a wide phylum of languages called Afro-Asiatic, one can wonder at what level this phylum lies on the etymological horizon. The reconstruction of this horizon, to some extent, should be found in the reconstruction of other related languages, at least of the closest families with respect to the process of dismemberment, in this case, Berber and Egyptian. Egyptian has the advantage of providing linguistic documentation that is as old as in Semitic. This means that the reconstruction of the proto-language of a language to which all the others are related goes beyond its own horizon. The situation of the Romance languages is a good illustration. If, for example, we take the etymological dictionaries of Spanish (1954ff.) and Catalan (1980), both by the same linguist (J. Coromines), their "entries" with respect to (Latin) etymology largely coincide. These "entries" can also be used, to a large extent, also for an etymological dictionary of French, Portuguese, Italian, etc. These, in turn, depend on the etymological dictionary of Latin, placed at a level above them, the dictionary of their "mother," from which these languages derive. Only the semantic development is different, given the independent development of their models. Semitic (original, morphemic, lexical) etymology, then, is valid for all the languages of the family in the same way. In fact, morpho-lexical coincidence is very strong, apart from the particular semantic development of each. This means that a good etymological dictionary of a language belonging to a well-defined derivational family is valid for all the others, from the aspect of reconstructing the phonetic sign and the basic seme, if it is possible to define it. It can even go right back to the proto-language and in this way become a sort of etymological dictionary for the whole phylum.[84] This also means that an etymological dictionary of the Semitic family can be undertaken even if we do not have good etymological dictionaries of each language, often used as an excuse to justify the lack of such a lexicographical tool. The new contributions possible from modern Semitic languages can help to complete and even refine an etymological Semitic dictionary begun without taking them into account. This can become the best starting-point for the construction of the etymological dictionaries of specific languages, especially modern languages, which, to be really useful, must first fix diachronic semantics, which arranges their lexicon, and then define the contributions of adstrates and substrates, that is to say, they must be "historical" dictionaries. Semantic development is the ultimate point of difference, given the basic morphological agreement that unites them all. While this semantic reconstruction is unavoidable in all the etymological-historical dictionaries of each Semitic language, it is felt even more intensely in the case of Arabic (see below) given its rich documentation.

In reality this is not exactly the case for the Semitic languages, in spite of the morphological and lexical coincidence among the members of the family, often compared to that of the Romance languages. But we cannot claim to reach the "Latin" of Semitic languages in the proto-language reconstructed etymologically, even if that were the ideal aim of etymological study or of the proto-language of a family of languages from a common trunk in a well-defined time and space and whose morpho-lexical agreement is so striking. This is an ideal that recedes further the more progress research makes in the reconstruction of the proto-languages wishing to take account of the etymology of linguistic families that have been separated from one another in a very remote state of development. As such, this development would be less fixed by distinctive characteristics, with their own degree of evolution/transformation of a common system, which would be the case, for example, in an etymological dictionary (the only type possible at the level of parallel historical documentation) of Semitic and Egyptian. Whatever the case, all etymological dictionaries of the various related families or of the reconstructed proto-languages (in our case, Egyptian, Berber, Chadic, Cushitic) must prove a high degree of agreement among them and especially open the way to a final proto-language, in this case Afro-Asiatic, which all the other derived languages must take into account, to the extent that such a reconstruction is possible today. We now have comprehensive tools of Afro-Asiatic that provide us with more abundant data and a more complete overall view of the phylum than any specialist in each of these families could previously propose. Thus, use of these tools (lexica and grammars), especially of Berber and Egyptian (to some extent, also reconstructed), is indispensable and must be taken into account. In this respect, Djakonoff,[85] who restricted himself to Semitic material (pp. 133, 136), as being the only one suitable at the time for a reconstruction of a Semitic proto-language, acknowledged that such an approach is completely unsatisfactory and even non-productive (p. 151). For some categories, especially primary nouns and the biconsonantal "bases," reference to Afro-Asiatic can prove to be useful.

In view of the deficiencies of other Afro-Asiatic languages and their lack of documentation, restricted as they are to the modern oral period, the reconstruction of Proto-Semitic on the basis of Common Semitic is no less possible or useful than the etymological reconstruction (dictionary) of Latin or Greek. The limitations of its linguistic horizon are offset by the closed nature and age of its literary material. In fact, Proto-Semitic reconstructed from Common Semitic becomes the surest approach to Proto-Afro-Asiatic, given its historical documentation, with the support of Egyptian texts. Besides, it is a perfectly organic and developed linguistic system, even if it is, in turn, the heir of another earlier system. It is more a rather late and innovative linguistic system, but, in any case, very stable.

In no way, then, can Semitics be set within a glottogonic perspective. However, in a very ideologically marked manner there has been a cultural but scientifically untenable doctrine that has recognized this original proto-language in a specific language, either Hebrew or Arabic, depending on tradition. Leaving aside the doctrinal reasons for this thesis,[86] even the "archaic" nature of Arabic within the Semitic languages, once accepted by many scholars as evident, today appears very debatable and debated. It seems clear that in many respects it is instead an innovative language.[87]

Excursus
ARABIC AND SEMITIC LEXICOGRAPHY

Arabic is certainly the modern Semitic language that is most complete from the aspect of phonetics (but on this topic see above p. 22 [Petráček]) and it preserves almost complete the original set found in South Arabian and Ugaritic. Apparently the result of a distinctive systematization, it can also be considered the most exact from the aspect of derived models. But it is certainly also the most innovative, the most "modern" one could say, from the semantic aspect. Accordingly, for the most complete catalogue possible of forms and combinations of the original Semitic lexicon, the Arabic dictionary can be a good starting-point. However, for an etymological semantics of the Semitic languages, which tries to establish the original semes as far as possible, the following semantic layers have to be left out of consideration, given that they are "culturally" late and clearly derived: (1) first the "Bedouin" layer, that is all semantics related to camels, tents, the desert as a habitat, etc.; (2) also the religious layer related to Islam and the Koran; (3) the military layer of the Arabic outfit, especially anything concerning the bow, the sword, the breast-plate, armor, etc.; (4) if it is not to be ignored completely, the semantic layer of "physiology," especially sexual, must be treated with considerable prudence given that often it follows its own paths as against the other languages of the family; (5) the semantic layer of Arabic "science," firstly medical but also astronomical, must be left aside; (6) similarly, one should be very hesitant toward the layer of names of animals and plants, especially such animals as the lion, gazelle, and horse, where metaphorical transposition plays such an important role and where loanwords are so common; (7) lastly, one must be very careful about its own semantics, typical and very developed, that defines the primitive Arabic social order; anyone familiar with the Arabic lexicon can find multiple names for groups of persons or their gait or allure, which correspond to the customs of that society. In this respect, certain culturally determined lexical "obsessions" are evident. From the semantic aspect, all these layers are an internal problem of the historical lexicography of Arabic, of its homophony/homonymy,[88] and should be explained from the social and cultural history of which the language is the tool of expression and provides a structure. They cannot be used as they are as a reflection of basic semes, but instead as derivations or transformations of semes defined by culturally developed usage. Of course, no language can be taken as a pure and sufficient witness of a proto-language and they all (let us say, for example, Akkadian, Syriac, Ethiopic) have their own semantic contour, but in these cases much simpler and more uniform and recognizable than in Arabic. After plunging into these abysses one emerges in lakes with calmer waters. In other words, whoever uses the Arabic lexicon as a starting-point for semantic comparison in Semitics can end up with a thesis like the one sketched above (see pp. 11ff., 37, 75ff. [Bohas]) that, if it were correct, would set Arabic outside any comparison with the other Semitic languages, leading to the formulation of an "Arabic" Semitism on the margins of Common Semitic. Of course, to reach Common Semitic, it is necessary to start from individual languages, and Arabic can be a good starting-point, as was said, but in that case some order has to be put into its historical semantic development, given that its enormous cultural and literary expansion has distanced it considerably from its origins. It could be said that science and poetry have "upset" (or rather "diversified") lexicography. This very "self-sufficient" richness, which, in turn, has created a sort of passion for the language among Arabic speakers,[89] perhaps explains the lack of interest in its lexicography, abundant and always alive, to develop an etymological treatment of the language. The axiom seems to be: Arabic is self-sufficient and has no need to refer to other sources.

3.2. *The Classification of the Semitic Languages*

To give a reliable answer to this problem it is necessary to start from a satisfactory classification of the Semitic languages that enables us to check the degree of innovation of each member of the family. First, it must be acknowledged that, unlike Amorite or Arabic innovation, that provided by the Modern South Arabian subfamily (from the aspects of the lexicon and of morphological structures) greatly complicates the horizon of the Semitic proto-language.[90]

I think that this question has to be considered in a perspective that is not purely linguistic (morphological) but also ethno-historical. This will enable us to sketch out a diagram that goes beyond pure representation as a "genealogical tree" to reach another in which space (a geographical map) and time (a genealogical tree) are superimposed, with geography and history combined in a socio-linguistic perspective.[91]

In this respect, reference must be made, first of all, even if only superficially, to the problem of the original home of the Semites. The old classical theory that located the "homeland" of the Semites in Arabia has been discarded and today an African origin is accepted as more likely. They formed part of a mass of peoples who, moving out of the heart of Africa, spread north and reached the Mediterranean coast and beyond in various places. The Semitic family, the spearhead of one of the expansive movements of peoples toward Asia through the Sinai peninsula, was the final break-up of the Afro-Asiatic group, as they are correctly named. Its members retained their linguistic system of clear and remarkable morphological and lexical similarities. This break-up would have happened in the late Neolithic (Chalcolithic) period.[92] The arrival of the Semites to the north of Syria (Middle Euphrates and Mount Bishri) can be dated to about the fourth millennium BCE, where it seems one must locate the furthest advance of their expansion from Africa and where they reached some stability and became lords of a region, once their march toward Mesopotamia had ended. In fact, it is at this period that the Semites appear in the history of the region, either as invaders or as gradually infiltrating people. This invasion shows that they really did arrive from a center of development/diffusion more to the west, that is, north of Syria. And it is also from there that later on, successive Amorite and Aramaean invasions and infiltrations left, to the detriment of their "brothers" already established in Mesopotamia and Syria-Palestine.

It is the period between the last break-up of Afro-Asiatic (Semitico-Berber) and the arrival of the Semites to the north of Syria, which is of particular interest to us, as the structuring of the Semitic proto-language can be dated to that period. This space can certainly be considered as the "hearth" of the Semitic people and of their language, but this center, just like a comet, has a wake, a "tail." As always happens with such "invasions," it is however always the head, the spearhead, that dictates the norm and in all probability leaves behind the ethnic elements that generated a dialectal development of the proto-language just when it becomes standardized. We do not know up to what point the center had an influence on the rearguard, from the political and linguistic aspects, then or at other times (possibly even the Hyksos movement must be considered in this perspective). The Aramaean and Arab invasions are the only ones to provide any data in this respect.

At the moment of the first of these historically attested invasions, their "brother" Semites, who had penetrated Mesopotamia several centuries earlier (Akkadians), as well as the (Neo-)Sumerians, who already lived there, called these invaders MARTU-*Amurru*, "Amorites" (meaning "westerners"). But according to the sketch outlined above, which places the Semite "hearth" in Syria, the Semites have always been "Amorites," like the creators of the kingdom of Agade. At a later period the "Aramaean" invaders could also be defined in the same way. But once the region occupied by the Semites in the course of the fourth to third millennia BCE had been stabilized, immigration and the process of a Semitic group being detached from the group of North Africa were complete. Later movements, recorded in written documents, would be internal (of Amorites—Aramaeans—Arabs).

Thus, it is from the "Amorite center" that a historical and geographical (ethnohistorical) classification of the languages of the Semitic peoples must be drawn up, without separating languages from their speakers. Today the bibliography on this matter is considerable,[93] and positions oscillate between (1) the classical division into five groups based on "geography" (i.e., on the cardinal points: East, West, South Semitic) and (3) the opposition between Central and peripheral Semitic, especially South Semitic, passing through (2) the postulate of a "central" branch as the origin of the whole classification or at least of the Northwest Semitic branch.

My own point of view, in line with what I have set out already, also postulates the existence of an original-central branch that could be defined as "Amorite" *avant la lettre*[94] or proto-Amorite (and, therefore, "western," the center being to the west as viewed by the Mesopotamians) from which the linguistic differentiation occurred, based on the geopolitical spread of the Semitic peoples, a diffusion that closes an historical circle, making them return as "Semites" to their African place of origin (the Ethiopic languages). See the diagram for the classification of the Semitic languages, at the end of this Chapter V, as proposed in the study cited. In my opinion, it is on the basis of the process implied that etymological research must be undertaken.

3.3.   *Phonetic Structure*

Coming now to the phonetic structure of the primary Semitic or proto-Semitic lexeme, I suppose in principle that it would be organized on a "resonance" based on binary or ternary articulation and low (anterior/posterior) or high (median) modulation [CvC-, CvCC-], linked to different alternations of morphemic (grammatical) expansion.[95] This phonetic structure makes many Semitic primary nouns (including the /CvCvC-/ type) seem secondary or expanded, that is, they would suppose a prior realization from which they derive. The base of the lexematic system must be the syllable, not the radical phoneme and its result, the supposed "root." This syllabic system must, besides, give place to the syntagmatic or grammatical realization, which is not only an internal expansion but conditions the structure of the syllabic base. We cannot present a non-grammatical system of "absolute" lexemes as a proto-language. This "state" is itself a syntagmatic result of the type /CvC-0/, which is also grammatical. The proto-language cannot be reconstructed for inflected languages like an agglutinative system of isolated lexemes, as I said above.

In fact, this means that instead of the biconsonantal/triconsonantal opposition as an alternative realization of the Semitic lexical proto-morpheme I propose a disyllabic morpheme (including the grammatical position) as the original realization of the base. Whether this proto-morpheme is biconsonantal or triconsonantal is completely secondary. Even the biconsonantal "roots" can be considered "potentially" triconsonantal, given their universal tendency to be realized as such, either by primary (vocalic [Voigt] or consonantal [gemination, doubling]) intensification or by secondary expansion (complementary morphemes).

As a result, following I. M. Djakonoff's thesis, which I adopt, the mono-consonantal bases are impossible because they cannot present a realizable degree /0/,[96] because a consonant cannot be realized without a vocalic modulation and a sequence of two successive vowels is forbidden in Semitic. This *a priori* is confirmed at the Proto-Semitic level by the absence of such nominal lexemes—even if some sporadic examples can be found (due to morphological reduction)—as well as at other levels of the phylum (see above pp. 19, 28f., 83). This is the case of functorial lexemes or the third lexical category of Bomhard-Kerns (pronouns and adverbs),[97] the only monosyllables with a fixed vowel. They represent the lexicalization of the functions and of their markers (/ba/, /ki/…) when they enter the system of inflected Semitic as relevant elements. It is only if, as in this case, the inflection is considered as an apophony or contrastive variant of the /Cv/ type with an original pre-inflected vowel and not as a morphemic suffix, that it would be possible to accept monoconsonantal primary lexemes. In any case, even for the primary state we must take account of the completed function of the base lexeme in the total or syntagmatic act of verbal communication.

The other lexical forms can be considered, in principle, either as having a secondary origin or else as loans from other linguistic systems.

On the other hand, the question of the "phonic" organization of the lexical sign plunges us into the abyss of glottogony, which classical (scholastic and structuralist) semantics of the "voice meaning *ad libitum*" or arbitrary skims over without committing itself, renouncing any semantic and phonetic implication. Even so, today, two closely related issues have been the subject of discussion: whether or not there is phonetic symbolism and the role of onomatopoeia in the origin of the original Semitic lexicon.

Onomatopoeia is universally accepted as generating primary lexemes in general linguistics.[98] Despite this, some Semitists tend to minimize its role (see above pp. 68, 70 [Voigt]), whereas others make it almost the only source of the production of the Semitic lexicon (see above Gazov-Ginsberg, as well as Bohas, Rosén, Heller-Botterweck). A middle position seems the most reasonable,[99] but some clarifications are required. First of all, it must be accepted that onomatopoeia (which is not a "root" but a consonantal-vocalic "polyphoneme" with a complex articulation, even if it can be analyzed phonetically) can coincide as a homophone with another non-onomato-poeic base, possibly the only admissible case of primary homophony. Often, this implies that the onomatopoeic base is not primary but introduced secondarily into the language or group of specific languages (this is particularly the case in Arabic, where the lexicon is full of "animal" onomatopoeias). It can even happen that different languages use different onomatopoeias for the same semiotic function or that they differ in the perception and reproduction of a natural sound.

In principle, onomatopoeia "means" nothing, semantically it is deictic in character, reproductive or imitative, a "phonogram" or "phonematopoeia" one could say. This can be seen from the numerous onomatopoeias I have just mentioned, used in Arabic for names of animals, especially camels, which reproduces particular sounds related in some way to these animals. It can be lexicalized, either as a noun ("tick," "tock," "drip") or as a verb ("to drip," "to thunder"), depending on the morphemic system in each language. All this happens as if man, by onomatopoeia, was trying to transform the sounds of the cosmos into language, in the same way that a painter or a sculptor tries to reproduce it in colors or forms. By creating this verbal sonority, man becomes the "sounding box" of his environment. This is the glottogonic vision, which is rather "romantic," and taken up once more in our time.[100]

But, going beyond this simple imitative use of onomatopoeia, since the nineteenth century there has been an attempt at least to introduce the "phonetic resonance" of certain symphonemes, the "articulatory combinations" or the "couples of phonetic features," as a more or less universal principle for the generation of the lexicon, termed "symbolic phonetics." In this way, the unity of the linguistic sign is recovered, since meaning derives from phonetic structure. In principle, semantics and phonology become a single item and this departs from the axiom of the sign as arbitrary, as stated by classical theory.[101]

Thus the etymological task would remain directed toward the research and the discovery of these "meaningful resonances" that in strict logic would lead to the reconstruction of a single proto-language. The differentiation of languages would then be due to a secondary diachronic process, even if one cannot exclude some difference of perception of certain "meaningful resonances" by the various groups of humankind, which could well be an important cause of language differentiation.

I have already touched on this issue when discussing in this regard the opinions of one of its modern defenders (see above pp. 82f.). And I have indicated my refusal to take this road, which for Semitics would make us penetrate an unverifiable fog of pure hypotheses contributing little to the empirical organization of its lexicon, confusing the diachronic levels of its development and generating the hypothesis of an original anomalous semantic lack of differentiation. It may be valid to use this approach in certain cases of what is called "expressive," strongly connotative language, and as such linked to states of the psyche that "express themselves" easily by spontaneously produced sounds.[102] But as a general principle of lexical production, it does not seem acceptable.

Generally speaking, in Semitic comparative study and etymology cannot be practiced at a glottogonic level. Even in the form of a modern mathematical formulation, it cannot be reconstructed, given the lack of a deictic monoconsonantal series that one would expect in line with this hypothesis, in spite of its obvious "economy" in the production of primary lexemes. In this sense it is clear that terms of *deixis* (pronouns, adverbs and functors) seem to be the oldest (pre-Semitic) "words" or lexical "bases."[103]

In any case, without making any glottogonic claims, one could sketch a certain diachronic/historical process in the origin of lexical signs in Semitic. From the fourth millennium, one could already engage in the analysis of discrete phonemes in Semitic (perhaps also Afro-Asiatic), a process that leads to phonetic writing. This phase would have been preceded, both in Semitic and in other families of languages, by a phase ("Proto-Afro-Asiatic") of "phonetics of resonance" in which the lexemes would not have yet acquired full phonetic fixed articulatory "discreteness."

It is in this sense that one can accept the concept of "phonetic resonance." It has no connection to "symbolic phonetic resonance," which I have just mentioned, being stripped of any semantic determinism of the "symbolic" type. To some extent it resumes Jusmanov's thesis of "diffuse sounds" (see above p. 54), Fraenkel's thesis of "consonantal series" (see above p. 59), and Bohas" "matrix" thesis (see above p. 12). For myself, however, this resonance is articulatory and syllabic, and affects the "word" as a complex phonological unit, not the isolated phonemes. It is a "symphonic" or composite and combined (biconsonantal or triconsonantal) articulation. That is, in the beginning the primary subject of phonetic change was the "word" and not the "phoneme."[104] It must be remembered that Proto-Semitic is already a clearly and distinctively articulatory language, as soon as it is accessible to us.

In fact, the origin of the phonological table of each language system is the result of a long and late process of differentiation. In the beginning, "words" are continuous resonances, more or less undifferentiated in terms of articulation, with the possibility of generating many allophones. Many elements are combined in this differentiation, including stress, tone, length, according to the prosodic system chosen by each language for its phonological development. Specifically, in languages with a tonic stress it seems to have a determinative function in the formation of discrete lexemes. It is perhaps stress that in the process of functional or grammatical derivation dissolves the "resonance" into clearly distinct points of articulation and other differentiating "features."[105] The texts from Ebla and, to some extent, the texts from Sumer and ancient Egypt,[106] from the third millennium, are fluctuating and inexact transcriptions of "lexical resonances" in allophonic phonologico-syllabic systems. The articulatory phonemes already existed; it is their phonological interpretation that remained undefined. The compulsory use of the alphabetical or acrophonical spelling to eliminate any doubts in the identification of the single phonemes is proof of the indistinct perception and delivery of sounds of identical or similar articulations in different phonetic systems.

As a summary, here is a phonetic model of the genesis of the "original" Semitic lexicon:

- *simple* articulatory resonance, deictic and functorial
- *binary* articulatory resonance + high/low "modular" resonance = /Ca:əC-/
- intensifications (*glides*)/expansions/derivations

- *sonorant ternary* articulatory resonance + *simple* high/low "modular" resonance: /Ca:ə SC-/, /Ca:əCS-/
- intensification (*glides*)/expansions/derivations
- *free ternary* articulatory resonance + *simple/binary* high/low "modular" resonance: /Ca:?C$^{(v)}$C-
- intensification (*glides*)/expansions/derivations[107]

In the process of phonological derivation/differentiation the "features" are introduced by binary oppositions (+/-) in each articulatory position (voiceless/voiced, lateral/0,...) and each modular position (front/back, nasal/0...). In this framework of the formation/derivation of the lexicon, the stable binary resonances, within a series of ternary resonances with related meaning, are defined by a pair of articulatory features that imply a third by the constraints of the grammatical system or from prosodic necessity, but elsewhere they do not occur in isolation nor do they form, as such, a "root" (or a "matrix"). As a result, allophonic variants are generated due to phonetic requirements (ternary resonance), without noticeable semantic determinism (against Ehret and other "complementarists"). On the other hand, the variation of the "phonetic resonance" does not necessarily imply a semantic variation, just like the reverse: the non-variation of the "resonance" does not ensure semantic univocity (for example, see the "root" /'-m-r/). Or again, in the case of original binary resonances, a tendency to internal intensification (morphological change) of the base is evident with the result of predictable systematic semantic variants. In fact, all the binary resonances tend to intensification, that is to ternary realization, as the typical morpheme of the Semitic family. It is precisely the "closed" syllabic structure that we claim to be the primitive structure of the Semitic base (/C$\underline{v}$C-/, /Cv$\underline{C}$-/ > /Cvw:yC-/, /CvC$_1$C$_1$-/ # /CxSC-/, /CvC$_1$C$_2$-/).

3.4. *The Semantic Component*

As for semantics, the other component of the lexeme, already discussed with respect to onomatopoeia and of which I have spoken at the beginning of this appraisal, the fact should be taken into account that usually one makes it revolve, in the comparativist and etymological perspective, around the definition of *basic* or *nuclear seme*, as proposed in structural semantics.[108] It is from this basic seme that one must find semantic derivations in other languages and not from transformations of the *stem* in each one of them. In this case it is a linguistic space peculiar to them and in which one can determine to the maximum the similarities of derivative patterns (or "semantic parallelism," according to Palache; see above p. 87), though it cannot be used to justify a different meaning for a primary lexeme.

Unlike the phonetic component, semantics is much more derivative and reconstructive.[109] This stems from the very nature of the signifying process and its referent. The latter (the object or "reality") is by nature polymorphic and "composite," which implies a possible and inevitable shift of "signified," of "meaning," imposed by the circumstances and interests of the speaker and his group. To the rigidity of the phonetic sign corresponds the flexibility of referential content, of the meaning, subject to a constant process of historical and socio-cultural differentiation, even in the case of what are termed "primary nouns."[110]

Referential differentiation, then, comes both from the polymorphism already mentioned of the thing referred to and from the polymorphism of relationships that the speaker/human subject can maintain with it. Thus, object and action are the two polymorphs due to their inner complexity and to their external expression.[111]

Now one would think that the basic seme should refer beyond these multiple references or meanings to the more complex and undefined "common" meaning that includes them all and from which they can be derived, that is, a sort of "maximal common denominator" (or rather a "minimal common multiple"), the result of componential analysis.[112] In fact, this kind of analysis comes from Hjelmslev and Jacobson, applied to phonology and even to synchronic semantic analysis. The problem arises when one wishes to apply it to etymological semantics.

In this area, I do not think that the "proto-language" originates from the accumulation of semantic "features" or "components of meaning" that formed the "common denominator," which then allowed many semantic derivations. Rather, derivation comes from a shift of meaning from a specific name that cannot be broken up (for example, an animal name), that functions usefully for the speaker. Its use or concrete functionality, for example, "meat," and not its more or less abstract semantic "features," "living," "male," "horned," etc., is what allows semantic development in the various languages.[113]

But this heuristic operation can become extremely speculative and nothing guarantees that semantic diversity should be realized by a process of specification (from a neutral and undefined reference to one that is more specific) and not by a process of "parallel" displacement of references within the same signifying and referential category. This is why I prefer to speak of "original seme" rather than of "basic seme," convinced that original Semitic semantics was, like any other, "concrete" and determined by the object referred in a specific social and cultural context.

Variation of this context can make the referent change with respect to the function to be performed, but it is always the concrete referent, the *"signifié."* If, for example, the Semitic primary noun /laḥm-/ has the meanings "grain," "bread," "meat" or "cow," this does not mean that its "basic meaning" is the generic or abstract "thing to eat, nourishment," covering all these meanings (*signifiés*). That would be to confuse function with meaning. I think that the original meaning has always been "concrete," even though it is difficult to determine what that was—here, social and cultural analysis has a great deal to say—and that the others correspond to semantic shifts due to their proper function effected by the referent in each community of speakers.

Thus, for example, in the scale of colors, the semantic differentiation of a single lexeme can depend not on an undefined base reference (for example, "reddish" > "red" // "yellow"), but rather on a shift of the perception of pure tones and their functional value.[114]

In any case, taking these details into account, the determination of the original or basic seme, at this primary level of reference, must be effected with some reservation and as a working hypothesis, the likelihood of which must be assessed in each case with respect to the evidence from the various languages and their diachronic and cultural level. In any case, this should be at the heart of the claim to "etymologize." From this point, one is faced with the central problem of etymological lexicography, the problem of "homonymy." One must, therefore, decide whether there are one or several lexemes (in this case, homographs) or whether, which amounts to the same thing, they can be ascribed to one and the same lexical source. It is a problem discussed in all the manuals of semantics and lexicography, even though their basic concern is the semantic arrangement of monolingual lexica of languages with living speakers.[115]

The problem of homonymy goes together with the problem of "change of meaning" that created it. As against the "regularity" and "predictability" of phonetic change, defended to excess by the neo-grammarians and today extensively revised, semantic change is more fluid and cannot be tested. Thus, after the difficulty we have noted in defining the original or basic seme, from meanings presumed to be primary in each language, at a second stage there comes the difficulty of determining the meanings created by processes of derivation, development, and later shifts. In principle there are two: *metonymy* or the aspectual expansion of the referent (part, quality, quantity, causality...) and *metaphor* or transposition in parallel of the referential reality.[116]

To the latter can be added, as a sort of conditioned metaphor, the syntagmatic transposition of the predicate (or verbal meaning) starting from the object. Furthermore, the lexicalization of metaphor or making it autonomous (loss of connection to the original seme) produces polysemy of the lexeme or "root" much more widely and deeply than in the case of metonymy. In any case, these are well-known processes of semantic derivation on which there is no need to insist.[117] They are the results both of the complexity of the reality to which reference is made and of the necessary economy that avoids indefinite expansion of the lexicon. Its counterpart is the unavoidable semantic ambiguity and obscurity of the etymological origin of lexemes.

In this respect, some questions must be asked. Can there be true homonyms (homographs-homophones) in a proto-language? Is an original ambiguous sign acceptable? Are homographs always secondary and derived? Certainly, etymology cannot attempt to resolve historical semantics, as Barr clearly saw. Rather, it should cease wherever the semantic relationship does not appear clearly. But it is very likely and even necessary to suppose that a relationship or motivation of semantic derivation did exist, even if we do not know which, if the axiom of the univocity of the lexical sign is accepted, as differentiating "sign" from "symbol."[118] But account must also be taken of the fact that the Semitic lexicon refers to pre-Proto-Semitic (Afro-Asiatic) stages when homonymy/polysemy could have already happened (e.g., by onomatopoeia or semantic shift) and are, therefore, inaccessible to (Proto-)Semitic etymology. Some degree of homonymy must, therefore, be presumed at this level.[119] The basic problem of the distinction between "etymological semantics" and "historical semantics" is that both developed precisely in opposite directions, one backward and the other forward.[120] Etymology moves in the "vertical" sense of the paradigm, whereas historical semantics moves in the "horizontal" sense of the syntagm, from contrasts of historical context. In order to read a text, this aspect is determinative, whereas etymology is almost pure "learning" and, therefore, a "useless" thing that one can disregard. It is not tied to the interpretation of a specific text, but to the determination of the neutral and "supra-contextual" meaning of the lexeme. This supposes a real process of semantic realization that, as the subject of purely academic comparative and analytical study, can serve to arrange and explain historical (diachronic) semantics, especially of texts without (living) speakers, for which the projection of simple (synchronic) historical semantics, starting from known languages, can become anachronistic. In this sense, Barr's opinion must be nuanced (see above p. 92). It is the process for which metaphorical lexicalization often means the end that etymology tries to revive. If it is true that a word (phonological component) means what it means (semantic component) in its own linguistic system (and even more, in a specific context) and not what it means in another,[121] it is no less true that all the individual multiple meanings are the product of semantic shifts that are not transferable to other systems. The clarification of their process of derivation can be decisive for the interpretation of new texts. One must be aware of the modest nature of the results of etymology, but also of its heuristic and historical value.

In this respect the various situations in which the lexeme can appear in the Semitic languages from the aspect of semantics are as follows: (1) the same lexeme with different semantic values; (2) the same semantic value expressed by different lexemes; (3) some lexemes nonexistent in certain languages or even in whole subfamilies; (4) some semantic values non-existent in certain languages.

Lastly, we have already seen various scholars pronounce on the topic of enantiosemy (see above pp. 46, 95f.), offering different suggestions. This happens especially in Arabic lexicography and must be considered in terms of the history of that language.[122] As I have said already, in this case the semantic organization of Arabic and its diachronic derivation (movement forward) are today more important and necessary than its etymological reduction (movement backward).

3.5. *The Dictionary*

In terms of function, the question has also often been raised of the ordering of the etymological lexicon: its own graphical sequence (and there are many such[123]), "alphabetical" sequence, phonetic (articulatory [Driver] or "by matrix" [Bohas]) sequence, or semantic sequence, by "field." The latter was chosen, for example, by Militarev-Kogan, and its advantages have been highlighted by several scholars.[124] They are obvious in the case of specific studies of cultural and socio-linguistic comparison. But for general use, a dictionary, especially if concise, arranged alphabetically, is a necessity that cannot be avoided, supported by the existence of similar tools for Indo-European, while a semantic arrangement is more "encyclopedic" in character.

To summarize, the following schematic table of the formation and organization of the Semitic lexicon can be proposed[125]—also valid for other language families—which includes the three fundamental types of lexical base: nouns, verbs and the deictic series:

Deixis:
- the "functorial" and pronominal series

Natural resonance:
- pure onomatopoeia:
- some human "preverbal" sounds" (> prim.nouns: /ˀab-/, /ˀəm-/...)

   - lexicalized animal sounds (> noun/verb)
   - lexicalized physical noises (> noun/verb)
   - natural-cultural onomatopoeia or sound symbolism
   - some primary nouns (?)

Arbitrary resonance:
   - intensified primary biconsonantal bases
         - object (> primary nouns)
         - action (> nouns/verbs)
   - expanded biconsonantal groups
   - primary triconsonantal bases
         - object (> primary nouns)
         - action (> nouns/verbs)
         - triconsonantal bases with an alternating third consonant

Of course, the most important part of the Semitic lexicon corresponds to arbitrary resonance, in line with the recognized nature of the lexematic sign. This primary resonance can be formed from "binary" or "ternary" consonantal epiphonemes (symphonemes) in proportion to the number of articulation features. Binaries tend toward "intensification" or "expansion," while ternaries tend to "alternation" or "variation" resulting in a generalized triconsonantal lexical system. This original resonance proves to be "monosyllabic" (pure or anaptyctic) in terms of "lexis," with one radical vocalic position and a second inflected (which produces grammatical disyllabism or polysyllabism). Full disyllabic lexical expansions (type /CvCvC-/) must be considered as apophonic or derivative. Etymology is concerned with these original resonances as signs or sememes.

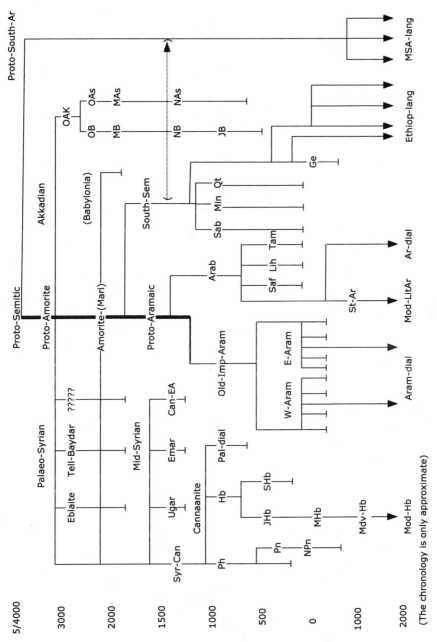

Classification diagram of the Semitic languages

(The chronology is only approximate)

ENDNOTES

Introduction

1. See, for example, S. Moscati, "Il biconsonantismo nelle lingue semitiche," *Biblica* 28 (1947), p. 113; J. Barr, *The Semantics of Biblical Language*, Oxford, 1961/1969, p. 288; J. H. Hospers, "A Hundred Years of Semitic Comparative Linguistics," in *Studia Biblica et Semitica* ..., 1966, p. 150; W. von Soden, "Ein semitisches Wurzelwörterbuch: Probleme und Möglichkeiten," *Or* 42 (1973), p. 142; W. Eilers, " Semitische Wurzeltheorie," in P. Fronzaroli, ed., *Atti del secondo congresso internazionale* ..., 1978, p. 125; J. Huehnergard, "New Directions in the Study of Semitic Languages," in J. S. Cooper and G. M. Schwartz, eds., *The Study of the Ancient Near East* ..., 1996, p. 263.

2. This bibliography can be consulted at the electronic address /www.telefonica.net/ web2/aulaorientalis/. It is updated regularly. See also G. del Olmo Lete, "Comparative Semitics: Classification and Reconstruction. An Organised Bibliography," *AuOr* 21, 2003, 97–138.

3. See M. A. Nowak and D. Krakauer, "The Evolution of Language," *Proceedings of the National Academy of Sciences* [Princeton] 96 (1999), pp. 8028–33; also, M. A. Nowak, D. Krakauer and D. Dress, "An error limit for the evolution of language," *Proceedings of the Royal Society* (London) 266 (1999), pp. 2131–36; M. A. Nowak, J. B. Plotkin and V. A. A. Jansen, "The evolution of syntactic communication," *Nature* 404 (March 30) (2000), pp. 495–98; A. S. Kaye in "Discussion" with B. S. J. Isserlin, "Some Aspects of the Present State of Hamito-Semitic Studies," in J. and Th. Bynon, eds., *Hamito-Semitica*, The Hague and Paris, 1975, p. 487. For a critique of the theory of glottogony see R. M. Voigt, *Die infirmen Verbaltypen des arabischen und das Biradikalismus-Problem*, AWLM, Veröfft. der Orient. Kommission B. XXXIX, Stuttgart, 1988, pp. 47–50 (the opinion was known already in the nineteenth century).

4. G. del Olmo Lete, "The Monoconsonantal Lexical Series in Semitic," *AuOr* 6 (1998), pp. 37–75.

5. G. del Olmo Lete, "The Semitic Personal Pronouns. A Preliminary Etymological Approach," in Y. Avishur, R. Deutsch, eds., *Michael. Historical, Epigraphical and Biblical Studies* ..., Tel Aviv-Jaffa, 1999, pp. 99–120.

6. G. del Olmo Lete, "Los numerales en semítico: ensayo de estudio etimológico," *Anuari de Filologia* 21/E (1998–1999), pp. 17–37.

7. See G. del Olmo Lete, "An Etymological and Comparative Semitic Dictionary Phonology versus Semantics: Questions of Method," *AuOr* 23 (2005), pp. 185–90; id., "The Biconsonantal Semitic Lexicon 1. The Series /ʾ-X/," *AuOr* 22 (2004), pp. 33–88; id., "The Biconsonantal Semitic

Lexicon 2. The Series /^{c}-X/," *AuOr* 22 (2006) (17–56); id., "The Biconsonantal Semitic Lexicon 3. The Series /B-X/" (in press).

8. See W. Eilers, "Semitische Wurzeltheorie," in P. Fronzaroli, ed., *Atti del secondo congresso internazionale* ..., Florence, 1978, pp. 125–26.

9. For a rather extreme solution see C. Ehret, "The origin of Third Consonants in Semitic Roots: An Internal Reconstruction (Applied to Arabic)," *JAL* 1 (1989), pp. 109–202.

10. See S. T. H. Hurwitz, *Root-determinatives in Semitic Speech. A Contribution to Semitic Philology*, New York, 1913, p. ix. For a more detailed explanation of my way of thinking in this regard cf. the forthcoming article "Phonetic Distribution in Semitic Binary Articulation Bases," paper delivered at the 13th Italian Meeting of Afro-Asiatic Linguistics, Udine, 21–24 May, 2007 (in press).

11. The question has been raised since the Middle Ages; see S. Moscati, "*Il biconsonantismo* ...," 1947, p. 114; S. Hurwitz, *Root-Determinatives* ..., 1913, p. 2.

12. On this topic see A. S. Kaye, in J. and Th. Bynon, eds., *Hamito-Semitica* ..., 1975, p. 486 ("General Discussion"). On Djakonoff's opinion concerning this topic see below p. 32.

Chapter 1

1. See the very detailed review of these three last works by R. M. Voigt, "Drei neue vergleichende semitische Werke," *WdO* 31 (2000–2001), pp. 165–89. The collective work edited by R. Hetzron, *The Semitic Languages*, London and New York, 1997, does not consider the question.

2. For this period, cf. now A. Maman, *Comparative Semitic Philology in the Middle Ages. From Sa^{c}dya Gaon to IBn Barūn (10th – 12th C.)*, Leiden/Boston 2004.

3. J. Cantineau, "Roots et schèmes," in *Mélanges offerts à William Marsais*..., Paris, 1950, pp. 119–24; id., "La notion de 'schème' et son altération dans diverses langues sémitiques," *Semitica* 3 (1950), pp. 73–83. The article by G. Hudson, "Arabic root and pattern morphology without tiers," *JL* 22 (1986), pp. 85–122, was not accessible.

4. In connection with Hebrew grammars see P. Cassuto, "Le classement dans les dictionnaires de l'hébreu," in P. Cassuto and P. Larcher, eds., *La sémitologie, aujourd'hui*, Aix-en-Provence, 2000, pp. 133–58.

5. See for example B. Spuler, *Semitistik*, HdO I/3, Leiden, 1964, pp. 8f.; H. Fleisch, *Traité de philologie arabe, I*, Beyrouth, 1990, pp. 247ff.; G. Goldenberg, "Principles of Semitic Word-Structure," in G. Goldenberg, S. Raz, eds., *Semitic and Cushitic Studies*, 1994, pp. 34–37, who cites other scholars (O'Leary [root, theme, stem], Starinin [root/affix], Buccellati [root-pattern]). On this topic see also the remarks by E. Ullendorff, "What is a Semitic Language?," in *Is Biblical Hebrew a Language?* ..., Wiesbaden, 1977, pp. 155–64 [158f.]; G. Douillet, "Le theme grammatical: stratégie et tactique," *Analyses, Théorie* 20 (1982), pp. 39–42; and A. Roman, "Sur l'origine de la diptosie en langue arabe," in P. Zemánek, ed., *Studies in Near Eastern Languages and Literatures ...*, Prague, 1996, pp. 515–34: "The syllabic system of the Semitic languages, reduced to only two syllables, namely /CV/ and /CVC/, has imposed the separation of the sub-set of consonant-phonemes, {C}, and of the sub-set of vowel-phonemes, {V}. This separation offered the Semitic languages a basic organization that they have realized by constructing on consonantal roots their systems of nomination and on vowels their systems of communication" (p. 516). A recent discussion of the organization of patterns in Semitic is provided by P. Ségéral, "Théorie de l'apophonie et organization des schèmes en sémitique," in J. Lecarme, J. Lowenstamm and U. Shlonsky, eds., *Research in Afroasiatic Grammar...*, Amsterdam and Philadelphia 2000, pp. 263–

99; J.F. Prunet, R. Béland, A. Idrissi, "The mental representation of Semitic words," *Linguistic Inquiry* 31 (2000), pp. 609–45; J. Fox, *Semitic Noun Patterns*, Winona Lake, Ind., 2003, pp. 1, 53, "is concerned with the internal pattern systems in the nouns" and their derivation (pp. 1–2), in the perspective of the "pattern-and-root" system set up by Cantineau (pp. 1, 53); this work (like most of the former) falls, then, in the field of morphology and so outside our present interest, the treatment of the root problem being rather cursory and elementary (chap. 4), sketched in function of the work's main concern, the Semitic inflectional patterns. These are laid out in chap. 8 and following, where the actual bearing of the book is to be found. In this regard it supplants Barth's classic work, although some linguistic areas like modern Aramaic and South-Ethiopic are disregarded. Otherwise, as is usual among American and West-European Semitists, it ignores Slav contributions almost completely, except for some of Djakonoff's. See also the studies by G. Bohas, below.

6. C. Reintges, "Egyptian Root-and-Pattern Morphology," *LinAeg* 4 (1994), pp. 213–44 [213, 240].

7. L. Galand, "Le comportement des schèmes et des racines dans l'évolution de la langue: exemples touaregs," in J. Bynon, ed., *Current Progress in Afro-Asiatic Linguistics...*, Amsterdam and Philadelphia, 1984, pp. 305–15. On Arabic see, for example, L. Drozdšk, "Towards Defining the Structural Level of the Stem in Arabic," *Orientalia Suecana* 16 (1967), pp. 85–95; and the studies by G. Bohas, below; for Modern Hebrew see M. Ephrat, "The psycholinguistic status of the root in Modern Hebrew," *FoL* 31, (1997), pp. 77–103; id., "Hebrew Morphology by Itself," *JNSL* 28, (2002), pp. 83–99; 29 (2002), pp. 55–65. For a new approach see J. Sanmartín, "The Semantic Potential of Bases ('roots') and Themes ('patterns'): a cognitive approach," *AuOr* 22 (2005), pp. 65–81.

8. I. M. Djakonoff, "Problems of Root Structure in Proto-Semitic," *ArOr* 38 (1970), pp. 453–77 (455).

9. I. M. Djakonoff, *Semito-Hamitic Languages: an essay in classification*, Moscow, 1965; id., *Jazyki drevnej Perednej Azii* [Languages of ancient Asia Minor], Moscow, 1967; id., *Afrasian Languages*, Moscow, 1988, pp. 42–56.

10. D. Cohen, "Problèmes de linguistique chamito-sémitique," *RES* 40 (1972), pp. 43–68 (see pp. 000 below).

11. D. Cohen, "À propos d'un dictionnaire des racines sémitiques," in P. Fronzaroli, ed., *Atti del secondo congresso internazionale...*, 1978, pp. 87–100 (88ff.). On this topic see the article by G. Bohas, "Et pourtant ils lisent …, " *LLMA* 3 (2002), pp. 11–28, who "shows" statistically that Arabic speakers are incapable of identifying a root and a pattern in a word (pp. 28).

12. P. Fronzaroli, "Problems of a Semitic Etymological Dictionary," in P. Fronzaroli, ed., *Studies on Semitic Lexicography*, Florence, 1973, pp. 1–17 (2–5).

13. K. Petráček, "La structure de la racine et la classification des langues chamito-sémitiques," *Phonetica Pragensia* 4 (1974), pp. 115–21.

14. S. S. Majzel," *Puti razvitija kornegovo fonda semitskih jazykov* [Types of derivation of the stock of Semitic roots], Moscow, 1983 (chap. 5: "The root in Semitic languages"; chap. 6: "The horizon of the theory on the origin of the Semitic root").

15. R.M. Voigt, *Die infirmen Verbaltypen des Arabischen und das Biradikalismus-Problem*, Stuttgart, 1988, pp. 17f., 36ff. For appraisal of this work see the reviews: *SO* 64 (1988), pp. 381–382 (T. Harviainen); *AcOr* 50 (1989), pp. 202–6 (J. Hämeen-Anttila); *AuOr* 7 (1989), pp. 151–52 (F. Corriente); *BiOr* 46 (1989), pp. 482–86 (L.O. Schuman); *ArOr* 58 (1990), pp. 290–91 (P. Zemánek); *Kratylos* 35 (1990), pp. 179–84 (F. Rundgren); *Islam* 68 (1991), pp. 129–32 (W. Fischer); *JRAS* (1990), pp. 141–44 (C. Holes); *JSS* 36 (1991), pp. 116–22 (W. von Soden); *RSO* 63 (1989), pp. 344–47 (O.

Durand); *WZKM* 81 (1991), pp. 260–64 (H. Hirsch); *WO* 23 (1992), pp. 187–93 (E.A. Knauf); *WO* 23 (1992), pp. 187–93 (E.A. Knauf); *Al-ᶜArabiyya* 28 (1993), pp. 158–59 (L. Edzard); *Lešonenu* 56 (1992), pp. 249–55 (J. Blau)].

16. See. H. Jungraithmayr, "On root augmentation in Hausa," *JAL* 9/2 (1970), pp. 83–88; id., "Reflections on the root structure in Chadohamitic (Chadic)," *Annales de l'Université d'Abidjan*, sér. H 1971, pp. 285–92.

17. G. M. Schramm, "Semitic Morpheme Structure Typology," in A. S. Kaye, ed., *Semitic Studies ...*, Wiesbaden, 1991, pp. 1402–08.

18. G. Bohas, "Le PCO et la structure des racines," in G. Bohas, ed., *Développements récents ...*, Damascus, 1993, pp. 9–44; essentially repeated in "Le PCO, la composition des racines et les conventions d'association," *BEO* 43 (1991), pp. 119–37 ; also G. Bohas, "Radical ou racine/ schème? L'organisation de la conjugaison syriaque, avant l'adoption de la racine," *Le Muséon* 116 (2003), pp. 343–76.

19. J. J. McCarthy, "Formal Problems in Semitic Phonology and Morphology," Diss. M.I.T., 1979/1982.

20. G. Bohas, "Diverses conceptions de la morphologie arabe," in G. Bohas, ed., *Développements récents ...*, 1993, pp. 45–59.

21. G. Bohas, *Matrices, Étymons, Roots. Éléments d'une théorie lexicologique du vocabulaire arabe*, Leuven, 1997; id., *Matrices et étymons. Développements de la théorie*, Lausanne, 2000. G. Bohas has directed and even co-edited the works of a school of Arabic-speaking students who follow his theories closely; see for example G. Bohas and A. Chekayri, "Les relations des racines bilitères en arabe," in R. Contini et al., *Semitica ...*, Turin, 1993, pp. 1–13; A. Chekayri, "La structure des racines en arabe," Ph.D. thesis, Univ. Paris VII, 1994; G. Bohas and S. Gharbaoui, "L'organisa- tion sémantique des matrices," in M. El Medlaoui, S. Gafaiti and F. Saa, eds., *Actes du premier congrès chamito-sémitique de Fès*, Fès, 1998, pp. 193–207; F. M. Dat, "Matrices et étymons. Mimo- phonie lexicale en hébreu biblique," Ph.D. diss., Univ. Lyon, 2002, this work was not accessible to me; id., "Matrices de traits et icons auditives en hébreu biblique," *LLMA* 4 (2003), pp. 87–118; for a very recent example see id., "La matrice de dénomination {[coronal], [dorsal]} en hébreu biblique: invariance et organisation conceptuelle," *LLMA* [Hommage à André Miquel] 3 (2002), pp. 59–83; L. Khatef, "Le croisements des étymons: organisation formelle et sémantique," *LLMA* 4 (2003), pp. 119–38; A. Saguer, "La matrice {[nasale], [coronale]}, "traction" en arabe. Première esquisse," *LLMA* 4 (2003), pp. 139–83.

22. G. Goldenberg, "Principles of Semitic Word-Structure," in G. Goldenberg and Sh. Raz, eds., *Semitic and Cushitic Studies*, Wiesbaden, 1994, pp. 29–64. In a recent study the same scholar touches upon and sums up the situation in relation to certain questions which concern us: (1) Linguistic study of genealogically related languages; (2) Semitic languages and the comparative method; (3) General-linguistic studies and the Semitic languages; see also G. Goldenberg, "Semitic Linguistics and General Study of Languages," in Sh. Izre'el, ed., *Semitic Linguistics: the state of the art at the turn of the twenty-first century* (IOS XX), Winona Lake, Ind., 2002, pp. 21–41; he also deals with morphological word-structure in "Word-Structure, Morphological Analysis, the Semitic Languages and Beyond," in P. Fronzaroli, P. Marrassini, eds., *Proceedings of the 10th Meeting of Hamito-Semitic (Afroasiatic) Linguistics* (Florence, 18–20, 2001) (QuSem 25), Florence 2006, pp. 169–93. See also *infra* Chap. IV, 1.25.

23. A. R. Bomhard, "The Root in Indo-European and Afroasiatic," in P. Zemánek, ed., *Stud- ies in Near Eastern Languages ...*, 1999, pp. 161–70.

24. D. Baggioni and P. Larcher, "Note sur la racine en indo-européen et en sémitique," in P. Cassuto and P. Larcher, eds., *La sémitologie, aujourd'hui ...*, 2000, pp. 121–31.

25. Cf. J. Sanmartín, "The Semantic potential of Bases ("root') and Themes ("patterns'): A cognitive approach," *AuOr* 23 (2005), pp. 65–81).

26. On this see R. M. Voigt, *Die infirmen Verbaltypen …*, 1988, pp. 164.

27. H. B. Rosén, "On 'Normal' Full Root Structure and its Historical Development," in A. Giacalone Ramat, O. Carruba and G. Bernini, eds., *Papers from the 7th International Conference …*, Amsterdam and Philadelphia, 1987, pp. 535–44.

28. See R. M. Voigt, *Die infirmen Verbaltypen …*, 1988, pp. 22.

29. On the other hand, the concept of "theme" seems to refer to the specific forms that the "stem" assumes. For C. Reintges, "Egyptian Root-and-Pattern Morphology," *LinAeg* 4 (1994), pp. 213, "stem" as against "root" "is a physically interpretable surface form," that is, an inter-digitated "pattern." For a slightly different approach see Sanmartín's article quoted in n. 6.; also J. Fox, *Semitic Noun Patterns*, Winona Lake, Ind., 2003, p. 34, who prefers "stirp" to "stem," dealing with verb derivation.

30. See P. Ségéral, "Théorie de l'apophonie et organisation des schèmes en sémitique," in J. Lecarme, J. Loewenstamm and U. Shlonsky, eds., *Research in Afroasiatic Grammar …*, 2000, pp. 263–99.

31. See W. U. Dressler, *Morphonology – The Dynamics of Derivation*, Ann Arbor, Mich., 1985, pp. 346f.; with the critique by G. Goldenberg, "Principles of Semitic Word-Structure," in G. Goldenberg and S. Raz, eds., *Semitic and Cushitic Studies*, Wiesbaden, 1994, pp. 52f.

32. See A. R. Bomhard, "The Root in Indo-European and Afroasiatic," in P. Zemánek, ed., *Studies in Near Eastern Languages …*, 1999, pp. 165ff.; D. Baggioni and P. Larcher, "Note sur la racine en indo-européen et en sémitique," in P. Cassuto and P. Larcher, *La sémitologie, aujourd'hui …*, 2000, pp. 128f.

33. See I. M. Djakonoff, "Problems of Root Structure in Proto-Semitic," *ArOr* 38 (1970), pp. 453–77 (458ff.); id., "On Root Structure in Proto-Semitic," in J. and Th. Bynon, eds., *Hamito-Semitica …*, 1975, pp. 133–53 (137f.); K. Petráček, "La structure de la racine et la classification des langues chamito-sémitiques," *Phonetica Pragensia* 4 (1974), pp. 115ff.

34. Cited by R. M. Voigt, *Die infirmen Verbaltypen …*, 1988, p. 24. See also I. M. Djakonoff, *Afrasian Languages*, Moscow, 1975, pp. 29–31. G. M. Gabučan, "K voprusu o strukture semitskogo slova (v svjazi s problemoj 'vnutrennej fleksii')" [On the problem of the structure of the word in Semitic in relation to the problem of "internal inflection"], in G. Š. Šarvatov, ed., *Semitskie jazyki …*, 1965[2], pp. 114–27, and G. M. Gabučan and A. A. Kovaljov, "O Probleme slova v cvete faktov araskogo litieraturnogo yazika" [On the problem of the word in the light of data from Arabic literature], in *idd.*, eds., *Arabska Filologija*, Moscow 1968, pp. 40–51, provide a collateral consideration of the concept of "word," determined by the problem of "internal inflection," especially of Arabic. Their starting-point is the article A. Mel'čuk, "O 'vnutrennej fleksii' v indo-evropejskih i semitskih jazikah" [On "internal inflection" in Indo-European and Semitic], *Voprosu jazikoznanija* 4 (1963), pp. 27–40.

Chapter 2

1. V. P. Starinin, *Struktura semitskogo slova. Preryvistye morfemy* [The structure of the Semitic word. Discontinuous morphemes], Moscow, 1963.

2. I. M. Djakonoff, "Problems of Root Structure in Proto-Semitic," *ArOr* 38 (1970), pp. 453–77; see also id., "On Root Structure in Proto-Semitic," in J. and Th. Bynon, eds., *Hamito-Semitica…*, 1975, pp. 133–53; I. M. Djakonoff et al., "Historical Comparative Vocabulary of Afrasian,"

SPJASt 2 (1993), pp. 5–6. The articles by A.G. Belova, "The Structure of the Semitic Root and the Morphological Semitic System" (Russ.), *Voprosy Jazykosnanija* 1 (1991), pp. 79–90; id., "Towards the problem of the Semitic Root Structure" (Russ.), in *History and Languages of Ancient Orient: I. M. Diakonoff Memorial Volume*, St. Petersburg 2002, pp. 29–36, were not accessible to me. Cf. also A.G. Belova, ""Les racines arabes homonymes comme résultat des changements historiques," in S. Leder et al., eds., *Studies in Arabic and Islam* (OLA 108), Leuven / Paris / Sterling, Va., 2002, pp. 349–56.

3. I. M. Djakonoff, *Semito-Hamitic Languages: An Essay in Classification*, Moscow 1965; id., *Jazyki drevnej Perednej Azii*, Moscow, 1967.

4. I. M. Djakonoff, *Afrasian Languages*, Moscow, 1988, pp. 42–56.

5. On this topic see J. J. McCarthy, "Formal Problems in Semitic Phonology and Morphology," Ph.D. diss., M.I.T., 1979, pp. 21ff.

6. G. del Olmo Lete, "The Monoconsonantal Lexical Series in Semitic," *AuOr* 16 (1998), pp. 37–75 (46–47).

7. This explanation needs to be revised; it seems contradictory that it is precisely the vowel /a/, the most clearly defined in the presupposed vowel system, which in this case is the unstable primitive vowel.

8. G. del Olmo Lete, "The Semitic Personal Pronouns. A Preliminary Etymological Approach," in Y. Avishur and R. Deutsch, eds., *MICHAEL. Historical, Epigraphical and Biblical Studies* …, 1999, pp. 99–120.

9. I. M. Djakonoff, « On Root Structure in Proto-Semitic," in J. and Th. Bynon, eds., *HamitoSemitica* …, 1975, pp. 133–53. See also A. Roman, "Sur l'origine de la diptosie en langue arabe," in P. Zemánek, ed., *Studies in Near Eastern Languages* … 1996, pp. 516, 523. See below n. 33.

10. I. M. Djakonoff, *Proto-Afrasian and Old Akkadian. A study in historical phonetics* (*Journal of Afroasiatic Languages* 4/1–2), Princeton, NY, 1991–92, especially chap. 4: "Proto-Afrasian Root Structure and the Sonants: Implications for Akkadian," and chap. 5: "Proto-Afrasian and Old Akkadian: Prosody: the Two Vowels of PAA."

11. I. M. Djakonoff, *Semito-Hamitic Languages: an essay in classification*, Moscow, 1965; id., *Jazyki drevnej Perednej Azii*, Moscow, 1967; id., *Afrasian Languages*, Moscow, 1988. In respect of the 1965 edition, D. O. Edzard, "Die semitohamitischen Sprachen in neuer Sicht," *RA* 61 (1967), pp. 137–49, in a long review, confined himself, in connection with the question we are discussing, ("2. Zur Rekonstruktion des ältesten Phonembestandes im Semitischen," pp. 145–47), to commenting on problems of phonology (see below) along with others that are more remote ("ergativity," "genre/nominal class").

12. K. Petráček, "La structure de la racine et la classification des langues chamitosémitiques ," *Phonetica Pragensia* 4 (1974), pp. 115–21 (115–16); id., "La racine en indo-européen et en chamito-sémitique et leurs perspectives comparatives," *AION* 42 (1982), pp. 381–402.

13. With regard to the period that concerns us, A. Cuny, *Invitation à l'étude des langues indoeuropéennes et des langues chamito-sémitiques*, Bordeaux, 1946, is very revealing of this trend; see also by the same author: *Recherches sur le vocalisme, le consonantisme et la formation des racines en 'nostratique' ancêtre de l'indo-européen et du chamito-sémitique*, Paris, 1943.

14. K. Petráček, "La méthodologie du chamito-sémitique comparé: état, problèmes, perspectives," in J. Bynon, ed., *Current Progress in Afro-Asiatic Linguistics* …, Amsterdam and Philadelphia, 1984, pp. 423–61.

15. K. Petráček, "La racine en sémitique d'après quelques travaux récents en russe," *ArOr* 53 (1985), pp. 171–73.

16. H. B. Rosén, "On 'Normal' Full Root Structure and Its Historical Development," in A. Giacalone Ramat, O. Carruba and G. Bernini, eds., *Papers from the 7th International Conference ...*, 1987, pp. 535–44.

17. V. Blažek, "Paralelní procesy ve vy´voji indoevropského a afroasijského korene" [Parallel processes in the development of the Indo-European and Afroasiatic root], *Jazykovedné Aktuality* 26/1–2 (1989), pp. 28–33.

18. A. R. Bomhard, "The Root in Indo-European and Afroasiatic," in P. Zemánek, ed., *Studies in Near Eastern Languages ...*, 1996, pp. 161–70. See also B. A. Dolgopolsky, "Struktura semitochamitskogo kornja v sravnitel'no-istoričeskom osvesčenii" [The structure of the Hamito-Semitic root in a comparative-historical perspective], *Voprosy Jazykosnanija* 1976, pp. 278–82; W. Vycichl, "The Origin of the Semitic Languages," in H. Jungrathmayr, W. W. Müller, eds., *Proceedings of the 4th International Hamito-Semitic Congress ...*, Amsterdam and Philadelphia, 1987, pp. 113–14 ("roots and skeletons," "the third radical").

19. E. Lipiński, *Semitic Languages. Outline of a Comparative Grammar*, OLA 80, Leuven, 1997, pp. 201–8; S. Moscati et al., *An Introduction to the Comparative...*, Wiesbaden, 1964, pp. 71–74, also devotes a paragraph to "Root morpheme". A last appraisal of this question is offered by J.A. Naudé, "The Consonantal Root in Semitic Languages," *JNSL* 29, 2003, pp. 15–32.

20. With regard to the opposition between consonant and vowel, usually accepted in all the textbooks on phonology, we can mention here the article by G. N. Clements, "Lieu d'articulation des consonnes et des voyelles: une théorie unifiée," in B. Laks and A. Rialland, eds., *Architecture des représentations phonologiques*, Paris, 1993, pp. 101–45. This new unified approach to phonetic articulation is in line with the importance of vocalism in lexematic analysis in Semitic.

21. B. Kienast, "Das System der zweiradikaligen Verben im Akkadischen (Ein Beitrag zur vergleichenden Semitistik)," *ZA* 21 (1962), pp. 138–55.

22. P. Fronzaroli, "Sull'elemento vocalico del lessema in semitico," *RSO* 38 (1963), pp. 119–29; also id., "Problems of a Semitic Etymological Dictionary," in P. Fronzaroli, ed., *Studies on Semitic Lexicography...*, 1973, p. 5. See below pp. 92ff.

23. A. M. Gazov-Ginsberg, "Semitskij koren' i obsčelingvisticeskaja teorija monovokalizma" [The Semitic root and the linguistic theory of monovocalism], in G. Š. Šarvatov, ed., *Semitskie jazyki ...*," 1965, pp. 200–4; id., "Sledy monovokalizma v semitskih vnegrammatičeskih glasnyh" [Traces of monovocalism in the extragrammatical vocalic system in Semitic], *Kratkie Šoobsčenija Instituta Narodov Azii* 86 (1965), pp. 90–96. For a critique of this see I. M. Djakonoff, "Problems of Root Structure in Proto-Semitic," *ArOr* 38 (1970), p. 454, n. 6. The theory had already been proposed, in a way, by L. Reinisch; see M. Fraenkel, *Zur Theorie der Lamed-He-Stämme*, Jerusalem, 1970, p. 13.

24. A. M. Gazov-Ginsberg, *Symvolizm prasiemitskoj fleksii. O bezuslobnoj motivirovannosti znaka* [The symbolism of inflection in Proto-Semitic: unconditioned motivated signs], Moscow, 1974. See also A. M. Gazov-Ginsberg, "Simvolika kratkosti i dolgoty v osnovah semitskih spjagaemyh form" [The symbolism of short versus long bases in conjugated forms in Semitic], *Palestinskij Sbornik* 19 (1969), pp. 45–55; A. M. Gazov-Ginsberg, "Simvolizm u::i kak vyračenie pola (roda) i razmerov v semitskih jazykah" [The u::i symbolism as an expression of type and height in the Semitic languages], *Palestinskij Sbornik* 21 (1970), pp. 100–10.

25. A. M. Gazov-Ginsberg, *Bil li jazyk izobrazitelen v svoih istokah ? (Svidetel'stvo prasiemitskogo zapasa kornej)* [Was language descriptive in origin?], Moscow, 1965.

26. A detailed reconstruction of a Proto-Afro-Asiatic system with five vowels, differentiated qualitatively and quantitatively, is carried out by Chr. Ehret, *Reconstructing Proto-Afroasiatic*, Berkeley, Calif., 1995, pp. 55–67.

27. On this see also I. M. Djakonoff, "On Root Structure in Proto-Semitic," in J. and Th. Bynon, eds., *Hamito-Semitica* ..., 1975, pp. 133–53; similarly, A. Ju. Militarev and L. Kogan, *Semitic Etymological Dictionary...*, 2000, pp. xlv–vi, liii, cxxiv–cxxv, cxxxvii–cxxxix A. R. Bomhard and J. C. Kerns, *The Nostratic Macrofamily*, Berlin and New York, 1994 pp. 107–8. For a critique of Djakonoff's vocalic theory see D. Cohen, "Problèmes de linguistique chamito-sémitique," *Revue des Études Slaves* 40 (1972), pp. 67–68. Following Djakonoff's footsteps and other authors' opinions, L. Kogan ("Observations on Proto-Semitic Vocalism," *AuOr* 23 [2005], pp. 131–67) has scrutinized radical and morphological Semitic vocalism arriving at the conclusion that "the original root-vocalism can be –at least in principle – reconstructed" (p. 164), but maybe it is not worthwhile, given the low rate of oppositions the Semitic lexicon exhibits in this connection (p. 165).

28. R. M. Voigt, *Die infirmen Verbaltypen des Arabischen und das Biradikalismus-Problem*, Stuttgart, 1988, p. 106.

29. Vl. Orel, "On Hamito-Semitic Morphology and Morphonology," *Orbis* 37 (1994), pp. 162–75. At the Afro-Asiatic level, the problem of radical vocalism is also studied (especially in connection with Chadic) by Vl. É. Orel and Ol. V. Stolbova, "K rekonstrukcii praafrazijskogo vokalizma 1–2; 3–4" [On the reconstruction of vocalism in proto-Afro-Asiatic], *Voprosy jazykoznanija* 5 (1989), pp. 66–84; 2 (1990), pp. 75–90; idd., *Hamito-Semitic Etymological Dictionary*, 2000, pp. xxi–xxiv; see A. R. Bomhard and J. C. Kerns, *The Nostratic Macrofamily*, 1994, p. 108.

30. A. G. Belova, "Struktura kornja v drevneegipetskom i semitskij jazykah" [The structure of the root in ancient Egyptian and the Semitic languages], in St. Pilaszewiez and J. Tulisow, eds., *Problemy języków Azij i Afriki* ..., 1987, pp. 275–82; id., "Sur la reconstruction du vocalisme afro-asiatique: quelques correspondances égypto-sémitiques," in H. G. Mukarovsky, ed., *Proceedings of the fifth international Hamito-Semitic congress* ..., 1990, Bd. 2, pp. 85–93; id., "La structure de la racine afroasiatique. Le cas d'extension phonétique," in E. Eberman et al., eds., *Komparative Afrikanistik* ..., 1992, pp. 15–20; on this see G. Takács, *Etymological Dictionary of Egyptian*, vol. I, Leiden, 1999, p. 394 ("The Law of Belova"). Also A.G. Belova, "Struktura semitskogo kornja i semitskaja morfologičeskaja sistema" [The structure of the Semitic root and the Semitic morphological system], in *Voprosy yazikoznanija* (1991), pp. 79–90; id., "K koprosu o strukture semitskogo kornja (komplementy i fonetičeskie rašyriteli)" (Toward the problem of the Semitic root structure (complements and phonetical extensions)," in *Istorija I jazykii drevnego vostoka: pamjati I.M. Djakonoff (History and Languages of Ancient Orient: I.M. Diakonoff Memorial Volumen)*, St. Petersburg 2002, pp. 29–36.

31. A. G. Belova, "Sur la reconstruction du vocalisme radical en arabe et en sémitique," in P. Zemánek, ed., *Studies in Near Eastern Languages* ..., 1996, pp. 81–88.

32. See A. G. Belova, "K voprosu o rekonstrukcii semitskogo kornevogo voakalizma" [Towards the reconstruction of radical vocalism in Semitic], *Voprosy Jazikoznanija* 6 (1993), pp. 28–56.

33. See T. Frolova, "The Reconstruction of the Vowel in the Proto-Semitic Verbal Base - $C_1C_2VC_3$-. The Evidence of Akkadian and Arabic," in *Fs. A. Militarev*, pp. 79–101. With a clearer effect on the Proto-Semitic perspective, she continues the work of J. Aro, *Die Vokalisierung des Grundstammes im semitischen Verbum*, Helsinki, 1964.

34. On this topic see A. Roman, "Sur l'origine de la diptosie en langue arabe," in P. Zemánek, ed., *Studies in Near Eastern Languages* ..., 1996, pp. 515–34; for him the "unités de nomination" have been imagined by man in relation to time: outside time, *res* (noun); within time, *modus* (verb) (p. 516). From the aspect of phonology, the *res* has a /CvCC/ structure, whereas the structure of the *modus* is /CvCvC/ (p. 523). For a different approach, see A. Gai, "Several Points of

Semitic and Akkadian Grammar," *Le Muséon* 114 (2001), pp. 1–2 ("1. The Root of a 'Primary Word'," against G. Buccellati [*A Structural Grammar of Babylonian*, Wiesbaden, 1996, 10.1] who considers that many (primary) Akkadian words are not derived from a "root."

35. Here we are speaking about "level zero" as defined by Djakonoff, not in the sense that "degree zero" has in Indo-European linguistics; see O. Szemerényi, *Einführung in die vergleichende Sprachwissenschaft*, Darmstadt, 1989³, pp. 116ff.; H. B. Rosén, "On 'Normal' Full Root Structure ... ," in A. Giacalone Ramat, O. Carruba and G. Bernini, eds., *Papers from the 7th International Conference ...*, 1987, p. 536.

36. Probably the first "grammatical" transformation, as the opposition object/action, has led the /QvTL/ type to become /Q(v)TvL/ > /QvT$\underline{v}$L/ (> *$qat\bar{a}lu$ in Akkadian and Hebrew), by virtue of the expressive nature of the action; afterward, the verbal morpheme /-QTvL/ is a result of this transformation. The alternation of the infinitive construct in Hebrew (/qotl-/ > /q^{e}tol/), as against the plurality of forms of *maṣdar* in Arabic, is a good model. But this very plurality, to be found in other Semitic languages, suggests that this is due to derivation. In any case, this transformation would take us to a Proto-Afro-Asiatic stage. See Sh. Armon-Lotem, "What Hebrew Early Verbs Teach Us about Root Infinitives," in *Proceedings of the Groningen Assembly ...*, Groningen, 1996, pp. 77–86; on the noun-verb relationship in general from the derivational point of view cf. J. Fox, *Semitic Noun Patterns*, Winona Lake, Ind., 2003, pp. 9, 25–30.

37. On this topic see D. Cohen, "À propos d'un dictionnaire des racines sémitiques," in P. Fronzaroli, ed., *Atti del secondo congresso internazionale ...*, Florence, 1978, pp. 93f.; W. Vycichl, "Le nom verbal du chamito-sémitique," in M. Pittau, ed., *Circolazioni culturali nel Mediterraneo antico ...*, Cagliari, 1994, pp. 255–62. For a classic discussion of the noun/verb question, see J. Barr, *The Semantics of Biblical Language*, Oxford, 1969, pp. 14f., 56f., 76, 84f., 97, 101, 104.

38. See for example B. Landsberger, "Die Gestalt der semitischen Wurzel," in *Atti del XIX Congresso Internazionale degli Orientalisti ...*," 1938, pp. 450–52: "die Nomina bei der Entstehung der Sprache in einer früheren Periode feste Gestalt annahmen als die Verba" (p. 452).

39. On this subject see the situation in Berber as set out by L. Galand, "Un nom de verbe d'état. Le témoignage du berbère," in H. G. Mukarovsky, ed., *Proceedings of the Fifth International Hamito-Semitic Congress ...*, 1990, Bd. I, pp. 123–38. English also includes, in this respect, a high degree of equivalence between nouns and verbs. On the functionality of substantives and adjectives, cf. J. Fox, *Semitic Noun Patterns*, Winona Lake, Ind., 2003, pp. 27f., with a slight different use of the "actantial" category.

40. On this topic, see J. Fox, "A Sequence of Vowel Shifts in Phoenician and Other Languages," *JNES* 55 (1996), pp. 37–47. Also one must take account of the original nominal (0/a) inflection in Akkadian; G. Garbini, *Le lingue semitiche. Studi di storia linguistica*, Naples, 1973, p. 153.

41. In this connection, a long vowel could be considered as "original" within the process of derivation from a short vowel and as a case of intensification with semantic function. In this way it belongs to the functional or grammatical level that we consider as "primary," as we have noted above.

42. See I. M. Djakonoff, "Opening Address," in J. and Th. Bynon, eds., *Hamito-Semitica...*, 1975, pp. 26, 34.

43. See J. Huehnergard, "New Directions in the Study of Semitic Languages," in J. S. Cooper and G. M. Schwartz, eds., *The Study of the Ancient Near East ...*, 1996, pp. 264f.

44. See A. Dolgopolsky, *From Proto-Semitic to Hebrew. Phonology. Etymological approach in a Hamito-Semitic perspective*, Milan, 1999.

Chapter 3

1. Cantineau "Le consonantisme du sémitique," *Semitica* 4 (1951–52), pp. 79–94.

2. J. Cantineau, *Cours de phonétique arabe*, 1946; id., "Esquisse d'une phonologie de l'arabe classique," *BSLP* 43 (1946), pp. 93–140; id., "Essai d'une phonologie de l'hébreu biblique," *BSLP* 46 (1950), pp. 82–122; in this context reference should also be made to H. Fleisch, "Études de phonétique arabe," *MUSJ* 18 (1949–50), pp. 233–37, which has been followed by several more modern studies on the phonology of this language which it would be tedious and of little use to mention here.

3. See the discussion in *GLECS* 5 (1960–1963), pp. 49–50 (A. Haudricourt-W. Leslau-M. Cohen).

4. For Hebrew see the similar diagram in G. É. Weil, "Trilitéralité fonctionnelle ou bilitéralité fondamentale des racines verbales hébraïques. Un essai d'analyse quantifié," *RHPhR* 59 (1979), p. 300; also Moscati, below and p. 48.

5. A. Martinet, "Remarques sur le consonantisme sémitique," *BSLP* 49 (1953), pp. 67–78.

6. S. Moscati, *Il sistema consonantico delle lingue semitiche*, Rome, 1954.

7. S. Moscati, ed., *An Introduction to the Comparative Grammar…*, 1964, pp. 22–46.

8. S. Moscati, *Prehistoria e storia del consonantismo ebraico antico*, ANL Memorie Scienze Morali Ser. VIII, vol. 5, 8, 1954, pp. 383–447. See also G. Garbini, "Il consonantismo dell'ebraico attraverso il tempo," AION 14 (1964), pp. 165–90; U. Rapallo, "Problemi di linguistica teorica relativi al consonantismo semítico con particolare riguardo al Medio-Ebraico e all'Aramaico Giudaico," *Archivio Glottologico Italiano*, 58 (1973), pp. 105–36.

9. W. Leslau, "The Semitic Phonetic System," in L. Kaiser, *Manual of Phonetics*, Amsterdam 1957, pp. 325–29. For a more profound discussion of the diachronic development of the phonological structure of particular Semitic languages, see the collective work edited by A. S. Kaye and P. T. Daniels [*Phonologies of Asia and Africa*, vol. 1 (Winona Lake, Ind., 1997)].

10. A. S. Kaye and P. T. Daniels, eds., *Phonologies of Asia and Africa*, vol. 1, Winona Lake, Ind., 1997.

11. R. C. Steiner, *The Case for Fricative-Laterals in Proto-Semitic*, New Haven, Conn., 1977. See also id., "Addenda to The Case for Fricative-Laterals in Proto-Semitic," in A. S. Kaye, ed., Semitic Studies in honor of Wolf Leslau …, vol. II, 1991, pp. 1499–513; R. M. Voigt, "Die Laterale im Semitischen," *WdO* 10 (1979), pp. 93–114; R. M. Voigt, "Die Laterale /ś, ṣ́, ź/ im Semitischen," *ZDMG* 142 (1992), pp. 37–52.

12. Studies such as the one by L. R. Shehadeh ("Some Observations of the Sibilants in the Second Millennium B.C.," in M. Golomb, *Working with no Data* [*Fs*. Lambdin], Winona Lake, Ind., 1987, pp. 229–46) are not concerned with the phonological value of such consonants but only with their graphic representation in the various dossiers documenting the period under consideration. Other studies are limited to one phoneme in a specific languáge. See, e.g., F. Corriente, "Ḍ-L Doublets in Classical Arabic as Evidence of the Process of Delateralization of ḍād and Development of Its Standard Reflex," JSS 23 (1978), pp. 50–55; recently G. Bohas, "Le statut du ḍād dans le lexique de l'arabe et ses implications," LLMA 1 (1999), pp. 13–28; S. Weninger, "Zur Realisation des ḍ (< *d̲) im Altäthiopischen," *WdO* 29 (1998), pp. 147–48; A.A. Ambros, "Some Observations on the Lexical Yield of the Arabic Consonants," *WZKM* 89 (1999), pp. 33–44.

13. A. R. Bomhard, "The Reconstruction of the Proto-Semitic Consonant System," in Y. L. Arbeitman, ed., *FUCUS. A Semitic/Afrasian Gathering …*, 1988, pp. 113–39.

14. A. Militarev, L. Kogan, *Semitic Etymological Dictionary* ... Vol I, Münster, 2000, pp. LXVII–CXXVIII.; Vol. II, Münster 2005, pp. LVII–LXV.

15. "Palatalization" (/x^y/), "labialization" (/x^w/) and other extensions ("emphatization" and "affrication") of the "sibilant" and "palatal" series (/š/, /ž/, /č/, /ǧ/ ...) or "(re)sonant/nasal" (/ ñ /), as well as the change of sonority evident in Modern South Arabian and Ethiopic, must also be considered as secondary processes, peculiar to those languages. Also to be taken into account is the "affricated" nature of the alveolar-dental series ("sibilants'), on which one can see the good discussion provided by R. Stempel, *Abriss einer historischen Grammatik der semitischen Sprachen*, Frankfurt-am-Main, 1999, pp. 52–54; also M.P. Streck, "Sibilants in Old Babylonian Texts of Hammurapi and the Governors in Qaṭṭunān," in ALSC, pp. 215–51.

16. G. Bohas, *Matrices, Étymons, Racines* ..., Leuven, 1997; id., *Matrices et étymons. Développements de la théorie* ..., Lausanne 2000.

17. A. Murtonen, "Brief Outline of Linguistic Analysis on an Empirical Basis," in P. Zemánek, ed., *Studies in Near Eastern Languages and Literatures*, 1996, pp. 393–414.

18. A. Murtonen, *Hebrew in its West Semitic Setting*, Part One. Part Two, Leiden, 1989/1990, pp. 9–55/1–96.

19. G. Garbini and O. Durand, *Introduzione alle lingue semitiche*, Brescia, 1994, pp. 75–90 (a very good summary); P. R. Bennett, *Comparative Semitic Linguistics. A Manual*, Winona Lake, Ind., 1998, pp. 5–12, 68–73 (an excellent description of concepts of general phonology; schematic with respect to Semitic; comparative paradigms); E. Lipiński, *Semitic Languages Outline of Comparative Grammar*, Leuven, 1997, pp. 96–177 (lengthy and well-documented description of the various categories of the Semitic phonological set; sketchy in respect of Semitic: comparative and historical); R. Stempel, *Abriss einer historischen Grammatik...*, 1999, pp. 42–68 (up-to-date and well-informed discussion); B. Kienast, *Historische Semitische Sprachwissenschaft*, Wiesbaden, 2001, pp. 25–31 (very brief); for the different Semitic languages, see A. S. Kaye and P. T. Daniels, eds., *Phonologies of Asia and Africa*, vol. 1 (Winona Lake, Ind., 1977), pp. 3–430. See also A. Torres Fernández "Sobre el consonantismo protosemítico," in *Homenaje al Profesor José María Fórneas Besteiro*, Granada 1994, vol. I, pp. 493–505; id., "Sobre el consonantismo protosemítico (II)," *MEAH* (Sección Hebreo) 54 (2005), pp. 3–26.

20. M. Cohen, *Essai comparatif sur le vocabulaire et la phonétique du chamito-sémitique*, Paris, 1947; see A. Zaborski, "La linguistique chamito-sémitique cinquante années après l'essai comparatif de Marcel Cohen," in M. Elmedlaoui, S. Gafaiti and F. Saa, eds., *Actes du 1er congrès Chamito-Sémitique de Fès* ..., 1998, pp. 23–35. See also, from the same period, A. Cuny, *Recherches sur le vocalisme, le consonantisme et la formation des racines en "nostratique," ancêtre de l'indo-européen et du chamito-sémitique*, Paris, 1943; id., *Invitation à l'étude comparative des langues indo-européennes et des langues chamito-sémitiques*, Bordeaux, 1946.

21. I. M. Djakonoff, *Afrasian Languages*, Moscow, 1988, pp. 34–40: "Chapter One: Phonology" [Bomhard 1988: 114 was unaware of this work]. For a critique of his suggestions in relation to the phonemes /p̣/, /š̱/ and /ś/ see D. O. Edzard, "Die semitohamitischen Sprachen in neuer Sicht," *RA* 61 (1967), pp. 137–49 [145–47] and D. Cohen, "Problèmes de linguistique chamito-sémitique," *RES* 40 (1972), pp. 43–68 [67–68], both of whom comment on the English edition of 1965.

22. I. M. Djakonoff, *Proto-Afrasian and Old Akkadian*, Princeton, N.J., 1990–91. See also I. Djakonoff, A. JU. Militarev, V. Porkhomosvsky and O. Stolbova, "On the Principles of Afrasian Phonological Reconstruction," *SPJASt* 1 (1993), pp. 7–15; A. Militarev and O. Stolbova, "First Approach to Comparative-Historical Phonology of Afrasian (consonantism)," in H. Mukarovsky, ed., *Proceedings of the Fifth International Hamito-Semitic Congress* ..., 1990, pp. 45–72.

23. K. Petráček, *Úvod do hamitosemitské (afroasijské) jazykovedy*. Dil. I/II [Introduction to Hamito-Semitic (Afro-Asiatic) linguistics]. Vol. I/II], Prague, 1989 [3.1.6.1.]; id., *Altägyptisch, Hamitosemitisch und ihre Beziehungen zu einigen Sprachfamilien in Afrika und Asien ...*, 1988 [2.2.1.2]. See also S. S. Majzel'," Puti razvitija kornegovo fonda semitskih jazykov [Types of basic derivation of Semitic roots], Moscow, 1983, pp. 111–18 ("Semitski Konsonantism").

24. A. R. Bomhard and J. C. Kerns, *The Nostratic Macrofamily ...*, 1994, pp. 91–108.

25. VL. E. Orel and Ol. V. Slobova, *Hamito-Semitic Etymological Dictionary...*, 1995, pp. xv–xxiv.

26. Chr. Ehret, *Reconstructing Proto-Afroasiatic (Proto-Afrasian). Vowels, Tone, Consonants, and Vocabulary*, Berkeley, Calif., 1995, pp. 7–14, 71–482.

27. G. Takács, *Etymological Dictionary of Egyptian*. Volume One. A *Phonological Introduction*, Leiden, 1999, pp. 49–322.

28. A. Dolgopolsky, *From Proto-Semitic to Hebrew Phonology. Etymological Approach in a Hamito-Semitic Perspective*, Milan, 1999. P For a general overview of this question see An. Zaborski, "Archaic Semantics in the Light of Hamito-Semitic," ZAH 7 (1994), pp. 234–44. See also M. Elmedlaoui, "Principes de la comparaison chamito-sémitique à la lumière du concept des classes phonologiques naturelles," *RFLO* 1 (1990), pp. 53–95.

29. J. H. Greenberg, "The Patterning of Root Morphemes in Semitic," *Word* 6 (1950), pp. 162–81. For a critical appraisal see P. Fronzaroli, "Statistical Methods in the Study of Ancient Near Eastern Languages," *Or* 42 (1973), pp. 97–113 (100–1). In line with this approach, H. A. Žvaniya, *Sovmestimost' soglasnyh v kornjah jazyka geéz* [The compatibility of root consonants in Geᶜez], Tbilisi, 1972, studies and quantifies consonantal incompatibility in classical Ethiopic. For Hebrew and Arabic see also M. Weitzman, "Statistical Patterns in Hebrew & Arabic Roots," JRAS 1987, pp. 15–22; id., "Hitpalgut ᶜiṣurim bašorašim ᶜibriyim wehiguyim" [The Distribution and Pronunciation of Hebrew Root Consonants], in *The 6th Hebrew Scientific European Congress*, Jerusalem, 1987, pp. 51–52. For a discussion of the problem at the morphemic level see J.-F. Prunet, "On the Validity of the Morpheme Structure Constraints," CJL 38 (1993), pp. 235–56 (esp. pp. 239f. where he discusses Greenberg's theory).

30. This may be a "proof" of primitive biliteralism (I-II) in opposition to the triliteral development (I–III, II–III)?

31. G. Herdan, "The Patterning of Semitic Verbal Roots Subjected to Combinatory Analysis," *Word* 18 (1962), pp. 262–68; cf. id., *The Calculus of Linguistic Observation*, London, 1962, pp. 47–55.

32. K. Petráček, "Die Inkompatibilität in der semitischen Wurzel in Sicht der Informationstheorie," *Rozenik Orientalistyzny* (Warsaw) 27 (1964), pp. 133–39; see also id., "Lingvistiká charakteristika semitského korene ve světle nych metod" [Linguistic characterization of the Semitic root according to new methods], *Slovo a slovocsnost* (Prague) 25 (1964), pp. 30–33. The study by M. Mrayati, "Statistical Studies of Arabic Language Roots," in *Applied Arabic Linguistics and Signal and Information Processing*, 1987, pp. 97–103, was not available to me.

33. K. Petráček, "Le dynamisme du système phonologique proto-sémitique et les problèmes de la phonologie chamito-sémitique," in J. and Th. Bynon, eds., *Hamito-Semitica ...*, 1975, pp. 161–68 (with discussion); see also K. Petráček, "Vers une conception dynamique du paradigme dans les études chamito-sémitiques," *MUSJ* 48 (1973–1974), pp. 155–63.

34. K. Petráček, "Nochmals über die Struktur der Wurzeln mit Pharyngalen im Altägyptischen und Semitischen und ihre Inkompatibilität," in Y. L. Arbeitman, ed., *FUCUS. A Semitic/ Afrasian Gathering ...*, 1988, pp. 371–77; see also K. Petráček, "Les laryngales en chamito-sémi-

tique. Essai de synthèse (résumé)," in H. Jungrathmayr and W. Müller, eds., *Proceedings of the 4th International Hamito-Semitic Congress* ..., Amsterdam and Philadelphia, 1987, pp. 65–71; K. Petráček, "Sur le rôle des modalités sonantiques dans l'élaboration de la racine sémitique," *Arabica* 34 (1987), pp. 106–10.

35. On this see K. Petráček, "Die Struktur der Altägyptischen Wurzelmorpheme mit Glottalen und Pharingalen," *ArOr* 37 (1969), pp. 341–44; C. Reintges "Egyptian Root-and-Pattern Morphology," *LinAeg* 4 (1994), pp. 213–44, on glides [/w/, /y/, /ʾ/, /r/] and the aleph in Egyptian, the OCP, monoconsonantalism, reduplication, the arrangement of the root and epenthesis; G. Conti, *Studi sul bilitterismo in semitico e in egiziano* ..., 1980, pp. 98ff. for biliteral bases in Egyptian.

36. R. M. Voigt, "Inkompatibilitäten und Diskrepanzen in der Sprache und das erste phonologische Inkompatibilitätsgesetz des Semitischen," *WdO* 12 (1981), pp. 136–72. See his bibliography and n. 48 for other works on specific languages (Bender, Krupa, Koskinen, Barkai ...); also, the bibliography cited by G. Conti, *Studi sul bilitterismo in semitico e in egiziano* ... 1980, p. 99, n. (2).

37. A. Zaborski, "Exceptionless Incompatibility Rules and Verbal Root Structure in Semitic," in G. Goldenberg and SH. Raz, eds., *Semitic and Cushitic Studies*, Wiesbaden, 1994, pp. 1–18; id., "Some Alleged Exceptions to Incompatibility Rules in Arabic Verbal Roots," in P. Zemánek, ed., *Studies in Near Eastern Languages* ..., Prague, 1996, pp. 631–58 (in fact this article had been written earlier). For the opposite view see C. Paradis and J.-F. Prunet, "On the Validity of Morpheme Structure Constraints," *CJL* 38 (1993), pp. 235–356, and the critique by G. Bohas, *Matrices, Étymons, Racines* ..., 1997, pp. 93–94, based on his own system.

38. See G. Bohas, "Le PCO et la structure des racines," in G. Bohas, ed., *Développements en linguistique arabe et sémitique*, Damascus, 1993, p. 10; reprinted in G. Bohas, "Le PCO, la composition des racines et les conventions d'association," BEO (De la grammaire de l'arabe aux grammaires des arabes) 43 (1991), pp. 119–37.

39. See J. J. McCarthy, "OCP Effects: Gemination and Antigemination," *Linguistic Inquiry* 17 (1986), pp. 207–63 [207]; id., "Formal Problems in Semitic Phonology and Morphology," Diss. M.I.T., 1979; W. Leben, "Suprasegmental Phonology," Diss. M.I.T., 1976; id., "The Representation of Tone," in V.M. Fromkin, ed., *Tone: A Linguistic Survey*, New York, 1978, pp. 177–219; J. Goldsmith, "Autosegmental Phonology," Diss. M.I.T., 1976.

40. G. Bohas, "A Diachronic Effect of OCP," *Linguistic Inquiry* 21/2 (1990), pp. 298–301 (see p. 298 for current research). For other details see J. Padgett, "OCP Subsidiary Features," *NELS* 22 (1992), pp. 335–46.

41. G. Bohas, "OCP et la persistance des représentations sous-jacentes," *Langues orientales anciennes. Philologie et linguistique* 4 (1993), pp. 35–40.

42. See R. M. Voigt, "Inkompatibilitäten und Diskrepanzen in der Sprache und das erste Inkompatibilitätsgesetz des Semitischen," *WdO* 12 (1981), pp. 136–72. See also M. Kenstowicz, "Gemination and Spirantization in Tigrinya," *Studies in Linguistic Science* 12 (1982), pp. 103–22); G. Goldenberg, "Principles of Semitic Word-Structure," in G. Goldenberg, S. Raz, eds., *Semitic and Cushitic Studies* ..., 1994, pp. 53 –55; L. E. Edzard, "The Obligatory Contour Principle and Dissimilation in Afroasiatic," *JAAL* 3 (1992), pp. 151–71; E. Buckley, "Tigrinya Root and the OCP," *PWPL* 31 (1997), pp. 19–51; see also C. Paradis and J.-FR. Prunet, "On the Validity of Morpheme Structure Constraints," *The Canadian Journal of Linguistics* 38 (1993), pp. 235–356.

43. See for example M. Kenstowicz, *Phonology in Generative Grammar*, Oxford, 1994; E. Martínez Celdrán, *Fonética*, Barcelona, 1994.

44. M. Halle, "Phonological Features," in W. Bright, ed., *Oxford International Encyclopaedia of Linguistics*, Oxford, 1991, pp. 207–12; M. Kenstowicz, *Phonology*, 1994, pp. 30, 464f., 516f. See also G. N. Clements "Lieu d'articulation des consonnes et des voyelles …," in B. Laks and A. Rialland, eds., *Architecture des représentations phonologiques*, Paris, 1993, pp. 103ff. (labial, coronal, dorsal, radical [pharyngeal]).

45. On this topic see the discussion in *GLECS* 5 (1960–1963), pp. 49–50 (A. Haudricourt-W. Leslau-M. Cohen); also E. E. Knudsen, "Cases of Free Variants in the Akkadian q Phoneme," *JCS* 15 (1961), pp. 88ff. ("What is an Emphatic Consonant?").

46. For a survey see R. Stempel, *Abriss einer historischen Grammatik …*, 1999, pp. 56–60; A. Faber, "On the Nature of Proto-Semitic *l," *JAOS* 109 (1989), pp. 33–36. On the various values of the Arabic phoneme /ḍ/ see, for example, W. L. Magee, "The Pronunciations of the Prelingual Mutes in Classical Arabic," *Word* 6 (1950), pp. 74–77.

47. See on the one hand I. M. Djakonoff, *Afrasian Languages*, Moscow, 1988, pp. 37f. A. J. Militarev and L. Kogan, *Semitic Etymological Dictionary …*, 2000, pp. XCIVff.; and on the other, P. Baldi, "Introduction: The Comparative Method," in P. Baldi, ed., *Linguistic Change and Reconstructing Methodology*, Berlin and New York, 1990, pp. 8f. ("a weakening process found in a number of languages"); R. M. Voigt, "Der Lautwandel $S^1 > H$ in wurzellosen Morphemen des Alt- und Neusüdarabischen," in G. Goldenberg and SH. Raz, eds., *Semitic and Cushitic Studies …*, 1994, pp. 19–28; id., "Drei vergleichende semitische Werke," *WdO* 31 (2000–2001), pp. 176ff.

48. As a response to Ružička see J. A. Emerton, "Some Notes on the Ugaritic Counterpart of the Arabic ghain," in G. E. Kadish and G. E. Freeman, eds., *Studies in Philology …*, Toronto, 1982, pp. 31–50. The possible change of /ẓ/ to /ġ/ in Ugaritic is a conditioned event; see J. Tropper, *Ugaritische Grammatik*, Münster, 2000, pp. 94, 114.

49. For the special phonetic nature of Egyptian /ʔ/ see G. Conti, *Studi sul bilitterismo in semitico e in egiziano …*, Florence, 1980, p. 102, as well as the remarks by L. Roussel, *La racine sémitique …*, 1952, p. 14, on the character and "warming-up nature" of the vowel, not of a true consonant (radical).

50. On this topic see for example the behavior of emphatics in Akkadian: E. E. Knudsen, art. cit. n. 45.

51. See R. Jacobson and M. Halle, *Fundamentals of Languages*, The Hague, 1980 4 (12 pairs); R. Jacobson, G. Fant and M. Halle, *Preliminaries to Speech Analysis, the Distinctive Features and their Correlates*, Cambridge, Mass., 1966. See below p. 82 for a critique of the use of this theory by Bohas.

52. See G. Bohas, *Matrices et étymons …*, 2000, pp. 139–49. See among other studies B. Morrison, *Wonderful Words. The Development of the Meaning of Hebrew antonyms from a Common Root. A study in countersense*, Johannesburg 1954; S. S. Al-Khamash, "Aḍdād - A Study of Homo-polysemous Oppositions in Arabic," Ph.D. diss., Indiana University, 1991.

53. On this topic see A. Murtonen, "Brief Outline of Linguistic Analysis on an Empirical Basis," in P. Zemánek, ed., *Studies in Near Eastern Languages …*, 1996, pp. 393f.

54. For the special behavior of this "emphatic" phoneme in Arabic see the excellent paper by J. Cantineau "Essai d'une phonologie de l'hébreu biblique," *BSLP* 46 (1950), pp. 94f.; for the dialectal variants in Arabic in this regard see C. Rabin, *Ancient West-Arabian*, London, 1951, pp. 125f.; E.E. Knudsen, "Cases of Free Variants in the Akkadian q Phoneme," *JCS* 15 (1961), p. 87 ("The substitution of phonetic [g] for ancient [q] is widely used in Arabic and attested in certain words in Akkadian"); also H. Blanc "Les deux prononciations du qôf d'après Avicenne," *Arabica* 13, 1966, 129–36; A. Zaborski, "Exceptionless Incompatibility Rules and Verbal Root Structure in Semitic," in G. Goldenberg and S. Raz, eds., *Semitic and Cushitic Studies …*, 1994, pp.

7f., and also p. 4 for a possible double pronunciation of original /g:ǧ/; also M. Sawaie, "Socio-linguistic Factors and Historical Linguistic Change: The Case of /q/ and Its Reflexes in Arabic Dialects," in R. M. Rammany and D. B. Parkinson, eds., *Investigating Arabic…*, 1994, pp. 15–39; A. S. Kaye, "Arabic Dialects and Maltese," in R. Hetzron, ed., *The Semitic Languages*, London and New York, 1997, pp. 270f. ("Qaaf"); P. Zemánek, "The Role of q in Arabic," *ArOr* 65 (1997), pp. 143–58; R. S. Mahadin, "Perspectives on the Arab Grammarian Description of the /q/ Sound," *ZAL* 34 (1997), pp. 31–52.

55. See G. Bohas, *Matrices et étymons …*, Lausanne, 2000, pp. 150f.

56. These series correspond to the "Korrelationspaar" and "Korrelationsbündel" of N. S. Trubetzkoy, *Grundzüge der Phonologie*, Göttingen 19776, pp. 75–80.

57. On this topic see E. Martínez Celdrán, *Fonética*, Barcelona, 1994, p. 162/168.

58. Cf. the summary provided by E. Martínez Celdrán, *Fonética*, pp. 159–242 (Los rasgos fonéticos segmentales), p. 181 (Resumen de los rasgos tradicionales).

59. On this see the alternation between *Indo-European /k/ and Vedic-Lithuanian /š/; O. Szemerényi, *Einführung in die vergleichende Sprachwissenschaft*, Darmstadt, 1990, p. 64.

60. A close and in some points divergent appraisal of my proposal can be found in A. Torres Fernández, "Sobre el consonantismo protosemítico (II)," *MEAH* (Hebrew section) 54 (2005), pp. 3–26.

Chapter 4

1. S. Th. Hurwitz, *Root-Determinatives in Semitic Speech. A Contribution to Semitic Philology*, New York, 1913 (reprint 1966).

2. S. Pappenheim [1802], W. Gesenius [1815], Fr[anz] Delitzsch [1838], Fr. Dietrich [1844], J. Fürst [1844], H. Ewald [1844], E. Meier [1845], M. Leguest [1858], J. Olshausen [1861], E. Renan [1861], Fr. Böttcher [1866/68], Fr.W.M. Philippi [1875], S. Fraenkel [1878], B. Stade [1879], E. König [1881], D.H. Müller [1884], Fr[iedrich] Delitzsch [1886], F. Praetorius [1888], P.A. de Lagarde [1889], A. Müller [1892], M. Lambert [1897], Th. Nöldeke [1898], J. Wellhausen [1899], A. Dillmann [1899], P. Haupt [1905f.], K. Ahrens [1910].

3. G. S. Colin, "Recherches sur les bases bilitères en arabe," *GLECS* 1 (1932), pp. 9–10; M. Gaudefroy-Demombynes, "Bases bilitères; pluriels internes, en arabe," *GLECS* 1 (1932), p. 11; E. Dhorme and M. Cohen, "Entretien sur la structure de la racine en chamito-sémitique," *GLECS* 2 (1934–1936), pp. 55–56. See also S. Strelcyn, "Les racines trilitères à première et troisième radi-cales identiques en hébreu," *GLECS* 4 (1945–1948), pp. 84–86; id., "Les racines trilitères à première et troisième radicales identiques dans les langues sémitiques de l'Ethiopie," *GLECS* 4 (1945–1948), pp. 86–88; id., "Les racines trilitères à première et deuxième radicales identiques, *GLECS* 4 (1945–1948), pp. 88–89. Lastly, a considerable number of lexemes from the semantic fields of animal names and anatomy from different AA languages witnessing the presence of prefixed, infixed and suffixed "root extenders" is presented by A. Militarev, "Root Extension and Root Formation in Semitic and Afrasian," *AuOr* 23 (2005), pp. 83–129.

4. H. B. Jušmanov, "*Struktura siemitskogo kornja*" [The structure of the root in Semitic], in *Raboty po obsčej fonetike, semitologii i arabskoj klassičeskoj morfologii* [Studies of general phonetics, Semitics and Classical Arabic morphology], Moscow, 1998, pp. 126–99. This study was initially a doctoral thesis defended in 1929 and first published in 1934 (*Struktura semitskogo korn'a i ee stadial'niy analiz* [Structure of the Semitic root and its analysis by stages], *Jazyk i myslenije* T.N.L.

1934). It seems to have been revised definitively at the end of the 1930s or the beginning of the 1940s. On this see p. 15 of A. G. Belova's introduction.

5. S. Moscati, "Il biconsonantalismo nelle lingue semitiche," *Biblica* 28 (1947), pp. 113–35; S. Moscati et al., *An Introduction to the Comparative Grammar ...*, 1964, pp. 159f. See also good, classic descriptions of the problem, for example, J. Barr, *Comparative Philology and the Text of the Old Testament*, Oxford, 1969, pp. 166ff.; P. R. Bennett, *Comparative Semitic Linguistics*, Winona Lake, Ind., 1998, pp. 62ff.

6. Gesenius, Renan, Delitzsch [Friedrich], Philippi, Lambert.

7. Brockelmann, Nöldeke, Haupt, Ružička, Möller, Ball, Meinhof.

8. A.-S. Marmarǧī, *Al-muᶜǧamiyyah al-ᶜarabiyya ᶜalā ǧaw" aṯ-ṯunā'iyyah wa-l-alsuniyyah as-sāmiyyah* [Arabic lexicography in the light of biliteralism and Semitic philology], Jerusalem, 1937. This book was unavailable to me. See also id., "Faḍl al-aṯ-ṯunā'iyyah ᶜalā-l-muᶜǧamīyyah" [The priority of biliterality in lexicography], *Maǧallat al-maǧmaᶜ al-ᶜilmī al-ᶜarabī* 28 (1953), pp. 542–51; 29 (1954), pp. 77–78.

9. See most recently A. M. R. Aristar, "The IIwy and the Vowel System of Proto-West Semitic," *AAL* 6/6 (1978–1979), pp. 209–25. On verbs with a third weak consonant, see for example J. Blau, "Marginalia Semitica III," *IOS* 7 (1977), pp. 14–32. ("4. Vestiges of a Bi-literal Origin of Verbs *III Y (W)* in Hebrew and Aramaic," pp. 27–29).

10. G. J. Botterweck, *Der Triliteralismus im Semitischen, erläutert an der Wurzel gl kl k.l*, BBB 3, Bonn, 1952; see J. Heller, "Neue Literatur zur Biliterismus-Frage," *ArOr* 27 (1959), pp. 678–82.

11. L. Roussel, *La racine sémitique vue de l'hébreu*, Nîmes, 1952.

12. B. Kienast, "Das System der zweiradikaligen Verben im Akkadischen (Ein Beitrag zur vergleichenden Semitistik)," *ZA* 21/55 (1962), pp. 138–55.

13. J. MacDonald, "New Thoughts on a Biliteral Origin for the Semitic Verb," *ALUOS* 5 (1963–1965), pp. 63–85.

14. W. von Soden, "*n* als Wurzelaugment im Semistischen," in id., *Bibel und Alter Orient*, 1985 (reprint of 1968), pp. 109–12. See also J. Sanmartín, "Über Regeln und Ausnahmen: Verhalten des vorkonsonantischen /n/ im 'Altsemitischen'," in M. Dietrich and O. Loretz, eds., *Vom Alten Orient zum Alten Testament. Festschrift für Wolfram Freiherrn von Soden...*, 1995, pp. 433–66.

15. See W. von Soden, *Grundriss der akkadischen Grammatik*, AnOr 33, Rome 1995², § 102 3).2: "Besonders oft beschreibt die zweikons. Basis lautmalende Geräusche..." (see Botterweck, above), "in anderen Fällen ist das *n* ein richtungsbestimmendes Element..."; see the critique by R. M. Voigt, *Die infirmen Verbaltypen*, Stuttgart, 1988, pp. 87f.

16. M. Fraenkel, *Zur Theorie der Lamed-He-Stämme*, Jerusalem, 1970. See also, id., *Zur Theorie der Ayin-Waw- und der Ayin-Jud-Stämme*, Jerusalem, 1970.

17. See P. Lacau, « Les verbes à troisième radicale faible ... (j) ou ... (w) en égyptien," *BIFAO* 52 (1953), pp. 7–50, a very interesting work for following the development of this Afro-Asiatic phenotype.

18. H. Wirth, *Der Aufgang der Menschheit*, 1928, p. 430 (cited by Fraenkel).

19. In the same vein, cf. his short brochure *Zur Theorie der Ayin-Waw- und der Ayin-Jud-Stämme*, 1970. These roots are also triconsonantal originally and the semi-vowels in question are weakened ancient labial or guttural consonants. The same year, F. I. Andersen, "Biconsonantal Byforms of Weak Hebrew Roots," *ZAW* 82 (1970), pp. 270–75, acknowledged the existence in Hebrew of biconsonantal roots, even though in some cases they are "alloroots" of triconsonan-

tal forms: "strong biconsonantal roots constitute a well-known set of morphemes in Northwest Semitic" (p. 272).

20. D. Cohen, "Problèmes de linguistique chamito-sémitique," *RES* 40 (1972), pp. 43–68; id., "Sémitique comparé," *AEPHE* (1975), pp. 265–75.

21. J. Kuryłowicz, *L'apophonie en sémitique*, Krakow 1961; id., *Studies in Semitic Grammar and Metrics*, Warsaw, 1972.

22. G. Jucquois, "Trois questions de linguistique sémitique," *Le Muséon* 86 (1973), pp. 475–97 (489–95: "La racine verbale en sémitique").

23. J. Lecerf, "Annonce d'une recherche en cours sur la structure des racines sémitiques," in P. Fronzaroli, ed., *Atti del secondo congresso ...*, 1978, pp. 173–74.

24. W. Eilers, "Semitische Wurzeltheorie," in P. Fronzaroli, ed., *op. cit.*, pp. 125–31.

25. See also W. Eilers, "Apokopierte Vollreduplikation," *Orientalia Suecana* 23–25 (1984–1986), pp. 85–95. And more generally, also W. Fischer, "Die Entstehung reduplizierter Wurzelmorpheme im Semitischen," in R. Contini, F. A. Pennacchietti and M. Tosco, eds., *Semitica. Serta philologica Constantino Tsereteli dicata*, Turin 1993, pp. 39–61. Another explanation of quadriliteral verbs in the spoken language (by expansion) is proposed by M. Kamil, "Zur Bildung der vierradikaligen Verben in den lebenden semitischen Sprachen," in *Studi orientalistici in onore di Giorgio Levi della Vida*, Volume I, Rome 1956, pp. 459–83.

26. These ideas are developed in his work, W. Eilers, *Die vergleichende semasiologische Methode in der Orientalistik*, Mainz 1974, pp. 21ff.

27. W. Eilers, "Die zweiradikalige Basis der semitischen Wurzel," in H. Jungrathmayr and W.W. Müller, eds., *Proceedings of the 4th International Hamito-Semitic Congress...*, 1987, pp. 511–24.

28. Z. Frajzyngier, "Notes on the R1R2R2 Stems in Semitic," *JSS* 24 (1979), pp. 1–12.

29. G. Conti, *Studi sul bilitterismo in semitico e in egiziano, 1. Il tema N1212*, QuSem 9, Florence 1980; see also Chr. Reintges, "Egyptian Root-and-Pattern Morphology," *LinAeg* 4 (1994), pp. 234f.

30. A. Ju Militarev, *Var'irovanie soglasnyh v semitskom korne* [Free variation of consonants in the Semitic root], Avtoreferat kand. Diss., Moscow 1973; id., "Čereduemost" i kombiniruemost" soglasnyh v trikonsonantnom arabskom korne" [Variation and incompatibility of consonants in the triconsonantal Arabic root], *Sbornik statej po vostočnomu jazykoznaniju* 1 (1973), pp. 58–60; id., "Issledonanie S.S. Majzelja v oblasti korneoblazobanija i semasiologii semitskih jazykov" [Study of the derivation and semasiology of the Semitic root according to S. S. Majzel'], *Narody Azii i Afriki* 1 (1973), pp. 114–21; id., "Razvitie vzgljadov na semitskij koren" [History of opinions on the root in Semitic], *Vostočnoie jazykoznanie*, Moscow 1977, pp. 19ff.; id., *Kornevye varianty v afrazijskih jazykah. Problemy rekonstrukcii* [Root variations in the Afro-Asiatic languages. Problems of reconstruction] (doctoral thesis), Moscow 1978, pp. 35–38.

31. S. S. Majzel," *Puti razvitija kornegovo fonda semitskih jazykov* [Types of derivation of the stock of Semitic roots], Moscow 1983 (Vstupitel'naja statja [Introduction by], A. J. Militarev, pp. 6–30). See also recently L. E. Kogan and A. J. Militarev, "O nekorotyh netrivial'nih semantičeskih perehodah v semitskih jasikah (novye materaly k izosemantičeskim rjadam Majzelja: anatomičeskaya leksika)" [On some important changes in the Semitic languages (new data for Maisel's isosemantic approach: anatomical vocabulary)], *Vestnik* (RGGU) 4 (2000), pp. 15–34.

32. We have to wait for the most recent works by Bohas (see below), which in his turn ignore those by Majzel'-Militarev.

33. K. Petráček, "La racine en sémitique d'après quelques travaux récents en russe," *ArOr* 53 (1985), pp. 171–73.

34. V. P. Starinin, *K voprosu o semantičeskom aspekte sravnitel'no-istoričeskogo jazykosnanija (izosemantičeskije rjady S. S. Majzelja)* [On the semantic aspect of comparative historical linguistics (the isosemantic approach of S. S. Majzel')], Moscow 1955.

35. H. B. Rosén, "On "Normal" Full Root Structure and its Historical Development," in A. Giacalone Ramat, O. Carruba and G. Bernini, eds., *Papers from the 7th International Conference ...,* 1987, pp. 535–44.

36. R. M. Voigt, *Die infirmen Verbaltypen des Arabischen und das Biradikalismus-Problem*, Stuttgart, 1988; cf. above 10, n. 15, for the reviews of this work.

37. See in this regard J. Fox, *Semitic Noun Patterns*, Winona Lake, Ind., 2003, pp. 54f.

38. Instead, M. Fraenkel (see pp. 000 above) sees these nouns as triconsonantal forms with the loss of the third consonant due to weakening (pp. 25, 37f.). M. M. Bravman, *Studies in Semitic Philology*, Leiden 1977, pp. 124–30, also considers them as triconsonantal.

39. On this see St. A. Kaufman, "Semitics: Direction and Re-Directions," in J. S. Cooper, G. M. Schwartz, eds., *The Study of the Ancient Near East ...,* 1996, p. 273.

40. C. Ehret, "The Origin of the Third Consonants in Semitic Roots: An Internal Reconstruction ," *Journal of Afroasiatic Languages* 1 (1989), pp. 109–202; C. Paradis, J.-F. Prunet, "On the Validity of Morpheme Structure Constraints," *The Canadian Journal of Linguistics* 38 (1993), pp. 241ff.

41. E. Lipiński, "Monosyllabic nominal and verbal roots in Semitic languages," in A. S. Kaye, ed., *Semitic Studies in Honor of Wolf Leslau...,*1991, pp. 927–30.

42. A. Zaborski, "Biconsonantal Roots and Triconsonantal Root Variation in Semitic: Solutions and Prospects," in A. S. Kaye, ed., *Semitic Studies in Honor of Wolf Leslau...,* 1991, pp. 1675–703 [with an extensive bibliography].

43. G. Bohas, "Le PCO, la composition des racines et les conventions d'association," *BEO* 43 (1991), pp. 119–35; essentially repeated in id., "Le PCO et la structure des racines," in G. Bohas, ed., *Développements récents en linguistique ...,* 1993, pp. 9–44.

44. G. Bohas, *Matrices, Étymons, Racines. Éléments d'une théorie lexicologique du vocabulaire arabe*, Leuven, 1997; id., *Matrices et étymons. Développements de la théorie*, Lausanne, 2000.

45. See G. Bohas, *Matrices et étymons ...,* 2000, p. 7; id., "Au-delà de la racine," in N. Anghelescu, N./A. Avram, eds., *Proceedings of the Colloquium on Arabic Linguistics*, Bucharest, 1995, pp. 29–45; id., "Pourquoi et comment se passer de la racine dans l'organisation du lexique arabe," *BSLP* 94, 1999, pp. 363–402.

46. A. R. Bomhard and J. C. Kerns, *The Nostratic Macrofamily*, 1994, pp. 109–11 ("Root Structure Patterning in Proto-Afroasiatic"); see *supra* Chap. II, n. 18.

47. D. Baggioni and P. Larcher, "Note sur la racine en indo-européen et en sémitique," in P. Cassuto and P. Larcher, eds., *La sémitologie, aujourd'hui...,* 2000, pp. 121–31.

48. Cf. G. Goldenberg, "Semitic Triradicalism and the Biradical Question," in G. Kahn, ed., *Semitic Studies in Honour of Edward Ullendorff*, Leiden/Boston 2005. For a more nuanced and broad (AA) morphological treatment of this problem see G. Gragg, "Morphology and Root Structure: a Beja Perspective," *AuOr* 23 (2005), pp. 23–33 ("... but there continue to be visible signs of RRR patterns still attracting what might be RR antecedents," p. 30). For the analogy constriction see G. Rubio, "Chasing the Semitic root: The Skeleton in the Closet," *ibd.*, pp. 45–63.

49. G. del Olmo Lete, "The Monoconsonantal Lexical Series in Semitic," *AuOr* 16 (1998), pp. 37–75.

50. It is interesting to see that "in this monoconsonantal series more than anywhere else it is thus possible to determine the significance of the syllable (/Cv/: onset and rhyme) as the actual starting point of the lexicographical (phonological and semantic) analysis" (*ibd.*, p. 38, and n. 4). The further subdivision of that unit into "consonant" and "vowel" is already an abstraction or a phonetic "compositional" analysis, useful but dangerously distorting (see above p. 49 above).

51. For a more detailed exposition of this approach, see the already quoted article of G. del Olmo Lete, "Phonetic Distribution in Semitic Binary Articulation Bases," paper delivered at the 13th Italian Meeting of Afro-Asiatic Linguistics, Udine, 21–24 May, 2007 (in press).

52. See J. Huehnergard, "New Directions in the Study of Semitic Languages," in J. S. Cooper and G. M. Schwartz, eds., *The Study of the Ancient Near East …*, 1996, p. 252: "while this is an insightful work, we may predict with confidence that it will not be the last word." For other appraisals of this work cf. above p. 10 n. 15.

53. In first position the vowel goes against the phonological rule that forbids the existence of syllables with an initial vowel. On the other hand, it is not possible to allow a radical vowel in third/fourth position, because this position has to support the vocalic morphemic and inflectional position (Djakonoff), belonging to the level of the "moneme" on a par with the thematic vowel or root consonants. In the biliteral moneme (/CvC-/) there is only room for the intensification in second or third position in a one-way projection. This means that expansion in third position (IIIy:w verbs) must be consonantal (but not in Fraenkel's sense), as shown by Ugaritic and Ethiopic, as opposed to the second position or expansion (*mediae vocalis* verbs) possibly effected by glide. Nevertheless, the degree 0 of the base could also be advocated in this case.

54. See also G. Greg, "Ge'ez (Ethiopic)," in R. Hetzron, ed., *The Semitic Languages*, London, 1997, p. 252, who speaks of "stem vowel."

55. On this topic see the works of M. Dat, a student of G. Bohas, cited above p. 12 n. 21.

56. Unfortunately I was not able to consult the article announced by G. Bohas and R. Serhane, "Conséquences lexicales de la décomposition de phonème en traits," where it is more than likely that this question was discussed in detail.

57. This can also be appreciated in the treatment of the semantics of verbal bases: if a derived base has the same meaning as the simple base it means that a secondary neutralization has occurred which has to be noted and explained.

58. Logically, it should be called "triplication" in the finished form, given that both the radical consonant and vowel-consonant must each provide a vowel: /dv-fv-f-/ // /dv-vv-f-/; this anomaly disappears with the glide.

Chapter 5

1. See, for example, L. Zgusta, *Manual of Lexicography*, The Hague and Paris, 1971; P. R. Lutzeier, *Lexikologie. Ein Arbeitsbuch*, Tübingen, 1995; of the many textbooks on semantics it is sufficient to mention S. Ullmann, *Semantics. An Introduction to the Science of Meaning*, Oxford, 1972; R. M. Kempson, *Semantic Theory*, Cambridge, 1977; J. Lyons, *Semantics I/II*, Cambridge, 1994; A. Wierzbicka, *Semantics. Primes and Universals*, Oxford and New York, 1991, very interesting for determining "semantic universals" and their etymology; although his interest is focused on the semantic category it is useful to take into account in etymological semantics the views proposed by G. Kleiber, *La sémantique du prototype. Catégories et sens lexical*, Paris, 1999; a short but excellent summary of the question, with a good bibliography, is provided by H. P. Scanlin, "The Study of Semantics in General," in W. R. Bodine, ed., *Linguistics in Biblical Hebrew*, Winona Lake, Ind., 1992, pp. 125–36. Similarly, for a brief survey of the historical aspect, see P.

Fronzaroli, "Studi sul lessico comune semitico I. – Oggetto e metodo della ricerca," *ANLR* VIII/ 19, fasc. 5–6, 1964, 155ff. For the comparative method in general, see O. Szemerényi, *Einführung in die vergleichende Sprachwissenschaft*, Darmstadt, 1989[3]; R. Katičić, *A Contribution to the General Theory of Comparative Linguistics*, The Hague, 1970; also the relevant suggestions of L. Bloomfield, *Language*, New York, 1961, pp. 297ff. ["The comparative method"]. For an historical outline of etymological studies and methods see Y. Malkiel, *Etymology*, Cambridge, 1993. – The general layout of methods and principles of historical-comparative reconstruction is taken for granted in this appraisal of specific disputed issues put forward by modern authors. They have to be looked for in the works quoted, e.g., by Szemerényi and Katičic. The problems involved here have been dealt with in the *Proceedings of the Barcelona Symposium on Comparative Semitics, 11/19–20/2004*, for example, W.R. Garr, "The Comparative Method in Semitic Linguistics," in *AuOr* 23 (2005), pp. 17–21; P. Fronzaroli, "Etymologies," *ibd.*, pp. 35–43.

2. Exceptions are E. Lipiński, *Semitic Languages* ..., Leuven, 1997, pp. 543–74 ("Lexicon," "Etymology" ...); and the manual by P. R. Bennett, *Comparative Semitic Languages...*, Winona Lake, Ind., 1998, focusing on lexicographical reconstruction.

3. H. Fleisch, *Traité de philologie arabe*, vol. I/II, Beirut, 1990, only provides a few pages (247– 59) on "La racine et son utilisation" and on "La question bilitère," but he does not deal with problems of semantics and etymology.

4. J. L. Palache, *Semantic Notes on the Hebrew Lexicon*, Leiden, 1959. In fact, the method was developed, even though it went unnoticed, by S. S. Majzel," *Put razvitiya kornevogo fonda semitskikh yasikov*, 1983, pp. 187ff. ("izosemantičeskije rjady"), see above p. 65. In chap. 17, Majzel" analyses fifteen examples of "semantic chains" (or "isosemantic rows"), common to Semitic and non-Semitic languages, and in chap. 18 he analyzes more extensively thirteen others peculiar to the Semitic languages. For an up-to-date development of his thesis see V. P. Starinin, *Kvoprosu o semantčeskom aspekte sravnitel'noistorčeskogo jazykosnanija (izosemantičeskije rjady S. S. Majzelja)* [On the semantic aspect of comparative-historical linguistics (the isosemantic approach of S. S. Majzel')] (Sovietskoje jazykoznanije 4), Moscow, 1955; L. E. Kogan, A. Yu. Militarev, "Nekorotikh netribiyalnikh semantitseckikh pieriejodakh b semitsskikh yasikakh (novi ie matierali k isosemantidskim riadam Maiselya: anatomidskaya liesika)" [Certain Non-trivial shifts in Semitic languages (new data for Maisel's isosemantic approach: anatomical vocabulary)], *Viestnik* (RGGU) 2000, pp. 15–34, where the authors analyze seven of the "semantic chains" in the various Semitic languages (parts of the body); revised version idd., "Non-trivial semantic shifts in Semitic. S. Maisel's "isosemantic series" applied to anatomic lexicon," in *Fs. Fronzaroli*, pp. 286–300; on this topic see also A. (Y), Militarev, L. Kogan, *Semitic Etymological Dictionary...*, Münster, 2000, pp. L; and W. Leslau, "Amharic Parallels to Semantic Developments in Biblical Hebrew," *EI* 20 (1975) (*Fs.* N. Glueck), pp. 113–16.

5. The title of the work was: *Etymologische en Semasiologische Studiën over het Hebreeuwsche (Semietische) lexicon onder vergelijking met Indogermaanschen talen*. The author worked on the manuscript until his death in the concentration camp of Theresienstadt, where he disappeared at the moment of liberation; cf. J. L. Palache, *Semantic Notes on the Hebrew Lexikon*, Leiden, 1959, Editor's Preface (R. J. Zwi Werblowsky, not H. Rabin, as M. Masson states, n. 1). See also J. Barr, *The Semantics of Biblical Language*, Oxford, 1969, pp. 118, 133 [302], who cites a study by Palache, which I have not been able to consult.

6. C. Cohen, "The "Held Method" for Comparative Semitic Philology," *JANES* 19 (1989), pp. 9–23 (principles four and seven). The method is directed more at philological interpretation of the text and exhibits the well-known distrust of etymology as a source of "meaning," as already expressed by J. Barr, in a systematic way. The article collects together the sixty-four "inter-dialectal distributions" proposed by Held.

7. On linguistic universals in general, see the well-known treatment by J. H. Greenberg, *Language Universals*, The Hague, 1966; and the collective works also edited by J. H. Greenberg, ed., *Universals of Languages*, Cambridge, Mass., 1966[2]; id., *Universals of Human Language*, 4 vols., Stanford, 1978. In the first of these works (*Universals of Languages*) the contributions by U. Weinreich, "On the Semantic Structure of Language" (pp. 142–216) and S. Ullmann, "Semantic Universals" (pp. 217–62) merit particular attention.

8. See E. Ullendorff, "Comparative Semitic," in G. Levi della Vida, ed., *Linguistica semitica: presente e futuro*, Rome, 1961, pp. 13–32.

9. H. Birkeland, "Some reflections on Semitic and structural semantics," in M. Halle, H. Lunt, H. McLean, C. H. van Schooneveld, eds., *For Roman Jakobson. Essays on the occasion of his sixtieth birthday…*, The Hague, 1956, pp. 44–51 (he defends the use of the structuralist method in Semitic linguistics, especially in phonology).

10. J. Barr, *The Semantics of Biblical Hebrew*, Oxford, 1961 (repr. 1969). Many other "biblical" scholars have also tackled this problem (Cremer; Snaith, Torrance, Pedersen, Macnicol, Oepke, Jacob, Gretner-Fichtner, Strathmann, Barth …) and Barr mentions them in passing.

11. J. Barr, *Comparative Philology and the Text of the Old Testament*, Oxford, 1968; the comments by S. Segert in "Hebrew Bible and Semitic Comparative Lexicography," *VTS* 17 (1969), pp. 204–11, have a similar approach.

12. These chains correspond to more or less universal archetypes of semantic derivation: they are not produced by the "throat" but by the "sensitive imagination" which perceives and treats reality in an allusive manner, given its pluriform nature and social conditioning. See in this connection A. Hurtviz, "Continuity and Innovation in Biblical Hebrew: The Case of 'Semantic Change' in Postexilic Writings," in T. Muraoka, ed., *Studies in Ancient Hebrew Semantics*, Louvain 1995, pp. 1–10.

13. See D. Cohen, *Dictionnaire des racines …*, Leuven, 1996, fasc. 6, pp. xiv.

14. See U. Eco, *Il Segno*, Milan, 1973, pp. 22ff., 132ff. Of course, the "semantic" plurality of the linguistic sign, in principle unlimited polysemy, dealt with by semantics as a theory of the ambiguous use of signs, is a diachronic and derived semantics.

15. J. F. A. Sawyer, *Semantics in Biblical Research. New methods of defining Hebrew words for salvation* (Studies in Biblical Theology II, 24), London, 1972; previously id., J. F. A. Sawyer, "Root-Meanings in Hebrew," *JSS* 12, 1967, 37–50; see also B. Kedar, *Biblische Semantik*, Stuttgart, 1981; P. Swiggers, "Recent Developments in Linguistic Semantics and Their Application to Biblical Hebrew," *ZAH* 6 (1993), pp. 211–25. See also C. Dohmen, " *napḫar mātāti šūt šannâ lišānu*. Zur Frage der Semantik in der Semitistik," *BN* 47 (1989), pp. 13–34, a good discussion of the problem in general in respect of semantic analysis of the lexeme /ġ/ᶜlm(t)/.

16. J. C. Greenfield, "Etymological Semantics," *ZAH* 6 (1993), pp. 26–37, with the critical response to this typological division by B. Albrektson, ibid., pp. 28–33.

17. J. Barr, "Etymology and the Old Testament," in A. S. van der Woude, ed., *Language and Meaning, Studies in Hebrew and Biblical Exegesis*, OTS 19, Leiden, 1974, pp. 1–28; see also J. Barr, "Scope and Problems in the Semantics of Classical Hebrew," *ZAH* 6 (1993), pp. 3–14, where there is a similar approach.

18. P. Fronzaroli, "Studi sul lessico comune semitico. I. Oggetto e metodo della ricerca. II. Anatomia e fisiologia," *ANLR* 19/5–6 (1964), pp. 155–72, 243–80.

19. P. Fronzaroli, "Réflexions sur la paléontologie linguistique," in A. Caquot and D. Cohen, eds., *Actes du premier congrès international…*, The Hague and Paris, 1974, pp. 173–80. See also P.

Fronzaroli and G. Garbini, "Paleontologia semitica: il patrimonio lessicale semitico commune," in R. Gusmani, J. Knobloch et al., ed., *Palaeontologia lingüística...*, Brescia 1977, pp. 155–69.

20. P. Fronzaroli, "Problems of a Semitic Etymological Dictionary," in P. Fronzaroli, ed., *Studies on Semitic Lexicography...*, Florence, 1973, pp. 1–24 [2, 17].

21. P. Fronzaroli, "On the Common Semitic Lexicon and its Ecological and Cultural Background," in J. and Th. Bynon, eds., *Hamito-Semitica,* The Hague and Paris, 1975, pp. 43–53. See above n. 18.

22. G. Bergsträsser, *Introduction to the Semitic Languages*, Winona Lake, Ind., 1988, pp. 209ff.

23. D. Cohen, "Le vocabulaire de base sémitique et le classement des dialectes méridionaux," *Semitica* 11 (1961), pp. 55–84.

24. P. Fronzaroli, G. Garbini, "Paleontologia Semitica: il patrimonio lessicale semitico commune," in R. Gusmani, J. Knobloch et al., eds., *Palaeontologia Linguistica...*, Brescia, 1977, pp. 155–72; see below p. 107.

25. C. T. Hodge, "The Linguistic Cycle," *Language Science* 13 (1970), pp. 1–7.

26. C. T. Hodge, "A Set of Postulates for Comparative Linguistics," in A. Makkai, V. B. Makkai, eds., *The First LACUS Forum ...*, Columbia, 1975, pp. 209–16. In spite of its title, R. Hetzron, "Two Principles of Genetic Reconstruction," *Lingua* 38, 1976, pp. 89–108, is more concerned with the principles governing the classification of (Semitic) languages: archaic heterogeneity and shared morpholexical innovation; see also id., "La division del langues sémitiques" in *APCILSChS*, pp. 181–94.

27. D. Cohen, "La lexicographie comparée," in P. Fronzaroli, ed., *Studies on Semitic Lexicography*, QuSem 2, Florence, 1973, pp. 183–208.

28. D. Cohen, "A propos d'un dictionnaire des racines sémitiques," in P. Fronzaroli, ed., *Atti del secondo Congresso internazionale ...*, Florence, 1978, pp. 87–100. See also l'Avant-propos to his *Dictionnaire des racines sémitiques ...*, Paris, La Haye and Leuven 1970, pp. vii–ix.

29. W. Eilers, *Die vergleichend-semasiologische Methode in der Orientalistik*, Wiesbaden 1974.

30. On this topic see most recently G. Bohas, "Du concret à l'abstrait, sur les deux rives de la Méditerranée," *LLMA* 3 (2002), pp. 85–105.

31. K. Petráček, "Le dynamisme du système phonologique proto-sémitique et les problèmes de la phonologie chamito-sémitique," in J. and Th. Bynon, eds., *Hamito-Semitica*, The Hague and Paris, 1975, pp. 161–68.

32. K. Petráček, "La méthodologie du chamito-sémitique comparé: état, problèmes, perspectives," in J. Bynon, ed., *Current Progress in Afro-Asiatic Linguistics*, Amsterdam and Philadelphia, 1984, pp. 423–61.

33. G. Garbini, "Problemi di metodo relativi alla comparazione linguistica semitica: cento anni dopo," *AION* 37 (1977), pp. 113–24; see previous n. and also id., "Configurazione dell'unità linguistica semitica," in *Le 'protolingue'...*, Brescia, 1965, pp. 119–38.

34. G. Garbini, *Le lingue semitiche. Studi di storia linguistica*, Naples, 1972.

35. See V. Pisani, "Indoeuropeo e camito-semitico," *AION* 3 (1949), pp. 333–39; also *supra* nn. 11–12 (his own paleontological linguistic analysis seems to fail here).

36. See specifically G. Garbini, O. Durand, *Introduzione alle lingue semitiche*, Brescia, 1994, pp. 15ff., 131ff.

37. P. Baldi, "Introduction: The Comparative Method," in P. Baldi, ed., *Linguistic Change and Reconstruction Methodology*, Berlin and New York, 1990, pp. 1–13.

38. S. J. Lieberman, "Summary report: Linguistic Change and Reconstruction in the Afro-Asiatic Languages," ibid., pp. 565–75. A more focused study by the same author, "The regularity of Sound Change: A Semitistic Perspective," ibid., pp. 697–721 (on the application of the modern comparative [Indo-European] method to the Semitic family, specifically in respect of the regularity of phonetic change, with the names for numbers ('one') as an example: "neither too irregular nor absolutely regular"; the existence of "biforms" must be acknowledged) (pp. 211ff.).

39. H. M. Hoenigswald, "Is the 'Comparative' Method General or Family-specific?," ibid. pp. 375–83.

40. W.S. LaSor, "Proto-Semitic: Is the Concept No Longer Valid?," *Maarav* 5–6 (1990), pp. 189–205.

41. M. Masson, "Quelques parallélismes sémantiques en relation avec la notion de 'couler,'" in A. S. Kaye, ed., *Semitic Studies...*, Wiesbaden, 1991, pp. 1024–41. He even suggests using "semantic parallelism" to resolve the problem of triliteral "roots" with two consonants in common (pp. 1039–41); see also id., "À propos des parallélismes sémantiques," *GLECS* 29–30, 1984–1986, pp. 221–43.

42. On this see the pattern proposed by G. Bohas, *Matrices et étymons...*, Lausanne, 2000, pp. 69ff., based on the seme "to strike" / "to cut."

43. A. Faber, "Innovation, Retention, and Language Comparison: An Introduction to Historical Comparative Linguistics," in W. R. Bodine, ed., *Linguistics in Biblical Hebrew...*, Winona Lake, Ind., 1992, pp. 191–207.

44. L. Edzard, *Polygenesis, Convergence, and Entropy; An Alternative Model of Linguistic Evolution Applied to Semitic Linguistics*, Wiesbaden, 1998. In spite of its title, a second publication edited by L. Edzard, *Tradition and Innovation. Norm and Deviation in Arabic and in Semitic Linguistics* (Wiesbaden, 1999), deals just with specific problems chiefly related to Arabic.

45. R. Voigt, "Rekonstruktion oder Konvergenz? Zur Methodik in den semitischen Sprachwissenschaft?," *OLZ* 97 (2002), pp. 5–26.

46. Cf. also pp. 28, 29, 35, 36f., 38!, 44–45, 48–50[!]. For further details see the review by Voigt cited in the preceding footnote.

47. The reference to "proto-Arabic/Turkish" cannot be taken seriously, not even as an example.

48. Cf. my article: "The Genetic Historical Classification of the Semitic Language," in L. Kogan ed., *Studia Semitica* (*Fs.* A. Militarev) (Orientalia: Papers of the Oriental Institute, 3), Moscow 2003, pp. 18–52; cf. *infra* p. 125.

49. Once again we can refer to Voigt's critique (above n. 45) for more details.

50. The survey in K. J. Cathcart ("Some Nineteenth and Twentieth Century Views on Comparative Semitic Lexicography," in M. Kropp, A. Wagner, eds., "*Schnittpunkt*" *Ugarit*, Frankfurt a. Main, 2000, pp. 1–8) is not relevant to our purpose. He established the success of Hincks, for the correlation between Hebrew and Akkadian that he suggested and developed as well as Dahood's, between Ugaritic and Hebrew. However, he is opposed to Barr's theses. A very good survey of the question of etymology, from the aspects of both phonology and semantics (even though focused on the relationship between Ugaritic and Arabic) is provided by F. Renfroe, *Arabic and Ugaritic Lexicography*, doctoral thesis. Yale University, 1989, pp. 7–28.

51. Baron Carra de Vaux, *Tableau des racines sémitiques (Arabe-Hébreu), accompagnées de comparaisons*, Paris, 1944.

52. V. M. Illič Svityč, *Opyt sravnenija nostratčeskih jazykov (semitohamitskij, karvel'skij, indo-evropejskij, ural'skij, dravidijskij, altajskij)* [Comparative essay on the Nostratic languages: Hamito-Semitic, Kartvelian, Indo-European, Uralic, Dravidian, Altaic], 3 vols., Moscow, 1971.

53. S. Levin, *Semitic and Indo-European. The Principal Etymologies with Observations on Afro-Asiatic*, Amsterdam and Philadelphia, 1995.

54. Cf. A. R. Bomhard, "Linguistic Methodology and Distant Linguistic Comparison," *Mother Tongue* 20 (1993), pp. 1–4, who sketches in summary fashion the principles of comparative studies in general and their application to the specific question of long-range comparison, in anticipation of his study of "Nostratic" (see below); A. R. Bomhard, J. C. Kerns, *The Nostratic Macrofamily. A Study in Distant Linguistic Relationship*, Berlin and New York, 1994.

55. For a general survey of Hamito-Semitic linguistics in recent years, not only from the aspect of lexicography, see A. Zaborski, "La linguistique chamito-sémitique cinquante années après l'essai comparatif de Marcel Cohen," in M. El Medlaoui, S. Gafaiti and F. Saa, eds., *Actes du 1er congrès Chamito-Sémitique de Fès …*, Fès, 1998, pp. 23–35.

56. M. Cohen, *Essai comparatif sur le vocabulaire et la phonétique du chamito-sémitique*, Paris, 1947.

57. See J. H. Greenberg, *The Languages of Africa*, Bloomington and The Hague, 1963 ("Afroasiatic Comparative Word List," pp. 51–64); C. T. Hodge, "Some Afroasiatic Etymologies," *Anthropological Linguistics* 10 (1968), pp. 19–39; O. Rössler, "Libysch-Hamitisch-Semitisch," *Oriens* 17 (1964), pp. 199–216; W. W. Müller, "Beiträge zur hamito-semitischen Wortvergleichung," in J. and Th. Bynon, eds., *Hamito-Semitica …*, The Hague and Paris, 1975, pp. 63–74 (with discussion).

58. See K. Petráček, "La méthodologie du chamito-sémitique comparé: état, problèmes, perspectives," in J. Bynon, ed., *Current Progress in Afro-Asiatic Linguistics*, Amsterdam and Philadelphia, 1984, pp. 423–61; see above. Also A. L. Kaye and P. T. Daniels, "Comparative Afroasiatic and General Linguistics," *Word* 43 (1992), pp. 429–58 (rev. art. of H. Jungrathmayr and W. W. Müller, eds., *Proceedings of the 4th International Hamito-Semitic Congress…*, Amsterdam and Philadelphia, 1987).

59. A. G. Belova, I. M. Djakonoff, et al., "Srvanitel'no-istoričeskii slavar' afrazijskih jaazykov. Vypyski 1–3" [historical and comparative Afro-Asiatic vocabulary], *PPPIK, XV GNS,* čast" …IV, Moscow, 1981 / *PPPIK, XVI GNS,* čast' III, Moscow, 1982 / *PPPIK, XIX GNS,* čast' III, Moscow, 1986.

60. I. M. Djakonoff et al., "Historical Comparative Vocabulary of Afrasian," *SPJASt* 2 (1993), pp. 5–28; *SPJASt* 3 (1994), pp. 5–26; *SPJASt* 4 (1995), pp. 7–38; *SPJASt* 5 (1995), pp. 5–32.

61. I. M. Djakonoff, "Project of a Comparative Historical Lexicon of Afroasian Languages," in P. Fronzaroli, ed., *Atti del secondo Congresso internazionale …*, Florence, pp. 43–44; id., "Letter to the Conference," in J. Bynon, ed., *Current Progress in Afro-Asiatic Linguistics …*, Amsterdam and Philadelphia, 1984, p. 3.

62. V. E. Orel and O. V. Stolbova, *Hamito-Semitic Dictionary. Materials for a Reconstruction*, Leiden, 1995.

63. See I. M. Djakonoff and L. Kogan, "Addenda et Corrigenda to Hamito-Semitic Etymological Dictionary by V. Orel and O. Stolbova," *ZDMG* 146 (1996), pp. 25–38; also I. M. Djakonoff, "Some Reflections on the Afrasian Linguistic Macrofamily," *JNES* 55 (1996), pp. 293–94; A. Zaborski, "La linguistique chamito-sémitique cinquante années …," pp. 27–28.

64. C. Ehret, *Reconstructing Proto-Afroasiatic (Proto-Afrasian). Vowels, Tone, Consonants, and Vocabulary*, Berkeley, 1995.

65. See A. Zaborski, *art. cit.*, p. 28: "all in all, I find that Ehret's dictionary is the worst of them all and is even harmful."

66. G. Takács, *Etymological Dictionary of Egyptian. Volume One. A Phonological Introduction. Volume Two. b-, p-, f-*, Leiden, 1999; see V. Blažek, "Etymological Dictionary of Egyptian" (Review Article, vol. I), *ArOr* 69 (2001), pp. 624–32; H. Satzinger, "Historische ägyptische Phonologie und die afroasiatische Komparatistik" (Rezensionsartikel), *WZKM* 93, 2003, 211–25.

67. On this see S. Segert, "Considerations on Semitic Comparative Lexicography," *ArOr* 28 (1960), pp. 470–80 ("Past and Future of Semitic Comparative Lexicon," pp. 470–80); D. Cohen, "La lexicographie comparée," in P. Fronzaroli, ed., *Studies on Semitic Lexicography*, Florence, 1973, pp. 183–208.

68. I. Guidi, "Della sede primitiva dei popoli semitici," *ANLM* 3 (1878–1879), pp. 566–615.

69. G. Bergsträsser, *Introduction to the Semitic Languages*, Winona Lake, Ind., 1988, pp. 209–23 ("Common-Semitic Words").

70. P. R. Bennett, *Comparative Semitic Linguistics. A Manual*, Winona Lake, Ind., 1998, pp. 127–249 ("Wordlist A I").

71. A. Guillaume, *Hebrew and Arabic Lexicography. A Comparative Study*, Leiden, 1965 (offprint from *Abr-Nahrain* 1–4 [1959–1965]). An example of a partial study is M. Held, "Studies in Comparative Semitic Lexicography," in H. Güterbock, T. Jacobsen, eds., *Studies in Honor of Benno Landsberger…*, Chicago, 1965, pp. 395–406 (on three Akkadian-Hebrew-Ugaritic lexemes). To a limited extent, the *Dictionary of the North-West Semitic Inscriptions*, Leiden, 1995, by J. Hoftijzer and K. Jongeling (the new edition of the old *Dictionnaire des inscriptions ouest-sémitiques*, Leiden, 1965, by C. Jean and J. Hoftijzer) can be considered a comparative dictionary, given that all the citations are listed under the same consonantal "root." Dictionaries of particular Semitic languages (e.g., Koehler-Baumgartner's of Hebrew and Aramaic and Leslau's of Geʿez and Gurage) offer comparative and even etymological material which can be very useful.

72. S. Segert, "Considerations on Semitic Comparative Lexicography," *ArOr* 28 (1960), pp. 470–80 (cf. *ZDMG* Suppl. I, Teil 2 [1969], pp. 714–17); P. Fronzaroli, "Problems of a Semitic Etymological Dictionary," in P. Fronzaroli, ed., *Studies on Semitic Lexicography*, Florence, 1973, p. 24 (on pp. 20–24 he provides a sample of the project); D. Cohen, "La lexicographie compare," ibid., pp. 202.

73. P. Fronzaroli, "Studi sul lessico comune semitico. I. Oggetto e metodo della ricerca. II. Anatomia e fisiologia," *ANLR* 19 (1964), pp. 155–72, 243–80; id., "Studi sul lessico comune semitico. III. I fenomeni naturali. IV. La religione," ibid. 20 (1965), pp. 135–50; 246–69; id., "Studi sul lessico comune semitico. V. La natura selvatica," ibid. 23 (1968), pp. 267–303; id., "Studi sul lessico comune semitico. VI. La natura domestica," ibid. 24 (1969), pp. 1–36; id., "Studi sul lessico comune semitico. VII. L'alimentazione," ibid. 26 (1971), pp. 603–42. Also P. Fronzaroli, "Il mare e i corsi d'acqua nel lessico comune semitico," *BALM* 8–9 (1966–1967), pp. 205–13; and his students, for example P. Marrassini, *Formazione del lessico dell'edilizia militare nel semitico di Siria*, Florence, 1971; and other studies limited to specific semantic fields in several languages.

74. See *art. cit.*, n. 61 [I. Past and Future of Semitic Comparative Lexikon]; also by the same author: "Tendenzen und Perspektiven der vergleichenden semitischen Sprachwissenschaft," in M. Fleischhammer, ed., *Studia Orientalia in memoriam Caroli Brockelmann*, Halle-Wittenberg, 1968, pp. 167–73 [p. 169 for Brockelmann's project]; id., "Hebrew Bible and Semitic Comparative Lexicography," *VTS* 17 (1969), pp. 204–11; S. Segert and J. R. Hall, "A Computer Program for Analysis of Words According to Their Meaning (Conceptual Analysis of Latin Equivalents for the Comparative Dictionary of Semitic Languages)," *Or* 42 (1973), pp. 149–52 [I. Preparation of the Materials for the Comparative Dictionary of Semitic Languages"].

75. S. Segert, "A Preliminary Report on a Comparative Lexicon of North-West Semitic Languages," in *Trudy dvadcat' pjatogo meždunarodnogo kongressa vostokovedov, Sekcija IV*[e] [Proceedings of the 25th International Congress of Orientalists. Section IV]..., Moscow, 1962, pp. 383–85; id., "Die Arbeit am vergleichenden Wörterbuch der semitischen Sprachen mit Hilfe des Computers IBM 1410," *ZDMG Suppl.* I/2 (1969), pp. 714–17; id., "Hebrew Bible and Semitic Comparative Lexicography," *VTS* 17 (1969), pp. 204–11.

76. S. Segert, "A Computer Program for Analysis of Words According to Their Meaning (Conceptual Analysis of Latin Equivalents for the Comparative Dictionary of Semitic Languages)," *Or* 42 (1973), pp. 149–57.

77. D. Cohen [F. Bron, A. Lonnet], *Dictionnaire des racines sémitiques ou attestées dans les langues sémitiques*, Paris, La Haye and Leuven 1970–. For a critique see W. von Soden, *Or* 42 (1973), pp. 142–48.

78. See D. Cohen, "La lexicographie comparée," in P. Fronzaroli, ed., *Studies on Semitic Lexicography*, Florence, 1973, pp. 202–3; id., "À propos d'un dictionnaire des racines sémitiques," in P. Fronzaroli, ed., *Atti del secondo congresso internazionale* ..., Florence, 1978, pp. 87–100; id., "Sémitique comparé," *AEPHE* 1975, pp. 265–75; id., "Racines," in J. Drouin, A. Roth, eds., *À la croisée des études libyco-berbères*, Paris, 1993, pp. 161–75. See also the introductions to fascicules 1 and 6 (vols. 1 and 2).

79. W. von Soden, "Ein semitisches Wurzelwörterbuch: Probleme und Möglichkeiten," *Or* 42 (1973), pp. 142–48.

80. A. (J.) Militarev and L. Kogan, *Semitic Etymological Dictionary.* Vol. I. *Anatomy of Man and Animals* (AOAT 278/1), Münster, 2000; Vol. II. *Animal Names* (AOAT 278/2), Münster 2005. The very interesting second thesis by A. J. Militarev, *Principy semitskoj prajazykovoj rekonstrukcii, etimologii i genetičeskoj klassifikacii* [Principles of Proto-Semitic reconstruction, etymology and genetic classification], Avtoreferat Diss. Rossijkij gosudarstvennyj gumanitarnyj Universitet 2001, could not be taken into consideration here. It reuses and reworks fundamentally the ideas sketched out in the introduction to the dictionary.

81. For a bibliography on "proto-language and reconstruction" see G. del Olmo Lete, "Comparative Semitics: Classification and Reconstruction. An Organized Bibliography," *AuOr* 20 (2003), pp. 95–135.

82. See Djakonoff's opinion, above; and in general on the reconstruction of Proto-Semitic, S. Moscati, "Sulla ricostruzione del protosemitico," *RSO* 35 (1960), pp. 1–10; K. Petráček, "La méthodologie du chamito-sémitique comparé: état, problemes, perspectives," in J. Bynon, *Current Progress in Afro-Asiatic Linguistics* ..., Amsterdam and Philadelphia 1984, pp. 423–61.

83. See M. Cohen, *Essai comparatif* ..., Paris, 1947, pp. 53–54. Something similar can be said in respect of the classification of languages. The opposition between the "generative" and "diffuse" methods is completely unreal. On this topic see G. del Olmo Lete, "The Genetic Historical Classification of the Semitic Languages. A Synthetic Approach," in L. Kogan, ed., *Studia Semitica (Fs. A. Ju. Militarev)*, Moscow 2003, pp. 18–52.

84. See the example of the etymological dictionary of Greek by E. Boisacq, *Dictionnaire étymologique de la langue grecque*, Heidelberg, 1950[4], which to some extent precedes Pokorny's Indo-European (etymological) dictionary, whereas the book with the same title by P. Chantraine (Paris 1968) is more of an "historical" dictionary.

85. I. M. Djakonoff, "On Root Structure in Proto-Semitic," in J. and Th. Bynon, eds., *Hamito-Semitica.* ..., The Hague and Paris, 1975, pp. 133–53; see also ibid. pp. 26; and id., "Problems of Root Structure in Proto-Semitic," *ArOr* 38 (1970), pp. 453, the basic essay that refers to Afro-Asiatic, even excluding it explicitly as unsuitable, late, not documented, etc.

86. For Hebrew see most recently S. Levin, "In what sense was Hebrew a primordial language?," *GL* 29 (1989), pp. 221–27; for Arabic, A. Roman, "De la langue arabe comme un modèle général de la formation des langues sémitiques," *Arabica* 28 (1981), pp. 127–61.

87. On this topic see K. Petráček, "La méthodologie du chamito-sémitique comparé: état, problèmes, perspectives," in J. Bynon, ed., *Current progress in Afro-Asiatic Linguistics …*, Amsterdam and Philadelphia, 1984, pp. 423–62 (426); A. Zaborski, "The Problem of Archaism in Classical Arabic" (summary), in H. Jankowskiego, ed., *Z mekki do poznania …*, Poznan´, 1998, pp. 282f.; A. Zaborski, "The Position of Arabic within the Semitic Dialect Continuum," in K. Dévényi and T. Iványi, eds., *Proceedings of the Colloquium on Arabic Grammar*, Budapest, 1991, pp. 365–75; Garbini's view, set out above, and in general the works provided by K. Dévényi and T. Iványi, eds., *Proceedings of the Colloquium on Arabic Lexicology and Lexicography Budapest, 1–7 September 1993*, Part I, Budapest, 1993.

88. See T. Theillig, "Polysemie im Arabischen: Beobachtungen am arabischen Verb," in D. Blohm, ed., *Studien zur arabischen Linguistik…*, Berlin, 1989, pp. 81–92. In fact, Semitic homophony, which seems so shocking, is to a large extent Arabic homophony, historically conditioned; see (P. Fronzaroli,) G. Garbini, "Paleontologia semitica: il patrimonio lessicale semitico comune alla luce dell'affinità linguistica camito-semitica [b)]," in R. Gusmani, J. Knobloch et al., eds., *Paleontologia linguistica …*, Brescia, 1977, pp. 167ff.; A. G. Belova, "Omonimija v arabskom korneslove i struktura semitskogo kornja" [Homonymy in radical Arabic words and the structure of the Semitic root], in *Jazyki Azii i Afrik*, Moscow, 1998, pp. 11–15; id., "Les racines arabes homonymes comme résultat des changements historiquess," in S. Leder, ed., *Studies in Arabic and Islam. Proceedings of the 19ᵗʰ Congress. Union Européenne des Arabisants et Islamisants, Halle 1998*, Leuven / Paris / Sterling, Va., 2002, pp. 349–56.

89. See (Fronzaroli -) Garbini, *art. cit.*, p. 164; S. Lieberman, "Summary Report: Linguistic Change and Reconstruction in the Afro-Asiatic languages," in P. Baldi, ed., *Linguistic Change…*, Berlin and New York, 1990, p. 576; P. Larcher, "Métamorphose de la linguistique arabe," in P. Cassuto and P. Larcher, eds., *La sémitologie, aujourd'hui…*, Aix-en-Provence 2000, p. 185.

90. This problem was the subject of my own study, cited in n. 83, to which I refer.

91. See K. Petráček, "La méthodologie du chamito-sémitique comparé: état, problèmes, perspectives," in J. Byron, ed., *Current Progress in Afro-Asiatic Linguistics…*, Amsterdam and Philadelphia, pp. 426f., 432, 434ff. (language as a diachronic-dynamic system).

92. On this subject see, for example, I. M. Djakonoff, "Some Reflections on the Afrasian Linguistic Macrofamily," *JNES* 55 (1996), pp. 293–94; E. Lipiński, *Semitic Languages*, Leuven, 1997, p. 43; A.R. Bomhard, "The Root in Indo-European and Afroasiatic," in P. Zemánek, ed., *Studies in Near Eastern Languages…*, Prague, 1999, pp. 161–70 (167).

93. On this topic see the bibliographical bulletin mentioned in n. 81.

94. This and other aspects of my "historico-genetic" proposal are laid out in the article, "The Genetic Historical Classification of the Semitic Languages. A Synthetic Approach," in L. Kogan, ed., *Studia Semitica (Fs. A. Ju. Militarev)*, Moscow 2003, pp. 18–52, on different bases from Garbini's, who must be acknowledged as the father and persistent defender of the "Amorite" thesis from a synchronic language perspective (see, for example, his book *Le lingue semitiche*, Naples, 1972, *passim*). It may seem "bizarre" to supporters of a grammatical-morphological approach, used to work with isoglosses and shared innovations (cf. *infra* Huehnergard, "Features of Central Semitic") as the last but ambiguous arguments. My proposal follows on the steps of the Russian school (Djakonoff and disciples) of which A. Militarev's paper, "Genetic Classification of the Semitic Family according to Lexicostatics" (to appear in *Proceedings of the II Workshop on Comparative Semitics, Sitges May 31 – June 2, 2006*) is another approach, method-

ologically very distant but with a similar result. In this perspective "Amorite" is a working hypothesis with solid historical support, although the linguistic witnesses are difficult to discern. The Mari material, on which the Paris team continues to work steadily, is a sure pledge. Canaanite and Aramaic are historically involved in this perspective in an inescapable way. In this connection, a subdivision of NWS into Aramaic/Ugaritic/Canaanite on the same level, as put forward by J. Fox (*Semitic Noun Patterns*, p. 49) is for me unacceptable and with difficulty can be labelled "genetic." Here the perspective of time depth and ethnical history is completely absent. As for Akkadian, I do not know of any serious Assyriologist who denies its branching into Babylonian and Assyrian, although this presents serious problems as an almost exclusively administrative language; cf. J. Huehnergard, "Semitic Languages," in *CANE*, 4, pp. 2118; id., "Proto-Semitic and Proto-Akkadian," in *ALSC*, pp. 4. In the long run however, if we assume "West"-Semitic to mean "Amorite," the two diagrams are not so apart from each other. For a very recent criticism and modification of Hetzron's diagram cf. J. Huehnergard, "Features of Central Semitic," in A. Gianto, ed., *Biblical and Oriental Essays in Memory of William L. Moran* (BibOr 48), Roma 2005, pp. 155–203. A completely different approach is advocated by F. Corriente, "The Phonemic System of Semitic from the Advantage Point of Arabic and its Dialectology," *AuOr* 23 (2005), pp. 169–73; previously in "On the degree of kinship between Arabic and Northwest Semitic," in *AIDA 5th Conference Proceedings*, Cadix 2003, pp. 187–294. Corriente denies the consistence of the Central Semitic subgrouping as supported by the scholars quoted who follow in Hetzron's footsteps. Furthermore, he insists on the importance of Arabic as a "diastratic" (dialectal) complex for Semitics.

95.   On this topic see A. Roman, "Sur l'origine de la diptosie en langue arabe," in P. Zemánek, ed., *Studies in Near Eastern Languages...*, Prague, 1996, pp. 516, 523.

96.   Once again, note that this concept has no connection with its Indo-European homonym; see O. Szemerényi, *Einführung in die vergleichende Sprachwissenschaft...*, Darmstadt, 1990³, pp. 116ff.

97.   See A. R. Bomhard and J.C. Kerns, *The Nostratic Macrofamily...*, Berlin and New York, 1994, p. 111.

98.   For basic information see S. Ullmann, *Semantics*, Oxford, 1972, pp. 82ff. See also A. M. Gazov-Ginsberg, "O stroenii zvukopodražatel'nyh semitskih kornej" [On the structure of onomatopoeic roots in Semitic], *Kratkie Šoobščenija Instituta Narodov Azii* 72 (1963), pp. 3–8.

99.   On this topic see P. Fronzaroli, "Problems of a Semitic Etymological Dictionary," in P. Fronzaroli, ed., *Studies on Semitic Lexicography...*, Florence, 1973, pp. 7f., who distinguishes between grammaticalized (old) and non-grammaticalized onomatopoeia.

100.   For a balanced judgment on this matter see J. Barr, *Comparative Philology...*, Oxford, 1968, pp. 273ff.

101.   On this topic see J. Lyons, *Semantics*, Volume I, London, 1978, pp. 100ff.

102.   On this topic see G. Conti, *Studi sul bilitterismo in semitico e in egiziano ...*, Florence, 1980, pp. 22, 28, 104ff., 111; also P. Fronzaroli, *art. cit.*, pp. 8. B. Landsberger, "Die Gestalt der semitischen Wurzel," in *Atti del XIX Congresso Internazionale...*, Rome, 1938, pp. 450–52, already seems to be going in this direction when he speaks of a "Bedeutungsnuancierung durch Lautnuancierung" and of the "Gefühlsbetontheit" ("warme" und "kalte" Wörter); even so, he provides an interesting survey. See also K. Brockelmann, "Semitischen Reimwortbildungen," *Zeitschrift für Semitistik und verwandte Gebiete* 5 (1927), pp. 6–38.

103.   See G. del Olmo Lete, "The Monoconsonantal Lexical Series in Semitic," *AuOr* 16 (1998), pp. 37–75, *passim*. For an evaluation of the linguistic phenomenon of *deixis*, see St. C. Levison, *Pragmatics*, Cambridge, 1983, pp. 54ff.

104.   On this topic see Ph. Baldi, "Introduction: The Comparative Method," in St. Baldi, ed., *Linguistic Change and Reconstruction Methodology...*, Berlin and New York, 1990, p. 10; St. J. Lieberman, "The Regularity of Sound Change: A Semitic Perspective," ibid., pp. 706ff., on the regularity of the phonetic changes of the neo-grammarians ("while one aspect of the language, the phonemes used to express a word, follows one set of rules, the other aspect, its vocabulary, follows another"); also A. Faber, "Innovation, Retention, and Language Comparison: An Introduction to Historical Comparative Linguistics," in W. R. Bodine, ed., *Linguistics in Biblical Hebrew...*, Winona Lake, Ind., 1992, pp. 199ff. on double articulation; J. Barr, *Comparative Philology...*, Oxford, 1968, p. 169 ("conceivably there were two sectors in Semitic vocabulary. The first was already in a fairly fixed form in the proto-Semitic period. The words of this sector will then appear in the historical languages in forms showing the normal correspondences. In the second sector, however, the root sequences were still not firm in the proto-Semitic period, and various branches developed their words independently later, through expansion of a vague common base"). For the problem in general see P. R. Bennett, *Comparative Semitic Linguistics...*, Winona Lake, Ind., 1998, pp. 26ff. ("Cognancy and Regularity"). For a general view of this topic see M. Y. Chen, "The Time Dimension: Contribution to a Theory of Sound Change," *Foundation of Languages* 8 (1977), pp. 457–98; W. S.-Y. Wang, ed., *The Lexicon of the Phonologic Change*, The Hague, 1977; J. Fisiak, ed., *Linguistic Change under Contact Conditions*, Berlin and New York, 1994; *infra* n. 109.

105.   In this connection the hypothesis can be made that it is the stress (anterior or posterior) which in turn makes the third (or first) position of triliteralism a more random character, giving rise to two fixed consonants with a third undefined or free structural element. This is where the variability of bases would come from. This different realization of the resonance in the third consonantal position, due to stress, can exist at any stage of the language at all, especially in illiterate societies, not only in the primitive stage. In this way new, late allophones are created, peculiar to each language.

106.   On this topic see M. Cohen, *Essai comparatif...*, Paris, 1947, pp. 73; G. Takács, *Etymological Dictionary of Egyptian...*, Leiden, 1999, pp. 49ff.

107.   For the concepts of intensity and expansion see above p. 3 and G. del Olmo Lete, "Phonetic Distribution in Semitic Binary Articulation Bases" (in press).

108.   See A. J. Greimas, *Sémantique structurelle. Recherche de méthode*, Paris, 1966, pp. 42ff. See also the distinctions provided by Masson above pp. 102f. (basic and collateral semes, nuclear and peripheral semes, concentric semes ...); and the reservations of J. Barr, *Semantics of Biblical Language ...*, Oxford, 1969, pp. 115ff. as well as the specific application on pp. 187ff.

109.   On this topic see D. Cohen, "À propos d'un dictionnaire des racines sémitiques," in P. Fronzaroli, ed., *Atti del secondo congresso ...*, Florence, 1978, pp. 99–100.

110.   The *"Primärwörter"* are in principle words of simple meaning and their possible polysemy is derived and denominative.

111.   On this see the "semantic models" of G. Bohas, *Matrices et étymons ...*, Lausanne, 2000, pp. 69ff., valid as a system of semantic derivation by "objective" expansion.

112.   See the outline provided on this subject by R. M. Kempson, *Semantic Theory*, Cambridge, 1995, pp. 83ff.; also, P. Fronzaroli, "Componential Analysis," *ZAH* 6 (1993), pp. 79–91; G. van Steenbergen, "Componential Analysis of Meaning and Cognitive Linguistics: Some Prospects for Biblical Hebrew Lexicology," *JNSL* 28 (2002), pp. 19–37.

113.   In favor of a specific meaning of the primitive or radical seme is, for example, L. Roussel, *La racine sémitique vue de l'hébreu*, Nimes, 1952, pp. 14 ("the meaning of a root is always, originally, very clear and very narrow. But, as soon as a theme is put into service, a thousand causes

(analogy, catachresis, etc.) […] increase the nuances and changes of meaning. We others, when we then and quite wrongly take the *average* of all these meanings, are led to give the root an extremely general meaning. The original meaning escapes us, that is all. This should encourage us not to assume homophonic roots too often"). Similarly, see J. Barr, *Comparative Philology…*, Oxford, 1968, pp. 290f. ("Meanings are not derived from a basic idea, or from a class of referents, but from the meanings of forms already found").

114. For an example from the aspect of "distinctive features" see P. Fronzaroli, "Paléontologie linguistique," in A. Caquot and D. Cohen, eds., *Actes du premier congrès…*, The Hague and Paris, 1974, pp. 175ff. On this topic see also the interesting semantic and etymological analysis by J. Sanmartín, "Semantisches über '*MR*/'Sehen' und '*MR*/'Sagen' im Ugaritischen," *UF* 5 (1973), pp. 263–70.

115. See above n. 1. This, for example is the direction taken by G. Kleiber, *La sémantique du prototype. Catégories et sens lexical*, Paris, 1999[2], as well as the theory of "family resemblance" (Wittgenstein), which he defends. For a summary see J. H. Hospers, "Polysemy and Homonymy," *ZAH* 6 (1993), pp. 114–23. A. Wierzbicka, *Semantics. Primes and Universals*, Oxford and New York, 1996, pp. 245ff.; and S. Ullmann, "Semantic Universals," in J. H. Greenberg, ed., *Universals of Languages*, Cambridge, Mass., 1966[2], pp. 230f. ("Synonymy, Polysemy, Homonymy"), are very critical of the category of "family resemblance."

116. For example see S. Ullmann, *Semantics*, Oxford, 1986, pp. 193ff., 211ff.; id., "Semantic Universals," in J. H. Greenberg, ed., *Universals of Languages*, Cambridge, Mass., 1966[2], pp. 238ff.; C. Watkins, "Etymologies, Equations, and Comparanda: Types and Values, Criteria for Judgement," in P. Baldi, ed., *Linguistic Change and Reconstruction Methodology…*, Berlin and New York, 1990, pp. 289–303; E. Cl. Traugott and R. B. Dasher, *Regularity in Semantic Change*, Cambridge, 2002 ("Mechanisms of Semantic Change: Metaphorization, Metonymization," pp. 27ff.).

117. See, for example. J. Lyons, *Semantics*, vol. 2, Cambridge, 1977, pp. 548ff.; S. Ullmann, *Semantics*, Oxford, 1986, pp. 193ff. (with bibliography). Add: W. Labov, "Il meccanismo dei mutamenti linguistici," *Rassegna Italiana di Sociologia* 9 (1968), pp. 277–300; E. Rubinstein, "On the Mechanism of Semantic Shift: Causation or Symmetric Locavility," *AAL* 3/7 (1976), pp. 1–10; and the collective work edited by P. Baldi, *Linguistic Change and Reconstruction Methodology*, Berlin and New York, 1990; cf. *supra* n. 96.

118. See above n. 14.

119. On this topic see C. Ehret's extreme theory (above p. 107) which considers Semitic roots to be the result of the confluence of a much more differentiated Proto-Afro-Asiatic phonetic set, in terms of both consonants and vowels. For example, according to him, each Semitic root can have about twenty Proto-Afro-Asiatic prototypes only through vocalic variation (!).

120. See J. Barr, *Semantics of Biblical Language*, Oxford, 1969, p. 109: "The main point is that the etymology of a word is not a statement about its meaning but about its history … and it is quite wrong to suppose that the etymology of a word is necessarily a guide either to its "proper" meaning in a later period or to its actual meaning in that period." "Words can only be intelligibly interpreted by what they meant at the time of their use…" (pp. 139f.); also pp. 102f., 107ff. and above, pp. 146ff. E. Lipiński, *Semitic Languages*, Leuven, 1997, pp. 543ff.

121. So J. Barr, *Comparative Philology…*, Oxford, 1968, p. 90.

122. To the usual bibliography provided by Arabists add the recent thesis of S. S. Al-Khamash, "Aḍdād – A study of homo-polysemous oppositions in Arabic," Ph.D. diss., Indiana University, 1991.

123. Cf. G. Lancioli, "Sull'ordine dei dizionari arabi classici," in *In memoria di Francesco Gabrieli…*, Rome, 1997, pp. 113–27; G. Bohas, N. Darfouf, "Contribution à la réorganisation du lexique

de l'arabe: les étymons non-ordonnés," *TL-LC* 5/1–2 (1993), pp. 55–103. See also S. Segert, "Considerations on Semitic Comparative Lexicography," *ArOr* 28 (1960), pp. 484ff. See also lastly G. del Olmo Lete, "The alphabetic sequence of a Ugaritic dictionary," *AuOr* 24 (2006), pp. 145–48.

124.   See V. Blažek, "Semitic Etymological Dictionary I," *ArOr* 69 (2001), pp. 495–510 (review-article of A. Militarev, L. Kogan, *Semitic Etymological Dictionary*); S. Segert, *art. cit.*, p. 479.

125.   See A. R. Bomhard, J. C. Kerns, *The Nostratic Macrofamily...,* Berlin and New York, 1994, p. 111; also A. R. Bomhard, "The Root in Indo-European and Afroasiatic," in P. Zemánek, ed., *Studies in Near Eastern Languages...,* Prague, 1996, p. 168.

BIBLIOGRAPHY

S. S. Al-Khamash, "Aḍḍād: A Study of Homo-polysemous Oppositions in Arabic," diss. Indiana University, 1991.

F. I. Andersen, "Biconsonantal Byforms of Weak Hebrew Roots," *ZAW* 82 (1970), pp. 270–75.

N. Anghelescu, and A. Avram, eds., *Proceedings of the Colloquium on Arabic Linguistics*, Bucharest, 1995.

Y. L. Arbeitman, ed., *FUCUS. A Semitic/Afrasian Gathering in Remembrance of Albert Ehrman* (ASThHLSc Series IV - Current Issues in Linguistic Theory, 58), Amsterdam and Philadelphia, 1988.

A. M. R. Aristar, "The IIwy and the Vowel System of Proto-West Semitic," *AAL* 6/6 (1979), pp. 1–17.

S. Armon-Lotem, "What Hebrew Early Verbs Teach Us about Root Infinitives," in *Proceedings of the Groningen Assembly on Language Acquisition...*, Groningen, 1996, pp. 77–86.

J. Aro, *Die Vokalisierung des Grundstammes im semitischen Verbum*, Helsinki, 1964.

Atti del XIX Congresso Internazionale degli Orientalisti, Roma 23–29 settembre 1935, Rome, 1938.

Y. Avishur and R. Deutsch, eds., *Michael. Historical, Epigraphical and Biblical Studies in Honor of Prof. Michael Heltzer*, Tel Aviv-Jaffa, 1999.

D. Baggioni and P. Larcher, "Note sur la racine en indo-européen et en sémitique," in P. Cassuto and P. Larcher, *La sémitologie, aujourd'hui...*, Aix-en-Provence, 2000, pp. 121–31.

A. G. Belova, "Struktura semitskogo kornja i semitskaja morfologičeskaja sistema" [The structure of the Semitic root and the Semitic morphological system], in *Voprosy yazikoznanija* (1991), pp. 79–90.

————, "Sur la reconstruction du vocalisme afroasiatic: quelques correspondences Égypto-Sémitiques," in H. G. Mukarowsky, ed., *Proceedings of the Fifth International Hamito-Semitic Congress...*, Vienna, 1992, pp. 85–93.

————, "La structure de la racine afroasiatique. Le cas d'extension phonétique," in E. Eberrmann, E. R. Sommerauer, and K. É. Thomanek, eds., *Komparative Afrikanistik...*, Vienna, 1992, pp. 15–20.

————, "K voprosu o rekonstrukcii semitskogo kornevogo vokalizma" [Towards the reconstruction of radical vocalism in Semitic], *Voprosy yazikoznanija* (1993), pp. 28–56.

————, "Sur la reconstruction du vocalisme radical en arabe et en sémitique," in P. Zemánek, ed., *Studies in Near Eastern Languages ...*, Prague, 1996, pp. 81–88.

————————, "Omonimija v arabskom korneslove i struktura semitskogo kornja" [Homonymy in radical Arabic words and the structure of the Semitic root], in *Jazyki Azii i Afriki*, Moscow 1998, pp. 11–15.

————————, "Les racines arabes homonymes comme résultat des changements historiquess," in S. Leder, ed., *Studies in Arabic and Islam. Proceedings of the 19th Congress. Union Européenne des Arabisants et Islamisants, Halle 1998*, Leuven /Paris /Sterling, Va., 2002, pp. 349–56.

————————, "K koprosu o strukture semitskogo kornja (komplementy i fonetičeskie rašyriteli)" (Towards the problem of the Semitic root structure (complements and phonetical extensions), in *Istorija I jazykii drevnego vostoka: pamjati I.M. Djakonoff (History and Languages of Ancient Orient: I.M. Diakonoff Memorial Volumen)*, St. Petersburg 2002, pp. 29–36.

A. G. Belova, I. M. Djakonoff, A. J. Militarev, V. J. Porhomovskij, O. V. Stolbova and A. S. Četveruhin, "Srvanitel'no-istoričeskii slavar' afrazijskih jazykov. Vypyski 1–3" [Historical and comparative Afro-Asiatic voçabulary] (PPPIK, XV GNS, Čast' IV, Moscow, 1981 / PPPIK, XVI GNS, Čast' III, Moscow, 1982 / PPPIK, XIX GNS, Čast' III), Moscow, 1986.

M. L. Bender, "Consonant Co-occurrence Restrictions in Afroasiatic Verb Roots," in P. Fronzaroli, ed., *Atti del secondo congreso internazionale di linguistica camito-semitica...*, Florence 1978, pp. 1–19.

P. R. Bennett, *Comparative Semitic Linguistics. A Manual*, Winona Lake, Ind., 1998.

G. Bergsträsser, *Einführung in die semitischen Sprachen*, Munich, 1928 (= *Introduction to the Semitic Languages*, Winona Lake, Ind., 1988).

H. Birkeland, "Some Reflections on Semitic and Structural Semantics," in M. Halle, H. Lunt, H. McLean, and C. H. van Schooneveld, eds., *For Roman Jakobson. Essays on the Occasion of His Sixtieth Birthday ...*, The Hague, 1956, pp. 44–51.

H. Blanc, "Les deux prononciations du *qāf* d'après Avicenne," *Arabica* 13 (1966), pp. 129–36.

J. Blau, "Marginalia Semitica III," *IOS* 7 (1977), pp. 14–32.

V. Blažek, "Paralelní procesy ve vy´voji indoevropského a afroasijského korene" [Parallel processes in the development of the Indo-European and Afro-Asiatic root], *Jazykovédné Aktuality* 26/1–2 (1989), pp. 28–33.

————————, "Semitic Etymological Dictionary I," *ArOr* 69 (2001), pp. 495–510 (review article of Militarev/Kogan).

————————, "Etymological Dictionary of Egyptian," *ArOr* 69 (2001), pp. 624–32 (review article of Takács).

D. Blohm, ed., *Studien zur arabischen Linguistik: Wolfgang Reuschel zum 65. Geburtstag*, Berlin, 1989.

L. Bloomfield, *Language*, New York, 1933.

W. R. Bodine, ed., *Linguistics in Biblical Hebrew*, Winona Lake, Ind., 1992.

G. Bohas, "A Diachronic Effect of OCP," *Linguistic Inquiry* 21/2 (1990), pp. 298–301.

————————, "Le OCP, la composition des racines et les conventions d'association," *BEO* (De la grammaire de l'arabe aux grammaires des arabes) 43 (1991), pp. 119–37.

————————, "La réalisation des racines bilitères en arabe," in R. Contini, F. A. Pennacchietti, and M. Tosco, eds., *Semitica. Serta philologica Constantino Tsereteli dicata*, Turin, 1993, pp. 11–13.

————————, "OCP et la persistance des représentations sous-jacentes," *Langues orientales anciennes. Philologie et linguistique, LOAPL* 4 (1993), pp. 35–40.

————, "Le PCO et la structure des racines," in G. Bohas, ed., *Développements récents en linguistique arabe et sémitique*, Damascus, 1993, pp. 9–44.

————, "Diverses conceptions de la morphologie arabe," in G. Bohas, ed., *Développements récents en linguistique arabe et sémitique*, Damascus, 1993, pp. 45–59.

————, "Au-delà de la racine," in N. Anghelescu and A. Avram, eds., *Proceedings of the Colloquium on Arabic Linguistics…*, Bucharest, 1995, pp. 29–45.

————, *Matrices, Étymons, Racines. Éléments d'une thérie lexicologique du vocabulaire arabe* (ORBIS / Supplementa, 8), Leuven, 1997.

————, "Pourquoi et comment se passer de la racine dans l'organisation du lexique arabe," *BSLP* 94 (1999), pp. 363–402.

————, "Le statut du *ḍād* dans le lexique de l'arabe et ses implications," *LLMA* 1 (1999), pp. 13–28.

————, *Matrices et étymons. Développements de la thèorie* (IELOA, 3), Lausanne, 2000.

————, "Et pourtant ils lisent …," *LLMA* 3 (Fs. A. Miquel) (2002), pp. 11–28.

————, "Du concret à l'abstrait, sur les deux rives de la Méditerranée," *LLMA* 3 (2002), pp. 85–105.

G. Bohas and A. Chekayri, "Les rélations des racines bilitères en arabe," in R. Contini, F. A. Pennacchietti, and M. Tosco, eds., *Semitica …*, Turin, 1993, pp. 1–13.

G. Bohas and N. Darfouf, "Contribution à la réorganisation du lexique de l'arabe: les étymons non-ordonnés," *TL-LC* 5/1–2 (1993), pp. 55–103.

G. Bohas and S. Gharbaoui, "L'organisation sémantique des matrices," in M. El Medlaoui, S. Gafaiti, and F. Saa, eds., *Actes du premier congrès chamito-sémitique de Fès*, Fès, 1998, pp. 193–207.

A. R. Bomhard, "The Reconstruction of the Proto-Semitic Consonant System," in Y. L. Arbeitman, ed., *FUCUS. A Semitic/Afrasian Gathering in Remembrance of Albert Ehrman* (AStThHLSc Series IV - Current Issues in Linguistic Theory, 58), Amsterdam and Philadelphia, 1988, pp. 113–39.

————, "Linguistic Methodology and Distant Linguistic Comparison," *Mother Tongue* 20 (1993), pp. 1–4.

————, "The Root in Indo-European and Afroasiatic," in P. Zemánek, ed., *Studies in Near Eastern Languages and Literatures. Memorial Volume of Karel Petráček*, Prague, 1996, pp. 161–70.

A. R. Bomhard and J. C. Kerns, *The Nostratic Macrofamily. A Study in Distant Linguistic Relationship* (TL-SM 74), Berlin and New York, 1994, pp. 91–111.

————, "Root Structure Patterning in Proto-Afroasiatic," in *idd.*, *The Nostratic Macrofamily 1994*, pp. 109–11.

G. J. Botterweck, *Der Triliteralismus im Semitischen, erläutert an der Wurzel gl kl ḳl* (BBB 3), Bonn, 1952.

A. A. Boulos, *The Arabic Triliteral Verb. A Comparative Study of Grammatical Concepts and Processes*, Beirut, 1965.

M. M. Bravman, "Bi-consonantal Nouns of Roots III *w* (ˀab, ˀaḫ, ḥam)," in *Studies in Semitic Philology* (StSLL, VI), Leiden, 1977, pp. 124–30.

W. Bright, ed., *Oxford International Encyclopaedia of Linguistics*, New York, 1991.

K. Brockelmann, "Semitische Reimwortbildungen," *Zeitschrift für Semitistik und verwandte Gebiete* 5 (1927), pp. 6–38.

E. Buckley, "Tigrinya Root and the OCP," *PWPL* 31 (1997), pp. 19–51.

J. Bynon, ed., *Current Progress in Afro-Asiatic Linguistics: Papers of the Third International Hamito-Semitic Congress* (AStThHLSc. Current Issues in Linguistic Theory), Amsterdam and Philadelphia, 1984, pp. 1–10.

J. Bynon and T. Bynon, eds., *Hamito-Semitica. Proceedings of the Colloquium Held by the Historical Section of the Historical Association (Great Britain) at the School of the Oriental and African Studies, University of London, on the 18th, 19th and 20th of March 1970* (Janua Linguarum, Series Practica, 200), The Hague and Paris, 1975.

J. Cantineau, *Cours de phonétique arabe*, Algers, 1941.

————, "Esquisse d'une phonologie de l'arabe classique," *BSLP* 43 (1946), pp. 93–140.

————, (a), "Essai d'une phonologie de l'hébreu biblique," *BSLP* 46 (1950), pp. 82–122.

————, (b), "Racines et schèmes," in *Mélanges offerts à William Marçais…*, Paris, 1950, pp. 119–24.

————, "La notion de 'schème' et son altération dans diverses langues sémitiques," *Semitica* 3 (1950), pp. 73–83.

————, "Le consonantisme du sémitique," *Semitica* 4 (1951–52), pp. 79–94.

A. Caquot and D. Cohen, eds., *Actes du premier congrès international de linguistique sémitique et chamito-sémitique. Paris 16–19 juillet 1969* (Janua Linguarum. Series Practica, 159), The Hague and Paris, 1974.

Carra de Vaux, Baron, *Tableau des racines sémitiques (Arabe-Hébreu). Accompagnées de comparaisons*, Paris, 1944.

P. Cassuto, "Le classement dans les dictionnaires de l'hébreu," in P. Cassuto and P. Larcher, eds., *La sémitologie, aujourd'hui …*, 2000, pp. 133–58.

P. Cassuto and P. Larcher, eds., *La sémitologie, aujourd'hui. Actes de la journée de l'École doctorale de l'Université de Provence du 29 Mai 1997* (Cercle linguistique d'Aix-en-Provence), Aix-en-Provence, 2000.

K. J. Cathcart, "Some Nineteenth and Twentieth Century Views on Comparative Lexicography," in M. Kropp and A. Wagner, eds., *'Schnittpunkt' Ugarit*, Frankfurt am Main 2000, pp. 1–8.

H. H. Cazelles, "Note sur le trilittéralité en sémitique," *GLECS* 6 (1952), pp. 10.

A. Chekayri, "La structure des racines en arabe," Ddiss. Univ. Paris VII, 1994.

M. Y. Chen, "The Time Dimension: Contribution to a Theory of Sound Change," *Foundation of Languages* 8 (1977), pp. 457–98.

G. N. Clements, "Lieu d'articulation des consonnes et des voyelles: une théorie unifiée," in B. Laks and A. Rialland, eds., *Architecture des représentations phonologiques*, 1993, pp. 101–45.

C. Cohen, "The 'Held Method' for Comparative Semitic Philology," *JANES* 19 (1989), pp. 9–23.

D. Cohen, "Le vocabulaire de base sémitique et le classement des dialectes méridionaux," *Semitica* 11 (1961), pp. 55–84.

————, [F. Bron and A. Lonnet], *Dictionnaire des racines sémitiques ou attestées dans les langues sémitiques*, Paris, La Haye and Leuven, 1970.

————, "Problèmes de linguistique chamito-sémitique," *Revue des Études Slaves* 40 (1972), pp. 43–68.

————, "La lexicographie comparée," in P. Fronzaroli, ed., *Studies on Semitic Lexicography*, (QuSem 2), Florence, 1973, pp. 183–208.

————, "Sémitique comparé" [Lecture on "The comparative lexicography of Semitic"], *AEPHE* (1975), pp. 265–75.

—————, "À propos d'un dictionnaire des racines sémitiques," in P. Fronzaroli, ed., *Atti del secondo congresso internazionale di linguistica camito-semitica. Firenze, 16–19 aprile 1974* (QuSem 5), Florence, 1978, pp. 87–100.

—————, "Racines," in J. Drouin and A. Roth, eds., *À la croisée des études libyco-berbères* (Mélanges offerts à Paulette Galand-Pernet et Lionel Galand), Paris, 1993, pp. 161–75.

M. Cohen, "Entretien sur la structure de la racine en chamito-sémitique," *GLECS* 2 (1934–1936), pp. 55–56.

—————, *Essai comparatif sur le vocabulaire et la phonétique du chamito-sémitique,* Paris, 1947.

G. S. Colin, "Recherches sur les bases bilitères en arabe," *GLECS* 1 (1932), pp. 9–10.

—————, "Incompatibilité consonantique dans les racines de l'arabe classique," *GLECS* 3 (1939–1944), pp. 61–62.

—————, "Les racines trilitères à première et troisième radicales identiques en arabe clasique," *GLECS* 4 (1948), pp. 82–83.

G. Conti, *Studi sul bilitterismo in semitico e in egiziano, 1. Il tema N1212* (QuSem 9), Florence, 1980.

R. Contini, F. A. Pennacchietti, and M. Tosco, eds., *Semitica. Serta philologica Constantino Tsereteli dicata,* Turin, 1993.

J. S. Cooper and G. M. Schwartz, eds., *The Study of the Ancient Near East in the Twenty-first Century. The William Foxwell Albright Centennial Conference,* Winona Lake, Ind., 1996.

F. Corriente, "*Ḍ-L* Doublets in Classical Arabic as Evidence of the Processus of Delateralization of *ḍād* and Development of Its Standard Reflex," *JSS* 23 (1978), pp. 50–55.

—————, "On the Degree of Kinship between Arabic and Northwest Semitic," in *AIDA 5th Conference Proceedings, 25–28 september 2002,* Cadix 2003, pp. 187–294.

—————, "The Phonemic System of Semitic from the Advantage Point of Arabic and Its Dialectology," *AuOr* 23 (2005), pp. 169–73.

A. Cuny, *Recherches sur le vocalisme, le consonantisme et la formation des racines en 'nostratique', ancêtre de l'indo-européen et du chamito-sémitique,* Paris, 1943.

—————, *Invitation à l'étude comparative des langues indo-européennes et des langues chamito-sémitiques,* Bordeaux, 1946.

F. M. Dat, *Matrices et étymons. Mimophonie lexicale en hébreu biblique,* Doct. thesis, Univ. Lyon, 2002.

—————, "La matrice de dénomination {[coronal], [dorsal]} en hébreu biblique: invariance et organisation conceptuelle," *LLMA* (Hommage à André Miquel) 3 (2002), pp. 59–83.

G. del Olmo Lete, "The Monoconsonantal Lexical Series in Semitic," *AuOr* 16 (1998), pp. 37–75.

—————, "The Semitic Personal Pronouns. A Preliminary Etymological Approach," in Y. Avishur and R. Deutsch, eds., *Michael. Historical, Epigraphical and Biblical Studies ...,* 1999, pp. 99–120.

—————, "Los numerales en semítico ensayo de estudio etimológico," *Anuari de Filologia* (Homenatge a la Dra. Teresa Martínez Sáiz) 21/E (1998–99), pp. 17–37.

—————, "The Genetic Historical Classification of the Semitic Languages. A Synthetic Approach," in L. Kogan, ed., *Studia Semitica,* pp. 18–52.

——————, "Comparative Semitics: Classification and Reconstruction. An Organised Bibliography," *AuOr* 21 (2003), pp. 97–138.

——————, "An Etymological and Comparative Semitic Dictionary Phonology versus Semantics: Questions of Method," *AuOr* 23 (2005), pp. 185–90.

——————, "The Biconsonantal Semitic Lexicon 1. The Series /'-X/," *AuOr* 22 (2004), pp. 33–88.

——————, "The Biconsonantal Semitic Lexicon 2. The Series /ᶜ-X/," *AuOr* 22 (2006), pp. 17–56.

——————, "The Biconsonantal Semitic Lexicon 3. The Series /B-X/" (in press).

——————, "The Alphabetic Sequence of a Ugaritic Dictionary," *AuOr* 24 (2006), pp. 145–48.

K. Dévényi and T. Iványi, eds., *Proceedings of the Colloquium on Arabic Grammar*, Budapest, 1991.

——————, eds., *Proceedings of the Colloquium on Arabic Lexicology and Lexicography Budapest, 1–7 September 1993*, Part I, Budapest, 1993.

E. Dhorme and M. Cohen, "Entretien sur la structure de la racine en chamito-sémitique," *GLECS* 2 (1934–1936), pp. 55–56.

M. Dietrich and O. Loretz, eds., *Vom Alten Orient zum Alten Testament. Festschrift für Wolfram Freiherrn von Soden ...* (AOAT, 240), Münster, 1995.

I. M. Djakonoff, *Semito-Hamitic Languages: An Essay in Classification*, Moscow, 1965.

——————, *Jazyki drevnej Perednej Azii* [Languages of Ancient Asia Minor] Moscow, 1967.

——————, "Problems of Root Structure in Proto-Semitic," *ArOr* 38 (1970), pp. 453–77.

——————, "On Root Structure in Proto-Semitic," in J. Bynon and T. Bynon, eds., *Hamito-Semitica...*, 1975, pp. 133–53.

——————, "Opening Address," in J. Bynon and T. Bynon, eds., *Hamito-Semitica ...*, 1975, pp. 26, 34.

——————, "Project of a Comparative Historical Lexicon of Afrasian Languages," in P. Fronzaroli, ed., *Atti del secondo Congresso ...*, 1978, pp. 43–44.

——————, "Letter to the Conference," in J. Bynon, ed., *Current Progress in Afro-Asiatic Linguistics ...*, 1984, pp. 1–10.

——————, *Afrasian Languages*, Moscow, 1988.

——————, *Proto-Afrasian and Old Akkadian. A Study in Historical Phonetics, Journal of Afroasiatic Languages*, 4/1–2, Princeton, N.J., 1991–1992.

——————, "On the Principles of Afrasian Phonological Reconstruction," *St. Petersburg Journal of African Studies* 1 (1993), pp. 7–15.

——————, "Some Reflections on the Afrasian Linguistic Macrofamily," *JNES* 55 (1996), pp. 293–94.

I. M. Djakonoff and L. Kogan, "Addenda and Corrigenda to Hamito-Semitic Etymological Dictionary," *ZDMG* 146 (1996), pp. 25–38.

I. Djakonoff, A. Militarev, V. Porkhomosvsky and O. Stolbova, "On the Principles of Afrasian Phonological Reconstruction," *SPJASt* 1 (1993), pp. 7–15.

I. M. Djakonoff et al., "Historical Comparative Vocabulary of Afrasian," *SPJASt* 2 (1993), pp. 5–28; 3 (1994), pp. 5–26; 4 (1995), pp. 7–38; 5 (1995), pp. 5–32.

C. Dohmen, "'*napḫar mātāti šūt šannâ lišānu*. Zur Frage der Semantik in den Semitistik," *BN* 47 (1989), pp. 13–34.

A. Dolgopolsky, "Struktura semito-chamitskogo kornja v sravnitel'no-istoričeskom osveščenii" [The structure of the Hamito-Semitic root in a comparative-historical perspective], *Voprosy Jazykosnanije* 1976, pp. 278–82.

———, *From Proto-Semitic to Hebrew. Phonology. Etymological Approach in a Hamito-Semitic Perspective*, Milan, 1999.

G. Douillet, "Le thème grammatical: stratégie et tactique," *Analyses, Théorie* 20 (1982), pp. 39–42

W. U. Dressler, *Morphonology. The Dynamics of Derivation*, Ann Arbor, Mich., 1985, pp. 346f.

J. Drouin and A. Roth, eds., *À la croisée des études libyco-berbères* (Mélanges offerts à Paulette Galand-Pernet et Lionel Galand), Paris, 1993.

L. Drozdšk, "Towards Defining the Structural Level of the Stem in Arabic," *Orientalia Suecana* 16 (1967), pp. 85–95.

E. Eberman et al., eds., *Komparative Afrikanistik. Sprach- geschichts- und literaturwissenschaftliche Aufsätze zu Ehren von Hans G. Mukarovsky...* (Veröffentlichungen des Instituts für Afrikanistik und Ägyptologie. Beiträge zur Afrikanistik 44), Vienna, 1992.

U. Eco, *Il Segno*, Milan, 1967.

D. O. Edzard, "Die semitohamitischen Sprachen in neuer Sicht," *RA* 61 (1967), pp. 137–49 [145–47].

L. E. Edzard, "The Obligatory Contour Principle and Dissimilation in Afroasiatic," *JAAL* 3 (1992), pp. 151–71.

———, *Polygenesis, Convergence, and Entropy; An Alternative Model of Linguistic Evolution Applied to Semitic Linguistics*, Wiesbaden, 1998.

———, *Tradition and Innovation. Norm and Deviation in Arabic and in Semitic Linguistics*, Wiesbaden, 1999.

C. Ehret, *Reconstructing Proto-Afroasiatic (Proto-Afrasian). Vowels, Tone, Consonants, and Vocabulary* (UCPL, 126), Berkeley, Calif., 1995.

———, "The origin of Third Consonants in Semitic Roots: An Internal Reconstruction (Applied to Arabic)," *JAL* 1 (1989), pp. 109–202.

———, *Reconstructing Proto-Afroasiatic (Proto-Afrasian). Vowels, Tone, Consonants, and Vocabulary* (UCPL 126), Berkeley, Calif., 1995.

W. Eilers, "Semitische Wurzeltheorie," in P. Fronzaroli, ed., *Atti del secondo congresso* ..., 1978, pp. 125–31.

———, *Die vergleichend-semasiologische Methode in der Orientalistik*, (AWLAbG-SKl. Jahrgang 1973, 10), Wiesbaden, 1974.

———, "Apokopierte Vollreduplikation," *Orientalia Suecana* 33–35 (1984–1986), pp. 85–95.

———, "Die zweiradikalige Basis der semitischen Wurzel," in H. Jungraithmayr and W. W. Müller, eds., *Proceedings of the 4th International Hamito-Semitic Congress ... 1987*, pp. 511–24.

———, "Zu Resch als Wurzeldeterminativ (r-)," *Orientalia Suecana* 36–37 (1987–88), pp. 39–45.

M. El Medlaoui, "Principes de la comparaison chamito-sémitique à la lumière du concept des classes phonologiques naturelles," *RFLO* 1 (1990), pp. 53–95.

M. El Medlaoui, S. Gafaiti, and F. Saa, eds., *Actes du 1er congrès Chamito-Sémitique de Fès, 12–13 mars 1997*, Fès, 1998.

J. A. Emerton, "Some Notes on the Ugaritic Counterpart of the Arabic *ghain*," in G. E. Kadish and G. E. Freeman, eds., *Studies in Philology in Honour of Ronald James Williams*, Toronto, 1982, pp. 31–50.

M. Ephratt, "The Psycholinguistic Status of the Root in Modern Hebrew," *FoL* 31 (1997), pp. 77–103.

Essays on the Occasion of the Seventieth Anniversary of the Dropsie College, Philadelphia, 1979.

A. Faber, "On the Nature of Proto-Semitic *l*," *JAOS* 109 (1989), pp. 33–36.

————, "Innovation, Retention, and Language Comparison: An Introduction to Historical Comparative Linguistics," in W. R. Bodine, ed., *Linguistics in Biblical Hebrew*, 1992, pp. 193ff.

W. Fischer, "Die Enstehung reduplizierter Wurzelmorpheme im Semitischen," in R. Contini, F. A. Pennacchietti, and M. Tosco, eds., *Semitica. Serta philologica Constantino Tsereteli dicata*, 1993, pp. 39–61.

J. A. Fishman, ed., *Readings in the Sociology of Language*, The Hague, 1968.

J. Fisiak, ed., *Linguistic Change under Contact Conditions* (TL/SM, 81), Berlin and New York, 1994.

H. Fleisch, *Introduction à l'étude des langues sémitiques. Éléments de bibliographie*, Paris, 1947.

————, "Études de phonétique arabe," *MUSJ* 18 (1949–50), pp. 233–37.

————, *Traité de philologie arabe, 1–2*, Beirut, 1990.

M. Fleischhammer, ed., *Studia Orientalia in memoriam Caroli Brockelmann* (WZMLU, XVII, 2/3), Halle-Wittenberg, 1968.

J. Fox, "A Sequence of Vowel Shifts in Phoenician and Other Languages," *JNES* 55 (1996), pp. 37–47.

————, *Semitic Noun Patterns* (HSS 52), Winona Lake, Ind., 2003.

M. Fraenkel, *Zur Theorie der Lamed-He Stämme, gleichzeitig ein Beitrag zur semitischen-indogermanischen Sprachverwandtschaft*, Jerusalem, 1970.

————, *Zur Theorie der Ayin-Waw – und der Ayin-Jud – Stämme*, Jerusalem, 1970.

Z. Frajzyngier, "Notes on the R1R2R2 Stems in Semitic," *JSS* 24 (1979), pp. 1–12.

H. Franke, ed., *Akten des vierundzwanzigsten internationalen Orientalisten-Kongresses München 28. August bis 4. September 1957*, Wiesbaden, 1959.

T. Frolova, "The Reconstruction of the Vowel in the PS Verbal Base /$C_1C_2VC_3$/. The Evidence of Akkadian and Arabic," in L. Kogan, ed., *Studia Semitica*, pp. 79–101.

V. M. Fromkin, ed., *Tone: A Linguistic Survey*, New York, 1978.

P. Fronzaroli, "Sull'elemento vocalico del lessema in semitico," *RSO* 38 (1963), pp. 119–29.

————, "Le origini dei Semiti come problema storico," *ANLR Classe di scienze morali, storiche e filologiche* 15 (1960), pp. 123–44.

————, "Studi sul lessico comune semitico. I. Oggetto e metodo della ricerca. II. Anatomia e fisiologia," *ANLR Classe di scienze morali, storiche e filologiche* 19 (1964), pp. 155–72, 243–80.

————, "Studi sul lessico comune semitico. III. I fenomeni naturali. IV. La religione," *ANLR Classe di scienze morali, storiche e filologiche* 20 (1965), pp. 135–50; 246–69.

————, "Studi sul lessico comune semitico. V. La natura selvatica," *ANLR Classe di scienze morali, storiche e filologiche* 23 (1968), pp. 267–303.

————, "Studi sul lessico comune semitico. VI. La natura domestica," *ANLR Classe di scienze morali, storiche e filologiche* 24 (1969), pp. 1–36.

————, "Studi sul lessico comune semitico. VII. L'alimentazione," *ANLR Classe di scienze morali, storiche e filologiche* 26, 1971 (1973), pp. 603–42.

————, "Il mare e i corsi d'acqua nel lessico comune semitico," *BALM* 8–9 (1966–67) (1968), pp. 205–13.

————, ed., *Studies on Semitic Lexicography*, QuSem 2, Florence, 1973.

————, "Problems of a Semitic Etymological Dictionary," in P. Fronzaroli, ed., *Studies on Semitic Lexicography* ...1973, pp. 1–24.

————, "Réflexions sur la paléontologie linguistique," in A. Caquot and D. Cohen, eds., *Actes du premier congrès international* ...1974, pp. 173–78.

————, "Statistical Methods in the Study of Ancient Near Eastern Languages," *Or* 42 (1973), pp. 97–113.

————, "Paléontologie linguistique," in A. Caquot and D. Cohen, eds., *Actes du premier congrès* ... 1974, pp. 175ff.

————, "On the Common Semitic Lexicon and Its Ecological and Cultural Background," in J. Bynon and T. Bynon, eds., *Hamito-Semitica...*,1975, pp. 43–53.

————, ed., *Atti del secondo Congresso internazionale di linguistica camito-semitica. Firenze, 16–19 aprile 1974* (QuSem, 4), Florence, 1978.

————, "Componential Analisis," *ZAH* 6 (1993), pp. 79–91.

————, "Etymologies," *AuOr* 23 (2005), pp. 35–43.

P. Fronzaroli and G. Garbini, "Paleontologia semitica: il patrimonio lessicale semitico commune," in R. Gusmani and J. Knobloch et al., eds., *Paleontologia linguistica: Atti del VI convegno internazionale di linguisti, Milan 1974*, Brescia, 1977, pp. 155–58 and 170–72.

P. Fronzaroli and P. Marrassini, eds., *Proceedings of the 10th Meeting of Hamito-Semitic (Afroasiatic) Linguistics (Florence, 18–20, 2001)* (QuSem 25), Florence 2006.

G. M. Gabučan, "K voprusu o strukture semitskogo slova (v svjazi s problemoj 'vnutrennej fleksii')" [On the problem of the structure of the word in Semitic in relation to the problem of 'internal inflection'], in G. Š. Šarvatov, ed., *Semitskije jazyki* ..., pp. 114–27.

G. M. Gabučan and A. A. Kovaljov, "O Probleme slova v cvete faktov arabskogo litieraturnogo yazika" [On the problem of the word in the light of data from Arabic literature], in *idd.*, eds., *Arabskaja Filologija*, Moscow, 1968, pp. 40–51.

A. Gai, "Several Points of Semitic and Akkadian Grammar," *Le Muséon* 114 (2001), pp. 1–13 [1. The Root of a 'Primary Word', pp. 1f.].

L. Galand, "Le comportement des schèmes et des racines dans l'évolution de la langue: exemples touaregs," in J. Bynon, ed., *Current Progress in Afro-Asiatic Linguistics* ..., 1984, pp. 305–15.

————, "Du nom au verbe d'état. La témoignage du berbère," in H. G. Mukarowsky, ed., *Proceedings of the Fifth International Hamito-Semitic Congress* ... 1990, pp. 123–38.

G. Garbini, *Il semitico di nord-ovest*, Quaderni della sezione linguistica degli Annali, 1, Naples, 1960.

————, "Il consonantismo dell'ebraico attraverso il tempo," *AION* 14 (1964), pp. 165–90.

————, "Configurazione dell'unità linguistica semitica," in *Le "protolingue"...* 1965, pp. 119–38.

————, *Le lingue semitiche. Studi di storia linguistica* (Pubblicazioni del seminario de semitistica. Ricerche, IX), Naples, 1972.

————, "Problemi di metodo relativi alla comparazione lingüística semitica: cento anni dopo," *AION* 37 (1977), pp. 113–24.

G. Garbini and O. Durand, *Introduzione alle lingue semitiche* (Studi sul Vicino Oriente antico, 2), Brescia, 1994, pp. 15ff., 131ff.

W. R. Garr, "The Comparative Method in Semitic Linguistics," in *AuOr* 23 (2005), pp. 17–21.

M. Gaudefroy-Demombynes, "Bases bilitères; pluriels internes, en arabe," *GLECS* 1 (1932), p. 11.

A. M. Gazov-Ginsberg, "Čeredovanije obsčesemitskih kornej tipa plpl, ppl -> n-pl" [Dissimilation of common Semitic roots of the type plpl, ppl -> n-pl], *Palestinskij Sbornik* 7 (1962), pp. 152–58.

―――――, "O stroenii zvukopodračatel'nyh semitskih kornej" [On the structure of onomatopoeic roots in Semitic], *Kratkie Šoobsčenija Instituta Narodov Azii* 72 (1963), pp. 3–8.

―――――, *Bil li jazyk izobrazitelen v svoih istokah? (Svidetel'stvo prasiemitskogo zapasa kornej)* [Was language descriptive in origin?], Moscow, 1965.

―――――, "Sledy monovokalizma v semitskih vnegrammatičeskih glasnyh" [Traces of monovocalism in the extragrammatical vocalic system in Semitic], *Kratkie Šoobscenija Instituta Narodov Azii* 86 (1965), pp. 90–96.

―――――, "Semitskij koren' i obsčelingvisticeskaja teorija monovokalizma" [The Semitic root and the linguistic theory of monovocalism], in G. Š. Šarvatov, ed., *Semitskie jazyki. Vypp. 2, casti. 1 & 2. Materialy Pervoj Konferencii po semitskim jazykam, 26–28 okt. 1964 / Semitic languages. Issue 2, pt. 1 & 2. Papers from the First Conference on Semitic languages, 26–28 oct. 1964*, Moscow, 1965[2], pp. 200–4.

―――――, "Simvolika kratkosti i dolgoty v osnovah semitskih spjagaemyh form" [The symbolism of short versus long bases in conjugated forms in Semitic], *Palestinskij Sbornik* 19 (1969), pp. 45–55.

―――――, "Simvolizm u::i kak vyračenie pola (roda) i razmerov v semitskih jazykah" [The symbolism u::i as an expression of sex and height in the Semitic languages], *Palestinskij Sbornik* 21 (1970), pp. 100–10.

―――――, *Symvolizm prasiemitskoj fleksii. O bezuslobnoj motivirovannosti znaka* [The symbolism of inflection in Proto-Semitic: unconditioned motivated signs], Moscow, 1974.

A. Giacalone Ramat, O. Carruba, and G. Bernini, eds., *Papers from the 7th International Conference on Historical Linguistics* (CILTh, 48), Amsterdam and Philadelphia, 1987.

A. Gianto, ed., *Biblical and Oriental Essays in Memory of William L. Moran* (BibOr 48), Roma 2005.

H. L. Ginsberg, "The Classification of the North-West Semitic Languages," in H. Franke, ed., *Akten des vierundzwanzigsten internationalen Orientalisten-Kongresses …*, 1959, pp. 256–57.

G. Goldenberg, "The Contribution of Semitic Languages to the Linguistic Thinking," *Ex Oriente Lux* 30 (1987–1988), pp. 107–15 (= *Studies in Semitic Linguistics*, Jerusalem 1998, pp. [1–9]).

―――――, "Principles of Semitic Word-Structure," in G. Goldenberg and S. Raz, eds., *Semitic and Cushitic Studies* 1994, pp. 29–64. (= *Studies in Semitic Linguistics*, Jerusalem, 1998, pp. 10–45).

―――――, "Semitic Linguistics and General Study of Languages," in Sh. Izre'el, ed., *Semitic Linguistics: The State of the Art at the Turn of the Twenty-first Century* (IOS XX), Winona Lake, Ind., 2002, pp. 21–41.

―――――, "Semitic Triradicalism and the Biradical Question," in G. Khan, ed., *Semitic Studies in Honor of Edward Ullendorff*, Leiden/Boston, 2005, pp. 7–25.

————, "Word-Structure, Morphological Analysis, the Semitic Languages and Beyond," in P. Fronzaroli and P. Marrassini, eds., *Proceedings of the 10th Meeting of Hamito-Semitic (Afroasiatic) Linguistics*, pp. 169–93.

G. Goldenberg and S. Raz, eds., *Semitic and Cushitic Studies*, Wiesbaden, 1994.

J. Goldsmith, "Autosegmental Phonology," diss. M.I.T., 1976.

M. Golomb, *'Working with no Data'. Semitic and Egyptian Studies Presented to Thomas O. Lambdin*, Winona Lake, Ind., 1987.

M. Goshen-Gottstein, "Comparative Semitics," in *Essays in Honor ... of the Dropsie University*, 1979, pp. 14ff.

————, "The Present State of Comparative Semitic Linguistics," in A. S. Kaye, ed., *Semitic Studies in Honor of Wolf Leslau...*, Wiesbaden, 1991, pp. 558–69.

G. Gragg, "Morphology and Root Structure: A Beja Perspective," *AuOr* 23 (2005), pp. 23–33.

J. H. Greenberg, "The Patterning of Root Morphemes in Semitic," *Word* 6 (1950), pp. 162–81.

————, *The Languages of Africa*, Bloomington and The Hague, 1963.

————, *Language Universals, with Special Reference to Feature Hierarchies* (Janua Linguarum, Series Minor, 59), The Hague, 1966.

————, ed., *Universals of Languages. Report of a Conference Held at Dobbs Ferry, New York, April 13–15, 1961*, Cambridge, Mass., 1966².

————, ed., *Universals of Human Language*, 4 vols., Stanford, 1978.

J. C. Greenfield, "Etymological Semantics," *ZAH* 6 (1993), pp. 26–37 ("Response to ...," by B. Albrektson, *ibid.*, pp. 28–33).

G. Greg, "Ge'ez (Ethiopic)," in R. Hetzron, ed., *The Semitic Languages*, London, 1997.

A. J. Greimas, *Sémantique structurelle. Recherche de méthode*, Paris, 1966.

I. Guidi, "Della sede primitiva dei popoli semitici," *ANLM. Classe di scienze morali, storiche e filologiche* 3, 1878–1879, pp. 566–615.

A. Guillaume, *Hebrew and Arabic Lexicography. A Comparative Study*, Leiden, 1965 (off-print from *Abr-Nahrain* 1–4, 1959–1965).

R. Gusmani, J. Knobloch et al., eds., *Palaeontologia linguistica: Atti del VI convegno internazionale di linguisti, Milano 1974*, Brescia, 1977.

H. Güterbock and T. Jacobsen, eds., *Studies in Honor of Benno Landsberger on His Seventy-fifth Birthday* (AS 16), Chicago, 1965.

M. Halle, "Phonological Features," in W. Bright, ed., *Oxford International Encyclopaedia of Linguistics*, 1991, pp. 207–12.

M. Halle, H. Lunt, H. McLean, and C. H. van Schooneveld, eds., *For Roman Jakobson. Essays on the Occasion of His Sixtieth Birthday ...*, The Hague, 1956.

A. Haudricourt, "La mutation des emphatiques en sémitique," *GLECS* 5 (1960–1963), pp. 49–50.

M. Held, "Studies in Comparative Semitic Lexicography," in H. G. Güterbock and T. Jacobsen, eds., *Studies in Honor of Benno Landsberger on his Seventy-fifth Birthday* (AS 16), Chicago, 1965, pp. 395–406.

J. Heller, "Neue Literatur zur Biliterismus-Frage," *ArOr* 27 (1959), pp. 678–82.

G. Herdan, "The Patterning of Semitic Verbal Roots Subjected to Combinatory Analysis," *Word* 18 (1962), pp. 262–68.

————, *The Calculus of Linguistic Observation*, London, 1962.

R. Hetzron, "La division del langues sémitiques," in *APCILSChS*, pp. 181–94

————, "Two Principles of Genetic Reconstruction," *Lingua* 38 (1976), pp. 89–108.

—————, ed., *The Semitic Languages*, London and New York, 1997.

C. T. Hodge, "Some Afroasiatic Etymologies," *Anthropological Linguistics* 10 (1968), pp. 19–39.

—————, "The Linguistic Cycle," *Language Sciences* 13 (1970), pp. 1–7.

—————, "A Set of Postulates of Comparative Linguistics," in A. Makkai and V. B. Makkai, eds., *The First LACUS Forum, 1974*, Columbia, 1975, pp. 209–16.

H. M. Hoenigswald, "Is the 'Comparative' Method General or Family-specific?" in P. Baldi, ed., *Linguistic Change and Reconstruction Methodology*, 1990, pp. 375–83.

J. Hoftijzer and K. Jongeling, *Dictionary of the North-West Semitic Inscriptions*, Vol. I/II (HdO I/21), Leiden, 1995 [new edition of the *Dictionnaire des inscriptions ouest-sémitiques*, Leiden, 1965, by C.-F. Jean and J. Hoftijzer].

J. H. Hospers, "A Hundred Years of Semitic Comparative Linguistics," in *Studia Biblica et Semitica Th. C. Vriezen dedicata*, 1966, pp. 138–51.

—————, "Polysemy and Homonymy," *ZAH* 6 (1993), pp. 114–23 (Response by A. Lemaire, pp. 124–27).

G. Hudson, "Arabic Root and Pattern Morphology without Tiers," *JL* 22 (1986), pp. 85–122.

J. Huehnergard, "New Directions in the Study of Semitic Languages," in J. S. Cooper and G. M. Schwartz, eds., *The Study of the Ancient Near East ... Albright Centennial Conference*, 1996, pp. 251–72.

—————, "Semitic Languages," in *CANE*, pp. 2117–34.

—————, "Proto-Semitic and Proto-Akkadian," in *ALSC*, pp. 1–18.

—————, "Features of Central Semitic," in A.Gianto, ed., *Biblical and Oriental Essays in Memory of William L. Moran*, pp. 155–203.

S. T. Hurwitz, *Root-Determinatives in Semitic Speech. A Contribution to Semitic Philology*, New York, 1913 [repr. 1966].

V. M. Illič Svityč, *Opyt sravnenija nostratičeskih jazykov (semitohamitskij, karvel'skij, indoevropejskij, ural'skij, dravidijskij, altajskij)* [Comparative essay on the Nostratic languages: Hamito-Semitic, Kartvelian, Indo-European, Uralic, Dravidian, Altaic], 3 vols., Moscow, 1971.

In memoria di Francesco Gabrieli (1904–1996) (*RSO*, Suppl. 2), Rome, 1997.

B. S. J. Isserlin, "Some Aspects of the Present State of Hamito-Semitic Studies," in J. Bynon and T. Bynon, eds., *Hamito-Semitica ...*, 1975, pp. 479–85 ("Discussion," pp. 485–92).

R. Jacobson, G. Fant, and M. Halle, *Preliminaries to Speech Analysis, the Distinctive Features and Their Correlates*, Cambridge, Mass., 1966.

R. Jacobson and M. Halle, *Fundamentals of Languages* (Janua Linguarum. Series Minor, 1), The Hague, 1990⁴.

H. Jankowskiego, ed., *Z mekki do poznania. Materia?y 5. Ogólnopolskiej Konferencji ...*, Poznan´, 1998.

Jazyki Azii i Afriki: tradicii, sovremennoe sostojanie i perpektivy issledovanij. Materialy conferencii (5–8 oktabrja 1998 g.), Moscow, 1998.

G. Jucquois, "Trois questions de linguistique sémitique," *Le Muséon* 86 (1973), pp. 489–95.

H. Jungraithmayr, "On Root Augmentation in Hausa," *JAL* 9 (1970), pp. 83–88.

—————, "Reflections on the Root Structure in Chadohamitic (Chadic)," *Annales de l'Unversité d'Abidjan*, sér. H 1971, pp. 285–92.

H. Jungraithmayr and W. W. Müller, eds., *Proceedings of the 4th International Hamito-Semitic Congress, Marburg, 20–22 September, 1983* (AStThHLSc - Series IV - Current Issues in Linguistic Theory, 44), Amsterdam and Philadelphia, 1987.

H. B. Jušmanov, "Struktura siemitskogo kornja" [The structure of the root in Semitic, in *Raboty po obščej fonetike, semitologii i arabskoj klassičeskoj morfologii* [Studies of general phonetics, Semitics and Classical Arabic morphology], Moscow, 1998, pp. 126–99.

G. E. Kadish and G. E. Freeman, eds., *Studies in Philology in Honour of Ronald James Williams*, Toronto, 1982.

L. Kaiser, *Manual of Phonetics*, Amsterdam, 1957 (repr. in *Fifty Years of Research. Selection of Articles on Semitic, Ethiopian Semitic and Cushitic*, Wiesbaden, 1988, pp. 21–25).

M. Kamil, "Zur Bildung der vierradikaligen Verben in den lebenden semitischen Sprachen," in *Studi orientalistici…*, 1956, pp. 459–83.

R. Katičic, *A Contribution to the General Theory of Comparative Linguistics*, The Hague, 1970.

S. A. Kaufman, "Semitics: Directions and Re-Directions," in J. S. Cooper and G. M. Schwartz, eds., *The Study of the Ancient Near East in the Twenty-First Century …*, 1996, pp. 273–82.

A. S. Kaye, ed., *Semitic Studies in Honor of Wolf Leslau …*, vol. I/II, Wiesbaden, 1991.

————, "Arabic Dialects and Maltese," in R. Hetzron, ed., *The Semitic Languages*, pp. 263–311.

A. S. Kaye and P. T. Daniels, "Comparative Afroasiatic and General Linguistics," *Word* 43 (1992), pp. 429–58.

————, eds., *Phonologies of Asia and Africa*, vol. I, Winona Lake, Ind., 1997.

H. M. Kechrida, "De la radicale 'R' dans les racines trilitères arabes," *Orientalia Suecana* 23–25 (1984–86), pp. 215–30.

B. Kedar, *Biblische Semantik*, Stuttgart, 1981.

R. M. Kempson, *Semantic Theory* (Cambridge Textbooks in Linguistics), Cambridge, 1977.

M. Kenstowicz, "Gemination and Spirantization in Tigrinya," *Studies in Linguistic Science* 12 (1982), pp. 103–22.

————, *Phonology in Generative Grammar*, Oxford, 1994.

B. Kienast, "Das System der zweiradikaligen Verben im Akkadischen (Ein Beitrag zur vergleichenden Semitistik)," *ZA* 21 (1962), pp. 138–55.

————, "Ugaritisch – Arabisch," in M. Kropp and A. Wagner, eds., *'Schnittpunkt' Ugarit*, 1999, pp. 59–68.

————, *Historische Semitische Sprachwissenschaft*, Wiesbaden, 2001.

G. Kleiber, *La sémantique du prototype. Catégories et sens lexical*, Paris, 1999.

E. E. Knudsen, "Cases of Free Variants in the Akkadian *q* Phoneme," *JCS* 15 (1961), pp. 84–90.

L. Kogan, ed., *Studia Semitica* [*Fs.* A. J. Militarev] (Orientalia: Papers of the Oriental Institute. Issue III), Moscow, 2003.

————, "Observations on Proto-Semitic Vocalism," *AuOr* 23 (2005), pp. 131–67.

L. E. Kogan and A. J. Militarev, "O nekorotyh netrivial'nih semantičeskih perehodah v semitskih jasikah (novye materaly k izosemantičeskim rjadam Majzelja: anatomičeskaya leksika)" [On some important changes in the Semitic languages (new data for Maisel's isosemantic approach: anatomical vocabulary)], *Vestnik* (RGGU) 4 (2000), pp. 15–34.

K. Koskinen, "Kompatibilität in den dreikonsonantigen hebräischen Wurzeln," *ZDMG* 114 (1964), pp. 16–58.

M. Kropp and A. Wagner, eds., *'Schnittpunkt' Ugarit* (Nordostafrikanisch / Westasiatische Studien, 2), Frankfurt am Main, 1999.

J. Kuryłowicz, *L'apophonie en sémitique*, Krakow, 1961.

——, *Studies in Semitic Grammar and Metrics*, Warsaw, 1972.

W. Labov, "Il meccanismo dei mutamenti linguistici," *Rassegna Italiana di Sociologia* 9 (1968), pp. 277–300.

P. Lacau, "Les verbes à troisième radicale faible ... (j) ou ... (w) en égyptien," *BIFAO* 52 (1953), pp. 7–50.

——, "Passifs dans les verbes à troisième radicale faible," *BIFAO* 52 (1953), pp. 51–56.

C. Laks and A. Rialland, eds., *Architecture des représentations phonologiques*, Paris, 1993.

G. Lancioli, "Sull'ordine dei dizionari arabi classici," in *In memoria di Francesco Gabrieli*, 1997, pp. 113–27.

D.Landsberger, "Die Gestalt der semitischen Wurzel," in *Atti del XIX Congresso Internazionale degli Orientalisti, Roma 23–29 settembre 1935*, Rome, 1938, pp. 450–52.

P. Larcher, "Métamorphose de la linguistique arabe," in Ph. Cassuto and P. Larcher, eds., *La sémitologie, aujourd'hui ...*, 2000, pp. 181–87.

W. S. LaSor, "Proto-semitic: Is the Concept no Longer Valid?" *Maarav* 5–6 (1990), pp. 189–205.

W. Leben, "Suprasegmental Phonoloy," diss. M.I.T., 1976.

——, "The Representation of Tone," in V. Fromkin, ed., *Tone: A Linguistic Survey*, New York, 1978, pp. 177–219.

J. Lecarme, J. Lowenstamm, and U. Shlonsky, eds., *Research in Afroasiatic Grammar. Papers from the Third Conference on Afroasiatic Languages, Sophia Antipolis, 1996*, Current Issues in Linguistic Theory, 202, Amsterdam and Philadelphia, 2000.

J. Lecerf, "Annonce d'une recherche en cours sur la structure des racines sémitiques," in P. Fronzaroli, ed., *Atti del secondo congresso ...*, 1978, pp. 173–74.

Le 'protolingue'. Atti del IV°. Convegno internazionale di linguisti... 1963, Brescia, 1965.

W. Leslau, "The Semitic Phonetic System," in L. Kaiser, *Manual of Phonetics*, 1988, pp. 21–25.

——, "Amharic Parallels to Semantic Developments in Biblical Hebrew," *EI* 20 (1975) *(Fs.* N. Glueck), pp. 113–16.

——, "The Position of Ethiopic in Semitic: Akkadian and Ethiopic," in H. Franke, ed., *Akten des vierundzwanzigsten internationalen Orientalisten-Kongresses*, 1959, pp. 251–53.

G. Levi della Vida, *Linguistica semitica: presente e futuro* (StSem 4), Rome, 1961.

S. Levin, "In What Sense Was Hebrew a Primordial Language?" *GL* 29 (1989), pp. 221–27.

——, *Semitic and Indo-European. The Principal Etymologies with Observations on Afro-Asiatic* (AStThHLSc. Series IV - Current Issues in Linguistic Theory, 129), Amsterdam and Philadelphia, 1995.

S. C. Levison, *Pragmatics*, Cambridge, 1983.

S. J. Lieberman, "Summary Report: Linguistic Change and Reconstruction in the Afro-Asiatic Languages," in Ph. Baldi, ed., *Linguistic Change and Reconstruction Methodology*, 1990, pp. 565–75.

————, "The Regularity of Sound Change: A Semitistic Perspective," in Ph. Baldi, ed., *Linguistic Change and Reconstruction Methodology*, 1990, pp. 697–721.

E. Lipiński, "Monosyllabic Nominal and Verbal Roots in Semitic Languages," in A. S. Kaye, ed., *Semitic Studies in Honor of Wolf Leslau...*,1991, pp. 927–930.

————, *Semitic Languages. Outline of a Comparative Grammar* (OLA 80), Leuven, 1997.

P. R. Lutzeier, *Lexikologie. Ein Arbeitsbuch*, Tübingen, 1995.

J. Lyons, *Semantics* I/II, Cambridge, 1994.

J. MacDonald, "New Thoughts on a Biliteral Origin for the Semitic Verb," *ALUOS* 5 (1963–1965), pp. 63–85.

W. L. Magee, "The Pronunciation of the Prelingual Mutes in Classical Arabic," *Word* 6 (1950), pp. 74–77.

R. S. Mahadin, "Perspectives on the Arab Grammarian Description of the /q/ Sound," *ZAL* 34 (1997), pp. 31–52.

S. S. Majzel', *Puti razvitija kornegovo fonda semitskih jazykov* [Types of derivation of the fund of Semitic roots], Moscow, 1983 (Vstupitel'naja statja [Introduction by] by A. Ju. Militarev, pp. 3–30).

A. Makkai and V. B. Makkai, eds., *The First LACUS Forum, 1974*, Columbia, 1975.

Y. Malkiel, *Etymology*, Cambridge, 1993.

A. Maman, *Comparative Semitic Philology in the Middle Ages. From Saʿdya Gaon to Ibn Barūn (10th – 12th C.)*, Leiden/Boston, 2004.

A.-S. Marmarǧī al-Rumanikī, *Hal al-ʿarabiyyat mantiqiyyat?* [Is Arabic a logical language?], Gʼunieh (Lebanon), 1947.

————, "Faḍl al-aṯ-tunāʼiyyah ʿalā-l-muʿǧamiyyah" [The priority of biliterality in lexicography], *Maǧallat al-maǧmaʿ al-ʿilmī al-ʿarabī* 28 (1953), pp. 542–51; 29 (1954), pp. 77–78.

————, *Al-muʿǧamiyyah al-ʿarabiyya ʿalā ḍawʼ aṯ-tunāʼiyyah wa-l-alsuniyyah as-sāmiyyah* [Arabic lexicography in the light of biliterality and Semitic philology], Jerusalem, 1937.

P. Marrassini, *Formazione del lessico dell'edilizia militare nel semitico di Siria* (QuSem 1), Florence, 1971.

A. Martinet, « Remarques sur le consonantisme sémitique », *BSLP* 49 (1953), pp. 67–78.

E. Martínez Celdrán, *Fonética*, Barcelona, 1994.

M. Masson, "À propos des parallélismes sémantiques," *GLECS* 29–30 (1984–86) (1989), pp. 221–43.

————, "Quelques palallélismes sémantiques en relation avec la notion de 'couler' », in A. S. Kaye, ed., *Semitic Studies in Honor of Wolf Leslau*, 1991, pp. 1024–41 [1039–41: "Contribution à la recherche sur les bilittèresV].

J. J. McCarthy, "Formal Problems in Semitic Phonology and Morphology," diss. M.I.T., 1979/1982.

————, "OCP Effects: Gemination and Antigemination," *Linguistic Inquiry* 17 (1986), pp. 207–63.

F. Meier, ed., *Westöstliche Abhandlungen Rudolf Tschudi zum siebzigsten ...*, Wiesbaden, 1954.

Mélanges offerts à William Marçais..., Paris, 1950.

I. A. Mel'čuk, "O 'vnutrennej fleksii' v indoevropejskih i semitskih jazikah" [On 'internal inflection' in Indo-European and Semitic], *Voprosu jazikoznanija* 4 (1963), pp. 27–40.

A. Ju. Militarev, *Var'irovanie soglasnyh v semitskom korne* [Free variation of consonants in the Semitic root], Avtoreferat kand. Diss. Moscow, 1973.

————, "Čereduemost' i kombiniruemost' soglasnyh v trikonsonantnom arabskom korne" [Variation and compatibility of consonants in the triconsonantal Arabic root], *Sbornik statej po vostočnomu jazsykoznaniju* 1 (1973), pp. 58–60.

————, "Issledonanie S. S. Majzelja v oblasti korneoblazobanija i semasiologii semitskih jazykob" [Study of the derivation and semasiology of the Semitic root according to S. S. Majzel'], *Narody Azii i Afriki* 1 (1973), pp. 114–21.

————, "Razvitie vzgljadov na semitskij koren" [History of opinions on the root in Semitic], *Vostočnie jazykoznanie*, Moscow, 1977, pp. 19ff.

————, *Kornevye varianty v afrazijskih jazykah. Problemy rekonstrukcii* [Root variations in the Afro-Asiatic languages. Problems of reconstruction], diss. Moscow, 1978, pp. 35–38.

————, *Principy semitskoj prajazykovoj rekonstrukcii, etimologii i genetičeskoj klassifikacii* [The principles of Proto-Semitic reconstruction, etymology and genetic classification], Avtoreferat Diss. Rossijkij gosudarstvennyj gumanitarnyj Universitet, 2001.

————, "Root Extension and Root Formation in Semitic and Afrasian," *AuOr* 23 (2005), pp. 83–129.

————, "Genetic Classification of the Semitic Family according to Lexico-statistics," in *Proceedings of the II Workshop on Comparative Semitics, Sitges May 31 – June 2, 2006)* (in the press)

A. Ju. Militarev and L. Kogan, *Semitic Etymological Dictionary*, Vol. I. *Anatomy of Man and Animals* (AOAT, 278/1), Münster, 2000; Vol. II. *Animal Names* (AOAT 278/2), Münster 2005.

A. Ju. Militarev and Ol. Stolbova, "First Approach to Comparative-Historical Phonology of Afrasian (consonantism)," in H. Mukarovsky, ed., *Proceedings of the Fifth International Hamito-Semitic Congress, Band. I: Hamito-Semitic, Berber, Chadic* (VIAÄUW), Vienna, 1990, pp. 45–72.

B. Morrison, *Wonderful Words. The Development of the Meaning of Hebrew Antonyms from a Common Root. A Study in Countersense*, Johannesburg, 1954.

S. Moscati, "Il biconsonantismo nelle lingue semitiche," *Biblica* 28 (1947), pp. 113–35.

————, *Il sistema consonantico delle lingue semitiche*, Rome, 1954.

————, "Preistoria e storia del consonantismo ebraico antico" (ANLR V/8), Rome, 1954, pp. 385–445.

————, "Sulla ricostruzione del protosemitico," *RSO* 35 (1960), pp. 1–10.

S. Moscati et al., *An Introduction to the Comparative Grammar of the Semitic Languages. Phonology and Morphology*, Wiesbaden, 1964.

M. Mrayati, "Statistical Studies of Arabic Language Roots," in *Applied Arabic Linguistics and Signal and Information Processing*, Hamshir Publishing 1987, pp. 97–103.

H. G. Mukarowsky, ed., *Proceedings of the Fifth International Hamito-Semitic Congress. Band I.: Hamito-Semitic, Berber, Chadic* (VIAÄUW. Beiträge zur Afrikanistik, 40), Vienna, 1990.

W. W. Müller, "Beiträge zur hamito-semitischen Wortvergleichung," in J. Bynon and T. Bynon, eds., *Hamito-Semitica*, 1975, pp. 63–74 [with discussion].

T. Muraoka, ed., *Studies in Ancient Hebrew Semantics*, Louvain, 1995.

A. Murtonen, "Brief Outline of Linguistic Analysis on an Empirical Basis," in P. Zemánek, ed., *Studies in Near Eastern Languages …*,1996, pp. 393–414.

————————, *Hebrew in its West Semitic Setting, Part One/Part Two, Part Three*, Leiden, 1989/1990.

M. A. Nowak and D. Krakauer, "The Evolution of Language," *Proceedings of the National Academy of Sciences* (Princeton) 96 (1999), pp. 8028–33.

M. A. Nowak, D. Krakauer, and D. Dress, "An Error Limit for the Evolution of Language," *Proceedings of the Royal Society* (London), 266 (1999), pp. 2131–36.

M. A. Nowak, J. B. Plotkin and V. A. A. Jansen, "The Evolution of Syntactic Communication," *Nature* 404 (March 30) (2000), pp. 495–98.

H. S. Nyberg, "Zur Entwicklung der mehr als dreikonsonantischen Stämme in den semitischen Sprachen," in Fr. Meier, ed., *Westöstliche Abhandlunge ...*, 1954, pp. 128–36.

V. E. Orel, "On Hamito-Semitic Morphology and Morphonology," *Orbis* 37 (1994), pp. 162–75.

V. E. Orel and O. V. Stolbova, "K rekonstrukcii praafrazijskogo vokalizma 1–2; 3–4" [On the reconstruction of vocalism in proto-Afro-Asiatic], *Voprosy jazykoznanija* 1989/5, pp. 66–84; 1990/2, pp. 75–90.

————————, *Hamito-Semitic Etymological Dictionary* (HdO I, 18), Leiden, 1995 [pp. XV-XXIV].

J. Padgett, "OCP Subsidiary Features," *NELS* 22 (1992), pp. 335–46.

J. L. Palache, *Semantic Notes on the Hebrew Lexikon*, Leiden, 1959.

C. Paradis and J.-F. Prunet, "On the Validity of Morpheme Structure Constraints," *The Canadian Journal of Linguistics* 38 (1993), pp. 235–356.

J. M. J. Paul Brauchet, "Notes on Semitic Philology," *CBQ* 10 (1948), pp. 315–17.

K. Petráček, "Die Struktur der semitischen Wurzelmorpheme und der Übergang ᶜain > ġain und ᶜain > r im Arabischen," *ArOr* 23 (1955), pp. 475–78.

————————, "Lingvistiká charakteristika semitského korŧene ve sveŧtle novyˆch metod" [Caractérisation linguistique de la racine sémitique d'après les nouvelles méthodes], *Slovo a slovocsnost* (Prague) 25 (1964), pp. 30–33.

————————, "Die Inkompatibilität in der semitischen Wurzel in Sicht der Informations- theorie," *Rozcnik Orientalistyzny* (Warsaw), 27 (1964), pp. 133–39.

————————, "Die Struktur der Altägyptischen Wurzelmorpheme mit Glottalen und Pharingalen," *ArOr* 37 (1969), pp. 341–44.

————————, "La structure de la racine et la classification des langues chamito-sémitiques," *Phonetica Pragensia* 4 (1974), pp. 115–21.

————————, "La méthodologie du chamito-sémitique comparé: état, problèmes, perspectives," in J. Bynon, *Current Progress in Afro-Asiatic Linguistics ...*, 1984, pp. 423–61.

————————, *Altägyptisch, Hamitosemitisch und ihre Beziehungen zu einigen Sprachfamilien in Afrika und Asien* (Acta Universitatis Carolinae. Philologica. Monographia XC – 1986), Prague, 1988.

————————, "Le dynamisme du système phonologique proto-sémitique et les problèmes de la phonologie chamito-sémitique," in J. Bynon and T. Bynon, eds., *Hamito-Semitica ...*, 1975, pp. 161–68.

————————, "Vers une conception dynamique du paradigme dans les études chamito-sémitiques," *MUSJ* 48 (1973–1974) (1977), pp. 155–63.

————————, "La racine en indoeuropéen et en chamitosémitique et leurs perspectives comparatives," *AION* 42 (1982), pp. 381–402.

————————, "La méthodologie du chamito-sémitique comparé: état, problèmes, perspectives," in J. Bynon, ed., *Current progress in Afro-Asiatic Linguistics ...*, 1984, pp. 423–62.

————, "La racine en sémitique d'après quelques travaux récents en russe," *ArOr* 53 (1985), pp. 171–73.

————, "Sur le rôle des modalités sonantiques dans l'élaboration de la racine en sémitique," *Arabica* 34 (1987), 106–10.

————, "Les laryngales en chamito-sémitique. Essai de synthèse (résumé)," in H. Jungraithmayr and W. W. Müller, eds., *Proceedings of the 4th International Hamito-Semitic Congress* ..., 1987, pp. 65–71.

————, "Nochmals über die Struktur der Wurzeln mit Pharingalen im Altägyptischen und Semitischen und ihre Inkompatibilität," in Y. L. Arbeitman, ed., *FUCUS. A Semitic/Afrasian Gathering* ..., 1988, pp. 371–77.

————, *Úvod do hamitosemitské (afroasijské) jazykovedy* [Introduction to Hamito-Semitic (Afro-Asiatic) linguistics], Prague, 1989.

J. J. Pia, "Multiply-tiered Vocalic Inventories: An Afroasiatic Trait," in J. Bynon, ed., *Current Progress in Afro-Asiatic Linguistics* ..., 1984, pp. 463–75.

S. Pilaszewiez and J. Tulisow, eds., *Problemy jezyków Azij i Afriki: materialy II Międzynarodowego Sympozium Warszawa-Kraków 10–15 listopada 1980*, Warszaw, 1987.

V. Pisani, "Indoeuropeo e camito-semitico," *AION* 3 (1949), pp. 333–39 (= *Saggi de linguistica storica*, Turin, 1959, pp. 71–78).

M. Pittau et al., eds., *Circolazioni culturali nel Mediterraneo antico. Atti del I Convegno Internazionale di Linguistica dell'area mediterranea, Sassari, 24–27 aprile 1991* (Sesta Giornata Camito-Semitica e Indoeuropea), Cagliari, 1994.

Proceedings of the Groningen Assembly on Language Acquisition Held at the University of Groningen, 7–9 September 1995, Groningen, 1996.

Prophètes, poètes et sages. Hommages à Edmond Jacob... = *RHPhR* 59 (1979), pp. 267–644.

C. Rabin, *Ancient West-Arabian*, London, 1951.

R. M. Rammany and D. B. Parkinson, eds., *Investigating Arabic: Linguistic, Pedagogical and Literary Studies in Honor of Ernest N. McCarus*, Columbus, Ohio, 1994.

C. Reintges, "Egyptian Root-and-Pattern Morphology," *LinAeg* 4 (1994), pp. 213, 240.

F. H. Renfroe, "Arabic and Ugaritic Lexicography," diss. Yale University, 1989.

G. Rinaldi, *Le lingue semitiche*, Turin, 1954.

A. Roman, "De la langue arabe comme un modèle général de la formation des langues sémitiques," *Arabica* 28 (1981), pp. 127–61.

————, "Sur l'origine de la diptosie en langue arabe," in P. Zemánek, ed., *Studies in Near Eastern Languages* ..., 1999, pp. 515–34.

H. B. Rosén, "On 'Normal' Full Root Structure and Its Historical Development," in A. Giacalone Ramat, O. Carruba, and G. Bernini, eds., *Papers from the 7th International Conference* ...,1987, pp. 535–44.

O. Rössler, "Libysch-Hamitisch-Semitisch," *Oriens* 17 (1964), pp. 199–216 (= *Gesammelte Schriften zur Semitohamitistik* (AOAT 287), München, 2001, pp. 499–516).

L. Roussel, *La racine sémitique vue de l'hébreu*, Publications de la société: 'Les amis de la Faculté des Lettres de Montpellier', 2, Nimes, 1952.

E. Rubinstein, "On the Mechanism of Semantic Shift: Causation or Symmetric Locavility," *AAL* 3/7 (1976), pp. 1–10.

G. Rubio, "Chasing the Semitic Root: The Skeleton in the Closet," *AuOr* 23 (2005), pp. 45–63.

F. Rundgren, *Über Bildungen mit s/s und n-, t- Determinative im Semitischen*, Uppsala, 1955.

J. Sanmartín, "Semantisches über '*MR*/'Sehen' und '*MR*/'Sagen' im Ugaritischen," *UF* 5 (1973), pp. 263–70.

————, "Über Regeln und Ausnahmen: Verhalten des vorkonsonantischen /n/ im 'Altsemitischen'," in M. Dietrich and O. Loretz, eds., *Vom Alten Orient zum Alten Testament ...*, 1995, pp. 433–66.

————, "The Semantic Potential of Bases ('root') and Themes ('patterns') : A Cognitive Approach," *AuOr* 23 (2005), pp. 65–81).

G. Š. Šarvatov, ed., *Semitskie jazyki. Vyp. 2, č. 1 & 2. Materialy Pervoj Konferencii po semitskim jazykam, 26–28 okt. 1964 / Semitic languages. Issue 2, pt. 1 & 2. Papers from the First Conference on Semitic languages, 26–28 Oct. 1964*, Moscow, 1965², pp. 114–27.

M. Sawaie, "Sociolinguistic Factors and Historical Linguistic Change: The Case of /q/ and Its Reflexes in Arabic Dialects," in R. M. Rammany and D. B. Parkinson, eds., *Investigating Arabic ...*, 1994, pp. 15–39.

J. F. A. Sawyer, *Semantics in Biblical Research. New methods of defining Hebrew words for salvation*, (Studies in Biblical Theology II/24), London, 1972.

H. P. Scanlin, "The Study of Semantics in General," in W. R. Bodine, ed., *Linguistics in Biblical Hebrew*, 1992, pp. 125–36.

G. M. Schramm, "Semitic Morpheme Structure Typology," in A. S. Kaye, ed., *Semitic Studies in Honor of Wolf Leslau ...*, 1991, pp. 1402–8.

P. Ségéral, "Théorie de l'apophonie et organisation des schémes en sémitique," in J. Lecarme, J. Lowenstamm, and U. Shlonsky, eds., *Research in Afroasiatic Grammar. Papers from the Third Conference on Afroasiatic Languages, Sophia Antipolis, 1996* (CILTh, 202), Amsterdam and Philadelphia, 2000, pp. 263–99.

S. Segert, "Considerations on Semitic Comparative Lexicography," *ArOr* 28 (1960), pp. 470–87 [= ZDMG Suppl. I, Teil 2, 1969, pp. 714–17].

————, "A Preliminary Report on a Comparative Lexicon of North-West Semitic Languages," in *Trudy dvadcat'pjatogo meždunarodnogo kongressa vostokovedov, 1, Sekeija IV. Semitologija, gebraistika u bublejaskaja archieologija...* Proceedings of the 25th International Congress of Orientalists. Section IV, Moscow, 1962, pp. 383–85.

————, "Tendenzen und Perspektiven der vergleichenden semitischen Sprachwissenschaft," in M. Fleischhammer, ed., *Studia Orientalia in memoriam Caroli Brockelmann* (WZMLU XVII, 2/3), Halle-Wittenberg, 1968, pp. 167–73.

————, "Hebrew Bible and Semitic Comparative Lexicography," *VTS* 17 (1969), pp. 204–11.

————, "Die Arbeit am vergleichenden Wörterbuch der semitischen Sprachen mit Hilfe des Computers IBM 1410," *ZDMG* Suppl. I/2 (1969), pp. 714–17.

————, "Hebrew Bible and Semitic Comparative Lexicography," *VTS* 17 (1969), pp. 204–11.

S. Segert and J. R. Hall, "A Computer Program for Analysis of Words according to Their Meaning (Conceptual Analysis of Latin Equivalents for the Comparative Dictionary of Semitic Languages)," *Or* 42 (1973), pp. 149–57.

L. R. Shehadeh, "Some Observations of the Sibilants in the Second Millennium B.C.," in M. Golomb, *'Working with no Data'. Semitic and Egyptian Studies presented to Thomas O. Lambdim*, Winona Lake, Ind., 1987, pp. 229–46.

J. A. Soggin, "Tracce di antiche causativi in š-realizzati como radici autonome in ebraico biblico," *AION* 15 (1965), pp. 17–30.

B. Spuler, *Semitistik* (HdO I/3), Leiden, 1964, pp. 3–25.

V. P. Starinin, *K voprosu o semantičeskom aspekte sravnitel'no-istoričeskogo jazykosnanija (izosemantičeskije rjady S. S. Majzelja)* [On the semantic aspect of comparative historical linguistics (the isosemantic approach of S. S. Majzel'] (Sovietskoje jazykoznanije 4), Moscow, 1955.

—————, *Struktura semitskogo slova. Preryvistye morfemy* [The structure of the Semitic word. Discontinuous morphemes], Moscow, 1963.

R. C. Steiner, *The Case of Fricative-Laterals in Proto-Semitic*, AOS, 59, New Haven, 1977.

—————, "Addenda to *The Case for Fricative-Laterals in Proto-Semitic*," in A. S. Kaye, ed., *Semitic Studies in honor of Wolf Leslau ...*, vol. II, Wiesbaden, 1991, pp. 1499–513.

R. Stempel, *Abriss einer historischen Grammatik der semitischen Sprachen* (Nordafrikanisch / Westasiatische Studien, 3), Frankfurt am Main, 1999.

M. P. Streck, "Sibilants in Old Babylonian Texts of Hammurapi and the Governors in Qaṭṭunān," in *ALSC*, pp. 215–51.

S. Strelcyn, "Les racines trilitères à première et troisième radicales identiques en hébreu," *GLECS* 4 (1945–1948), pp. 84–86.

—————, "Les racines trilitères à première et troisième radicales identiques dans les langues sémitique de l'Éthiopie," *GLECS* 4 (1945–1948), pp. 86–88.

—————, "Les racines trilitères à première et deuxième radicales identiques ," *GLECS* 4 (1945–1948), pp. 88–89.

Studia Biblica et Semitica Th. C. Vriezen dedicata, Wageningen, 1966.

Studi orientalistici in onore di Giorgio Levi della Vida, t. I (Pubblicazioni dell'Istituto per l'Oriente, 52), Rome, 1956.

P. Swiggers, "Recent Developments in Linguistic Semantics and Their Application to Biblical Hebrew," *ZAH* 6 (1993), pp. 211–25.

O. Szemerényi, *Einführung in die vergleichende Sprachwissenschaft*, Darmstadt, 1990[4].

G. Takács, *Etymological Dictionary of Egyptian. Volume One. A Phonological Introduction* (HdO I/48), Leiden, 1999.

The 6th Hebrew Scientific European Congress, Jerusalem, 1987.

T. Theillig, "Polysemie im Arabischen: Beobachtungen am arabischen Verb," in D. Blohm, ed., *Studien zur arabischen Linguistik ...*, 1989, pp. 81–92.

A. Torres Fernández, "Sobre el consonantismo protosemítico (II), *MEAH* (Hebrew section) 54 (2005), pp. 3–26.

E. C. Traugott and R. B. Dasher, *Regularity in Semantic Change*, Cambridge Studies in Linguistics, 96, Cambridge, 2002.

J. Tropper, *Ugaritische Grammatik* (AOAT 273), Münster, 2000.

N. S. Trubetzkoy, *Grundzüge der Phonologie*, Göttingen, 1977[6].

Trudy dvadcat' pjatogo meždunarodnogo kongressa vostokovedov, Sekcija IV. Semitologija, gebraistika i biblejskaja arheologija... [Proceedings of the 25th International Congress of Orientalists. Section IV. Hebrew and Semitic Studies and Biblical Archaeology], Moscow, 1962.

E. Ullendorff, "Comparative Semitics," in G. Levi della Vida, *Linguistica semitica: presente e futuro* (StSem, 4), Rome, 1961, pp. 13–32.

—————, "What is a Semitic Language (?) (A Problem of Linguistic Identification)," *Or* 27 (1958), pp. 66–75.

—————, *Is Biblical Hebrew a Language? Studies in Semitic Languages and Civilizations*, Wiesbaden, 1977.

S. Ullmann, *Semantics. An Introduction to the Science of Meaning*, Oxford, 1972.

——————, "Semantic Universals," in J. H. Greenberg, ed., *Universals of Languages*, 1966, pp. 217–62).

A. S. van der Woude, ed., *Language and Meaning, Studies in Hebrew and Biblical Exegesis* (OTS 19), Leiden, 1974.

G. van Steenbergen, "Componential Analysis of Meaning and Cognitive Linguistics: Some Prospects for Biblical Hebrew Lexicology," *JNSL* 28 (2002), pp. 19–37.

R. M. Voigt, "Die Laterale im Semitischen," *WdO* 10 (1979), pp. 93–114.

——————, "Die Laterale /ś, š, ź / im Semitischen," *ZDMG* 142 (1992), pp. 37–52.

——————, "Inkompatibilitäten und Diskrepanzen in der Sprache und das erste phonologische Inkompatibilitätsgesetz des Semitischen," *WdO* 12 (1981), pp. 136–72.

——————, *Die infirmen Verbaltypen des Arabischen und das Biradikalismus-Problem* (AWLM, Veröff. der Orient. Komission, 39), Stuttgart, 1988.

——————, "Der Lautwandel $S^1 > H$ in wurzellosen Morphemen des Alt- und Neusüdarabischen," in G. Goldenberg and S. Raz, eds., *Semitic and Cushitic Studies*, Wiesbaden, 1994, pp. 19–28.

——————, "Drei vergleichende semitische Werke," *WdO* 31, 2000–2001, pp. 165–89 (review of Lipiński, Stempel, Bennet).

W. von Soden, *Grundriss der akkadischen Grammatik*, AnOr, 33, Rome, 1952, 1995².

——————, "Ein semitisches Wurzelwörterbuch: Probleme und Möglichkeiten," *Or* 42 (1973), pp. 142–48.

——————, "*n* als Wurzelaugment im Semitischen," in *Bibel und Alter Orient*, Berlin, 1985, pp. 109–12 (repr. of 1968 edition).

W. Vycichl, "Les études chamito-sémitiques à l'Université de Fribourg et le 'lamékhitique'," in A. Caquot and D. Cohen, eds., *Actes du Premier Congrès International ...*, 1974, pp. 60–67.

——————, "L'état actuel des études chamito-sémitiques," in P. Fronzaroli, ed., *Atti del secondo congresso internazionale ...*,1978, pp. 63–76.

——————, "The Origin of the Semitic Languages," in H. Jungraithmayr and W. W. Müller, eds., *Proceedings of the 4th International Hamito-Semitic Congress ...*, 1987, pp. 109–21.

——————, Le nom verbal du chamito-sémitique," in M. Pittau, ed., *I Convegno Internazionale di Linguistica ...*, 1994, pp. 255–62.

W. S.-Y. Wang, ed., *The Lexicon of the Phonologic Change*, The Hague, 1977.

C. Watkins, "Etymologies, Equations, and Comparanda: Types and Values, Criteria for Judgement," in Ph. Baldi, ed., *Linguistic Change and Reconstruction Methodology ...*1990, pp. 289–303.

G. É. Weil, "Trilitéralité fonctionelle ou bilitéralité fondamentale des racines verbales hébraïques. Un essai d'analyse quantifié," *RHPhR* [*Prophètes, poètes and sages*. Hommages à Edmond Jacob] 59 (1979), pp. 281–311.

U. Weinreich, "On the Semantic Structure of Language," in J. H. Greenberg, ed., *Universals of Languages*, 1966, pp. 142–216.

M. P. Weitzman, "Statistical Patterns in Hebrew & Arabic Roots," *JRAS* (1987), pp. 15–22.

——————, "Hitpalgut ᶜiṣurim bešoršim ᶜibriyim wehiguyim" [The Distribution and Pronunciation of Hebrew Root Consonants], in *The 6th Hebrew Scientific European Congress*, Jerusalem, 1987, pp. 51–52.

S. Weninger, "Zur Realisation des ḍ (< *ḏ) im Altäthiopischen," *WdO* 29 (1998), pp. 147–48.

A. Wierzbicka, *Semantics. Primes and Universals*, Oxford and New York, 1991.

A. Zaborski, "Prefixes, Root-determinatives and the Problem of Biconsonantal Roots in Semitic," *Folia Orientalia* 11 (1969), pp. 307–13.

——————, "Biconsonantal Verbal Roots in Semitic," *Prace Jezykoznawcze* 35 (1971), pp. 51–96.

——————, "Biconsonantal Roots and Triconsonantal Root Variation in Semitic: Solutions and Prospects," in A. S. Kaye, ed., *Semitic Studies in Honor of Wolf Leslau...*, 1991, pp. 1675–703.

——————, "The Position of Arabic within the Semitic Dialect Continuum," in K. Dévényi and T. Iványi, eds., *Proceedings of the Colloquium on Arabic Grammar*, Budapest, 1991, pp. 365–75.

——————, "Exceptionless Incompatibility Rules and Verbal Root Structure in Semitic," in G. Goldenberg and S. Raz, eds., *Semitic and Cushitic Studies* ...,1994, pp. 1–18.

——————, "Archaic Semitic in the Light of Hamito-Semitic," *ZAH* 7 (1994), pp. 234–44.

——————, Roots," in P. Zemánek, ed., *Studies in Near Eastern Languages and Literatures* ...,1996, pp. 631–58.

——————, "La linguistique chamito-sémitique cinquante années après l'essai comparative de Marcel Cohen," in M. El Medlaoui, S. Gafaiti, and F. Saa, eds., *Actes du 1er congrès Chamito-Sémitique de Fès, 12–13 mars 1997*, Fès, 1998, pp. 23–35.

——————, "Problem archaizmu klasyzcnego jezyka arabskiego" [The problem of archaism in Classical Arabic], in H. Jankowski, ed., *Z Mekki do Poznania. Materialy 5. Ogólnopolskiej Konferencji* [From Mecca to Poznan – Proceedings of the 5th Conference of Polish Arabists], Poznan, 1998, pp. 269–83 ('Eng. summary', pp. 282f.).

——————, "Comparative Semitic Studies: *status quaestionis*," in *PBSCS* (*AuOr* 23, 2005), pp. 9–15.

P. Zemánek, ed., *Studies in Near Eastern Languages and Literatures. Memorial Volume of K. Petrácek*, Prague, 1996.

——————, "The Role of *q* in Arabic," *ArOr* 65 (1997), pp. 143–58.

L. Zgusta, *Manual of Lexicography*, The Hague and Paris, 1971.

H. A. Žvaniya, *Sovmestimost' soglasnyh v kornjah jazyka geéz* [The compatibility of root consonants in Ge^cez, in Georgian with a summary in Russian], Tbilisi, 1972.

GLOSSARY

Actant/Actancial: in structural linguistics the functional implication of the syntactical elements or verbal "arguments" of the discourse.

Afro-Asiatic: *phylon* or super-family of languages comprising Semitic, Egyptian, Berber, Chadic, and Cushitic families (= Hamito-Semitic).

Allophone: phonetic variant of a lexeme produced within the frame of the homorganic articulatory phonemes without semantic change.

Allothesis/Metathesis: intended partial modifications of the consonantal components of a root involving also semantic change (Majzel'). See "consonantal alternation."

Antefix: the fronting of an element with no recognized grammatical function, as opposed to prefix (Roussel).

Apophony: change in the vocalic pattern of a base as a means of functional and semantic variation.

Approximant: class of consonantal phonemes of an articulatory friction type less pronounced than in proper fricatives; there is a trendency to place them on the same level as the sonants and semiconsonants.

Aspirate: see "spirant."

Association of the margins: a way of explaining the genesis of lexical morphemes and roots by "remplissage" (= padding) (triliterals), diffusion, and glide (biliterals) starting from the marginal components (C_1/C_3) (Yip), instead of by directional association (C1/C2) (McCarthy).

Base: the original empirical form of any lexical item, comprising all its phonological elements, consonants as well as sonants (vowels) (p. 19); the concept, as well as that of its correlates (root, stem, theme) may vary depending on the scholar. See "root," "stem," "theme."

Biconsonantal cell: fixed element which, according to Jušmanov, is composed of two consonants; it appears in various combinations without necessarily forming a root.

Common Semitic: the stock of roots and lexemes common to at least two languages of different branches of the Semitic family.

Consonantal alternation: Majzel's presumed process of root variation, without semantic change, produced by contact among the Afro-Asiatic dialectal groups.

Continuant: class of consonantal phoneme, also called "fricative" or "spirant," produced by the semi-opened articulation of the sounding organs.

Continuous/Discontinuous root/morpheme: said of the lexical unit as formed by the sequence of all its phonological components (set of consonants and of vowels) or just by one of them.

Degree zero: in Djakonoff's system, the state of the primary noun without inflectional ending. This meaning does not match that of the Indo-European grammar.

Diachronic: see "synchronic."

Diffuse phoneme: original but not clear-cut sound articulation that explains its interchangeability as a source of root variation.

Directional association : a way of explaining root expansion from left to right in the sequence of its components.

Enantiosemy : principle of semantic shift according to which a seme changes by polarity into its opposite, generating antonymy.

Epenthesis/Glide : interposition of a sound into a phonetic chain, mainly called "glide" in the case of semiconsonants.

Expansion: a way of explaining the genesis of new (triconsonantal) roots from simpler (biconsonantal) roots by the affixation of new elements, chiefly by suffixation.

Free association: theory according to which there are different ways (e.g., expansion, epenthesis, glide) to explain the development of roots (Guersell/Loewenstamm).

Fricative/Affricate: sort of consonantal phonemes produced by the narrowing of the phonic organs, called also "spirants," "constrictive" or "continuants"; when combined with an occlusive mode of articulation, the affricate sound is generated.

Glottogony/Glottogonic: the intended historical linguistic reconstruction from the very first origin of universal human language.

Government Theory: a way of explaining the development of morphemes and (biliteral) roots by the determination exerted on each other by the phonetic segments of the base according to their linear distribution (Kaye-Loewenstamm).

Hamito-Semitic: older and less appropriate labelling for Afro-Asiatic.

Homophony/Homography: the coincidence in sound or writing of a lexeme with different semantic values, generating in this way different kinds of homonymy and polysemy.

Inflectional position: position taken in a lexeme by the inflectional morphemes, usually an ending or final position.

Intensification: mono-articulatory lengthening or strengthening of a phoneme, mostly in biconsonantal bases, given way spontaneously to its doubling or (re)duplication.

Interdigitation : interposition of the different sound sets (consonantal and vocalic) to produce a concrete base or morphological pattern. See "continuous"/ "discontinuous."

Isosemantic/Bisemantic: said of the coincidence in meaning or otherwise of different bases sharing the same phonetic cluster.

Lautsymbolism: see "symbolic phonetics."

Matrix : in Bohas' analysis the last and most original element of a lexeme, "a non-ordered combination of two areas of articulation," upon which etymon and root are built up, most recently taken as formed by a pair of "phonetic features."

Mimophonic: see "symbolic phonetics."

Moneme: the simplest and indivisible lexical unity with a specific semantic load. Voigt considers root and pattern as monemes whose intersection produces morphemes.

Monemization/Monemisierung: descending linguistic analysis or etymological process, according to the "one-dimensional layering" of discourse, namely, from sentence through morpheme, moneme, phoneme, distinctive feature" (Voigt). See "morphemization."

Mono-/Bi-/Tri-consonantal: this labelling refers to the consonantal (graphemic and phonetic) skeleton of the Semitic lexemes that defines the root.

Mono-morphemic: the empirical basic lexical unity (either etymon or base) of its entire phonetic components, consonantal and vocalic.

Morpheme/Morphematics: aside from the conventional linguistic definition (lexical or grammatical morphs), some authors take morpheme as the different pattern developments a moneme can assume.

Morphemization/Morphemisierung: ascending linguistic analysis or historical reconstruction process, according to the "one-dimensional layering" of the discourse, namely from distinctive feature through phoneme, moneme, morpheme, sentence" (Voigt). See "monemization."

Morpho-syntagm: in opposition to root, it implies "base" and "inflectional position."

OCP ("Obligatory Contour Principle"): phonetic principle forbidding the contiguous sequence of identical consonantal elements.

One-dimensional layering: ordering of the linguistic material according to the descending sequence: "sentence, morpheme, moneme, phoneme, distinctive feature" (Voigt).

Paradigm, paradigmatic: in structural linguistics plane of the associative (semantic) concatenation of the linguistic elements. See "syntagm, syntagmatic."

Pattern: lexical/morphological phenotype resulting from the intersection (interdigitation) of the consonantal radical skeleton and the vocalic melody

(Cantineau), sometimes called "template," reserving the label "pattern" for the generic distribution (simple and expanded) of the consonantal root.

Phonetic feature: one of the (two) modular or articulatory aspects that shapes a phoneme.

Phonotactic: said of the conditions or constraints imposed by phonetic compatibility peculiar to each language.

Plereme: radical (moneme) or derivational (morpheme) constituent element of the linguistic unit in the plane of semantics.

Pre-Proto-Afro-Asiatic/[Hamito-Semitic]: hypothetical and controversial level of linguistic reconstruction that relates the Afro-Asiatic phylum with the Indo-European, called also "Nostratic" level.

Pre-Proto-Semitic: level of reconstruction of the Semitic languages that goes beyond the branching of this family from the Afro-Asiatic phylum. See "Proto-Afro-Asiatic."

Proto-Afro-Asiatic: level of reconstruction of the whole Afro-Asiatic phylum from which the forms of its different languages can be explained. See "Pre-Proto-Semitic."

Proto-morphosyntax/grammar: the level of original inflectional organization of the linguistic material, as a part or in parallel with the radical lexical organization.

Proto-phoneme: according to Gazov-Ginsberg, the original base whose consonantal component, phonetically rich and stable, acts on the radical monovowel to develop a complex apophonic inflectional system.

Proto-Semitic: level of reconstruction of the Semitic family from which the forms of its different languages can be explained. This level should find correspondence but not necessarily coincidence with the proto-level of the other Afro-Asiatic families.

Quadripositional: refers to the position held by the thematic vowel in the /yqtl/ form of the triliteral root /yqtvl/ (Voigt).

Radical: alternative designation for "root"; sometimes used for one of its phonetic components.

Radical integration: manner of completing the triliteral pattern by different expansion ways (Conti).

Resonance: characterization of the phonetic fluid organization of the radical lexeme, based on binary or ternary consonantal articulation and monovocalic modulation.

Root: the so-called consonantal skeleton of the radical lexeme, as such an abstraction. See "pattern," "base," "stem," "theme."

Root variation: said of roots having two consonants in common with the same or different meaning.

Semantic chain: the sequence of semantic derivation shifts from an original meaning, witnessed independently in different languages.

Semantics (etymological/historical): the reconstruction of the original meaning of a base and its diachronic or historic developments in the different languages.

Spirant: sort of consonantal phonemes, also called fricatives, produced by the narrowing of the sounding channel with a rubbing effect of the air flow, to be distinguished from aspirate, sort of occlusive consonant followed by a velar or ovular puff.

SSR ("Strong Semantic Relationship"): total homonymy or close semantic relationship between two lexemes.

Stem: sometimes a label for "root" or "base," mainly as a source of the derivation system and in this sense the opposite of "root." See "base," "pattern," "root," "theme."

Symbolic phonetics (/semantics): spontaneous semantic charge granted to simple sounds ("meaningful resonance") as the source of generating roots and bases; to be distinguished from "onomatopoeia."

Synchronic/Diachronic: in structural linguistics the levels of simultaneity of succession at which a linguistic element is considered.

Syntagm/Syntagmatic: plane of the linear (phrase, phonetics) concatenation of the linguistic elements; see "paradigm, paradigmatic."

Systemzwang: constraint imposed in word formation by the analogy with the dominant morphological system (Kienast).

Theme: radical element to which the inflectional system is joined, otherwise equivalent to "pattern." See "base," "pattern," "root," "stem."

Transposition/Metathesis: change of position of an element of the phonetic chain determined by affinity or incompatibility with the others.

Unmotivated vowel: the so-called original radical vowel not dependent on the apophonic derivation system.

WSR ("Weak Semantic Relationship"): partial homonymy or distant semantic relationship between two lexemes.

SPECIFIED TABLE OF CONTENTS